W9-BSF-326

*"Mother Donit fore the Best"*

Asylum class of small children.
*Courtesy of the Parsons Child and Family Center, Albany, New York.*

# "Mother Donit fore the Best"

## Correspondence of a Nineteenth-Century Orphan Asylum

### Judith A. Dulberger

Syracuse University Press

Copyright © 1996 by Syracuse University Press
Syracuse, New York 13244-5160
*All Rights Reserved*

First Edition 1996

96  97  98  99  00  01        6  5  4  3  2  1

The paper used in this publication meets the minimum requirements of American National Standard for Information Sciences—Permanence of Paper for Printed Library Materials, ANSI Z39.48-1984. ∞™

**Library of Congress Cataloging-in-Publication Data**
Dulberger, Judith A.
Mother donit fore the best : correspondence of a nineteenth-
century orphan asylum / Judith A. Dulberger. — 1st ed.
p.   cm.
Includes bibliographical references and index.
ISBN 0-8156-2696-7 (cloth : alk. paper). — ISBN 0-8156-0341-X
(pbk. : alk. paper)
1. Albany Orphan Asylum.   2. Orphanages—New York (State)—Albany—
History—19th century.   3. Orphans—New York (State)—Albany—
Correspondence.   4. Foster children—New York (State)—Albany—
Correspondence.   I. Title.
HV995.A32A533   1996
362.7'32'0974743—dc20              95-40038

*Manufactured in the United States of America*

*O how much better you will be to get a good schooling dont you think so. mother donit fore the best, so hurry & learn so you can be a clark some day & I will be so glad to see that day come.*

Judith A. Dulberger is a graduate of the Doctor of Arts program in American History at Carnegie Mellon University. She spent many years in Albany, New York, working in the field of historic preservation and now operates an independent consulting firm in Youngstown, Ohio, that specializes in cultural resource management, historical agency consultation, and public history education.

# Contents

# Illustrations

# Preface

The idea for this book was hatched nearly ten years ago at my dissertation prospectus review. The introduction of these letters is now long overdue. More than the story of institutionalized child care of the late nineteenth century of which they are a part, these letters speak both to the intellect and to the heart. More than simple historical fact, they relate the range and depth of emotions experienced by families of the late nineteenth century torn apart by poverty, sickness, and death. More than an accounting of the tyranny of asylum life, they reveal a story of friendship, intimacy, mutual attachments, and refuge. They portray the asylum from a new perspective, one in which legislative mandates, daily routine, and institutional policy take second place to the realities and human consequences of poverty in late-nineteenth-century America.

Letters for this volume were selected from over five hundred case files preserved in the records of the Parsons Child and Family Center, formerly the Albany Orphan Asylum, in Albany, New York. The collection is currently maintained in the Manuscripts and Special Collections Division of the New York State Library. For the most part, the correspondence presented here dates from the period of the 1880s and 1890s, a time at which the Albany Orphan Asylum functioned as a large congregate-care institution. At the height of its operating history in the mid-1890s, the Albany asylum ranked fifteenth in order of size within New York State's network of more than two hundred state-subsidized private homes for children. During this period it provided refuge each year to more than six hundred children within the confines of the asylum and oversight, or more precisely an early version of aftercare, to an additional six hundred children placed out on indenture.

The case files from which the letters of this volume have been extracted varied widely in terms of size and content. There were single files that contained as many as two hundred letters, and others that included only a letter or two or a bit of paperwork on an individual child. Biographical information was pieced together from detailed registration books that, though not always complete, provided information on a child's age, parentage, the names and number of siblings, the date and circumstances of admission, and the date and condition of discharge.

The decision to include certain cases and exclude others proved difficult, as each story somehow deserved to be told. A few simple criteria were employed in sifting through the material. Some letters from parents who wrote inquiring about their children were selected because they seemed to best illustrate a variety of life circumstances confronting poor families of the late nineteenth century—single parenting, desertion, chronic illness, illegitimacy, irregularity of work, and marital discord. Others appear here because of their poignant depiction of the consequences of familial separation and loss. Still others address significant points regarding parental attachment, attitudes, and expectations. Letters from foster parents have made their way into this volume primarily because of their remarkable, often detailed, descriptions of the behavioral problems of indentured children as well as the problems inherent in the indenture process itself. The children's correspondence, in turn, tells a great deal regarding sibling relations and, more particularly, the strong and persistent emotional attachments of the children to their "keeper."

The letters themselves, from parents, children, and foster-care providers, have been presented with as few changes as possible. To make them more readable, however, I have added punctuation when necessary, as it is almost universally omitted from these letters. Editing has been done as well to shorten very lengthy passages, but only when such extracts would not diminish the meaning or effect of a particular message. For reasons of confidentiality, surnames of children and families have been changed.

Finally, these letters exist largely because of the efforts of one man, Albert Fuller, who as superintendent of the Albany Orphan Asylum from 1879 until his death in 1893 proved a prolific correspondent and a scrupulous recordkeeper. Fuller was a singular man operating in an era before the professionalization of social work and child welfare. It was a time in which the character, attitude, and personal frame of reference of the individual alone, as superintendent or administrator, determined under what set of rules an institution would operate and what a child's (or parent's) lasting impression of the asylum might be.

Of course, the Albany asylum is a single case, one of many among the hundreds of institutional alternatives available in the closing decades of the nineteenth century. Yet the parents, children, and foster parents whose words appear in the following pages encountered a range of life circumstances. Their backgrounds varied in terms of geographical location, educational level, ethnicity, occupation, and marital status. In view of the diversity of the people involved, what seems most striking is the similarity of expression, response, and motivation revealed in their letters. As a body of evidence, the asylum correspondence suggests, perhaps more than anything else, the existence of an underlying set of parental values and aspirations among the poor that may help refashion some of our class-based theories regarding family dynamics in past societies. Certainly, if the correspondence accomplishes nothing else, it will begin to recast the story of the asylum in more realistic and human terms.

I want to acknowledge my appreciation and indebtedness to a number of individuals who helped in the completion of this work. First of all, I would like to thank members of my original dissertation review committee. John Modell, Richard Schoenwald, Edwin Fenton, and Peter Stearns each offered sound direction and encouragement over the years. Richard Schoenwald, especially, took the time to read numerous revisions of this text and his enthusiasm never seemed to diminish as months of initial preparation turned into years. It is to his memory, as mentor and friend, that I dedicate this book.

I wish also to thank James Corsaro, Kathleen Lawson, and other staff members of the Manuscripts and Special Collections Division of the New York State Library who eagerly provided assistance throughout the course of this project and whose many hours of photocopying considerably reduced my need to travel to and from Albany. I also mention John Modell again here for generously providing financial assistance for what proved to be quite formidable photocopy expenses. Lynn Pauquette of the Parsons Child and Family Center also was quite helpful, particularly in the location and identification of photographic materials presented here. I also wish to thank my mother, Irene Botch, whose persistent research efforts helped uncover a number of photographic images that may have otherwise been overlooked. And my thanks also go to Jon Crispin of Amherst, Massachusetts, who did a fine job photographing original materials from three different repositories. I am also, most especially, deeply grateful to my husband, Reid, whose quiet encouragement made this book a reality and whose computer skills eased the process of preparing the final manuscript.

Last, I want to acknowledge the children and families of the asylum whose humble but poignant words have reached out from the not-so-distant past. They have not only touched my heart but broadened my understanding of poverty and its tragic consequences for children, for parents, and for families not only one hundred years ago but today as well.

*"Mother Donit fore the Best"*

# Introduction

L ate nineteenth-century America was a time of unprecedented material progress. In many respects it was quite literally a "gilded" age. History recounts a quarter century or more of increased productivity and conspicuous consumption, an era of big business, technological innovation, vast fortunes, and endless opportunity. It was a moment in time when everyman seemed successful inventor, entrepreneur, and pioneer all rolled into one. Opulence reigned. Works of architectural splendor transformed the landscape of both town and country. Rags to riches myths became countless realities and accumulation of wealth and social climbing preoccupied a whole new class of society.

## A Precarious Life

Yet a dark and often tragic side disfigured the glittering facade of this golden era. For if the late nineteenth century prevailed as a time of fantastic wealth and opportunity, it was equally an era of extreme poverty and material deprivation. Chronic unemployment, overcrowding, hazardous workplaces, rampant disease, and untimely death characterized the experiences of a vast underbelly of American society comprised of those dependent on the still-emerging system of wage labor for their sustenance. The more pessimistic writers of the time sullenly characterized the late nineteenth century, perhaps aptly, as a time of prolonged economic depression with only brief interruptions. Financial panics and depressions of a greater or lesser severity did, in fact, occur in every decade following the Civil War.[1]

Despite the economic vacillations of the times, the material wealth of the country exploded in the closing decades of the nineteenth century and the standard of living maintained a steady rise. Economic stability and social mobility did not elude an expanding class of "middle" Americans. The simple yet tragic catch remained, however, that the rich had little trouble getting

1

richer, some of them infinitely so, while the poor ended up with little or nothing. Just "getting a living" proved a challenge. The rising national affluence left scant impression on those who were impoverished.

The paradox of progress, as Henry George wrote, was its attendant poverty. Tramping made its appearance along with the locomotive, and the almshouse, prison, and asylum accompanied sprawling middle-class suburbs, grandiose banking houses, and belching, thundering furnaces of the steel mill. Squalor and affluence coexisted, often separated by little more than an alley, a residential boulevard, or a commercial thoroughfare.[2]

Although the progress, and certainly the affluence, was unprecedented in the American past, the poverty itself was nothing new. As early as the 1790s, in large cities such as New York and Philadelphia, the poor presented not only a visible but a continuous social crisis. Their plight was seasonal at best and by the mid-nineteenth century outdoor relief, the almshouse, and transiency had already become common strategies for survival. Many, if not most, laborers and skilled journeymen, especially those with families, lived in poverty or on its edge. Their material lives were spartan or worse, and chances for upward mobility, even a marginal economic stability, remained severely restricted, held hostage as they were to the vagaries of weather, accident, disease, and economic downturn.[3]

Poverty was no merely urban phenomenon, however. Even by the mid-nineteenth century the life of the farm laborer had become precarious, especially in the Northeast, where land productivity had declined and land itself was scarce. A significant decrease in home manufacturing perhaps contributed most to the rise of rural poverty in the early part of the century, as families lost an important source of supplementary income to the shops and factories from which they now were forced to purchase many household goods. Agricultural mechanization in the latter part of the century only exacerbated the problem. Along with technological progress came increased farm size and productive capacity, but also a reduced need for manpower and a steady dislocation of the workforce. Seasonal labor became the norm, leaving the migrant worker with a hand-to-mouth existence, often compelled to beg, steal, or rely on the poorhouse from one season to the next. Throughout the century periodic crop failures, drought, falling prices, and chronic indebtedness only added to the uncertainty of their lives.[4]

If job insecurity was commonplace in the emerging system of wage labor, it had become part and parcel of the structure of working-class life by the end of the nineteenth century. Massive immigration, overstocked urban labor markets, strikes, layoffs, and "technological redundancy" at times threatened the very foundation of working-class life.[5] A tragic mixture of cyclical unemployment, seasonal unemployment, and structural unemployment left few workers able to count on a full-time pay check year round. Irregular work, low wages, and periodic dependence on private charity, outdoor relief, or public institutions became chronic. When steady work presented itself, workers were more often than not subjected to backbreaking labor, intensive fast-paced schedules, monotonous work routines, and the unsafe, even hazardous, conditions of the workplace. It was a way of life played out day to day not only in the squalid tenements of large metropolitan centers, but in the crowded, unsanitary streets of small industrial towns, and amid the scattered huts and ramshackle "homes" of migratory workers and farm laborers in the otherwise bucolic settings of the American countryside.[6]

Everyone was vulnerable. There were no safety nets when calamity struck. No one escaped the fear of poverty, for it was always present or nearby. At one moment work might be plentiful with labor in demand. The next moment the working-class family would be mired in poverty. The unskilled laborer, in particular, could be thrown out of work at any time, not just when the snow fell. Work often went hand-in-hand with "looking for work." Arrangements with employers were generally short and casual and competition for unskilled and unsavory tasks such as hauling, digging, sawing, piling, shoveling, and scavenging could be fierce. The laborer who was hired for a week, a day, or just a few hours could be terminated at any time with no explanation and no recourse but to resume the search for work.[7]

In the face of such uncertainty the cash earnings of wives and children became indispensable to a family's survival. As early as the mid-nineteenth century one of the main characteristics of the life style of the unskilled laborer was, in fact, his inability to support his family "unassisted." His income fell short by as much as one-third, making a man's family in effect his primary, perhaps his only, safety net in an era before the advent of systematic social welfare. Needs and circumstances might change as families passed through a variety of life stages from marriage through old age. Still, they tended to depend most on the financial contribution of wives, and less so on the earnings of children, for basic sustenance, if not survival.[8]

But what happened to those families suddenly devoid of their primary— or secondary—source of income? What circumstances faced women, often young mothers, left without male support on account of death, desertion, illness, or injury? And what of fathers forced by maternal loss into the dual role of major breadwinner and primary caretaker? Widowhood or single-parenting, in its suddenness, its very essence, spelled impoverishment. Both men and women struggled with the consequences, but unlike their male counterparts, women had fewer employment options, confined as they were to a male-dominated patriarchal economy. The first and last resort for many of these single mothers was often the poorhouse or a day-to-day existence piecing together outdoor relief with employment of any kind—sewing, washing, put-out work, peddling, even prostitution. Their husbands had worked the hardest at the least healthy jobs, dying relatively young in mines, in steel mills, and on railroads, stricken with consumption, pneumonia, and a variety of industrial diseases. Many of those who survived simply walked out, turning their backs on their families, unable to bear the physical and mental strain of gnawing poverty and constant struggle.[9]

As a consequence, in an era when divorce was uncommon, a large proportion of single women with children lived by themselves with no means of support save their own labor and ingenuity. For the most part, these poor widows and deserted mothers had few of the resources available to single parents today. They had little or no savings, no pension or social security of any kind and, until after the turn of the century, usually no insurance. The chronic lack of work and low, unpredictable wages made it impossible to accumulate savings, to purchase even the barest necessities for keeping house, or to pay for the support of their children.

Survival strategies for these single mothers took many forms. For some, providing lodging in their homes assured a regular, if meager, income. That is, of course, if they had a home at all, and most did not. The majority turned instead to domestic service, which offered by far the greatest, sometimes the only, opportunity for steady employment and a livable wage. It was, in fact, one of the very few forms of work in the late nineteenth century that made it possible for unskilled women to be continuously self-supporting. Unfortunately, the unwritten credo that "women with children need not apply" left thousands of mothers faced with a serious dilemma: to starve or to separate. The nature of domestic service in the nineteenth century meant "living in" with another family, not simply working out day to day; there would be room enough for the mother, as servant, but certainly not for her dependent children. An infant still at the breast might stay for a time, but the others would be placed out on indenture, sent to live with relatives, or taken, sometimes by force, to the orphan asylum or other institutions.[10]

Single fathers faced equally tragic circumstances. A high maternal mortality rate in the late nineteenth century often plunged men into early widowerhood. But single parenting among fathers also came about as a result of maternal desertion, mental illness, or incompetence, and no less so because of marital separation. Although single mothers far outnumbered single fathers in the closing decades of the nineteenth century, the percentage of fathers raising or attempting to raise small children alone was not insubstantial and their dilemma no less severe. They had small children and they had no work, or when they had work they had no one to watch the children. For many, it proved a vicious and frustrating circle from which there seemed to be no escape.[11]

## Welfare Options and Attitudes: Relief or Control?

To say there were no safety nets for the working poor of the last century is not to suggest that their plight was ignored by the larger society. It was not; in fact, the poor consumed great intellectual and material energy throughout the century. Sectarian and nonsectarian charitable organizations flourished. Public and private welfare institutions in every state housed thousands of the aged, the needy, the sick, and the unemployed. Legislative mandates went hand in hand with movements to "save the children" and to remove them from the influences of pauperism. Public outdoor relief was dispensed in cash or in kind, at least for a time. In periods of great distress, usually during severe economic depressions, local governments not only opened soup kitchens and distributed wood, coal, food, and clothing to the needy but sometimes answered the call, however haltingly, for public works projects ("Bread or Work") as a strategy for getting the masses of unemployed back to work.

Much of this seemingly heroic effort languished, however, as reformers, charity workers, institution builders, and spokesmen for state and municipal governments wrestled with the perennial question of culpability. Possibly more energy was expended on developing categories of "worthiness" and segregating the various populations of dependent poor from the general populace, and from one another, than on resolving immediate problems of hunger, hopelessness, and utter destitution.[12] Debates flared among those in the nascent welfare professions about how much charity was too much. "Shall we raise the standards of our charitable giving so high that it becomes desirable in the eyes of the poor," they would ask themselves and one another, "or should we keep it at a grade so low that it will be sought only in extreme poverty." The lexicon of nineteenth-century reform did not include the term "less eligibility," but the concept today differs little from the prevailing attitude of the times: that the dollar amount of relief dispensed should not exceed the lowest-paid job available.[13] Throughout the late nineteenth century a widely dissimilar corps of welfare reformers, providers, and practitioners heartily agreed on the philosophical tenet of restrictive relief. They did so perhaps more out of fear than out of simple meanness. Despite a general consensus over the need to stem the tide of chronic dependency, however, differences continually split the community of the reform-minded over the more immediate issue of how best to dispense aid.

As both public and private charity expanded throughout the late nineteenth century so too did the number and variety of methods, theories, plans, programs, and initiatives to reduce or eradicate a growing national problem. The most controversial of these schemes by far was the large, congregate-care institution—orphan home, poorhouse, reformatory, and insane asylum. During the latter half of the nineteenth century the states constructed hundreds of these massive rehabilitative, later custodial, facilities for the poor, the criminal, and the insane, and in the process created equally elaborate and complex bureaucracies to administer them.

In New York State, the most prolific of late-nineteenth-century institution builders, the social welfare bureaucracy reached beyond the public realm to maintain oversight not only of the state's own institutional creations but of state-subsidized private charitable efforts as well. In the 1890s, the New York State Board of Charities, established thirty years previous, found itself saddled with the responsibility of filing reports each year on more than two hundred privately run orphan asylums, reformatories, industrial schools, and "homes for the friendless." This was only a small fraction of the board's overall responsibilities, which included maintenance and operation of the state's own expanding system of insane asylums and homes for the feeble-minded, its reformatories and custodial institutions, and its homes and schools for deaf, blind, and crippled children.[14]

While all this institutional and bureaucratic growth was taking place, community-based networks of private charitable associations and agencies, in contrast, were being prodded to cut back and to eliminate waste and duplication in the relief process. Reformers preached a simple message: charity had to be organized, scientific, and unsentimental. The aptly named Charity Organization Society first reared its head in large metropolitan centers in the 1870s and 1880s and later found a place in smaller communities around the country. The concept of "scientific charity" was really nothing new; in a sense the movement itself was nothing more than a sophisticated version of the old-style friendly visiting of midcentury. In its ideal application, the overriding goal of scientific charity was neither the "giving" nor the provision of material relief. Rather, the objective was to "organize," to coordinate, to investigate, and to counsel. In the end, the movement failed largely because it succeeded so well in creating suspicions, hostilities, and rivalry among local relief organizations and because, ultimately, it offered little tangible assistance to those most in need.[15]

In both the public and private realms humanitarian instincts somehow got lost. Many have ventured to theorize that humanitarianism, in fact, had no part in the late-nineteenth-century relief question at all. Rather, the charity organization and relief society, the almshouse and asylum, the reformatory and prison, all interconnected somehow in a grand scheme, conscious or unconscious, subtle or direct, intentional or by happenstance, to control the masses, "to promote the stability of society at a moment when traditional ideas and practices appeared outmoded, constricted, and ineffective." Fear, anxiety, even panic accompanied the disintegration of community life in late-eighteenth-century America. As the new century progressed, immigration, industrialization, the explosive growth of cities, and the simultaneous opening and settling of the Western frontier added to a sometimes chronic sense of apprehension. In many instances, the response took the form of an almost frantic search for order, for the constancy of the past, and for new and palatable hierarchies of social relations. [16]

A number of historians have speculated that a new moral and social control tradition emerged from this almost century-long quest for order, a tradition many suggest is with us yet today. [17] The seeds of this tradition are said to have taken root in the private charitable organizations and public relief agencies of the late nineteenth century that together sought to mold, to manipulate, and to uplift the masses of working poor into paragons of middle-class virtue. Public welfare reform, with its predominating institutional focus, however, far outdistanced private efforts to manage the poor. The massive welfare institutions of the era, in fact, proved the very consummation of social and moral control, at least in their inception. The orphan asylums and mental hospitals especially, but even the almshouse and the penitentiary, incorporated within the confines of their walls the essence of social order. Here the deviant and dependent classes could be removed from contact with the general populace, rehabilitated, reconstituted, and spit back out on society as models of right and righteous behavior. Moral and social uplift soon proved an unattainable goal, however, as public institutions of all kinds and categories evolved into massive custodial facilities with little to inspire the imagination. Only the hulking edifices that had transformed the cultural landscape remained, painful and expensive reminders of the failures of nearly a century of social engineering. [18]

Nineteenth-century charitable and welfare reform, then, was conceived as little more than a mechanism to control the masses, to elevate them in mind and spirit, and to restore them to independence, or so the theory goes. Whatever the underlying motivation, the truth is that the poor found themselves stuck with an array of social welfare options that, though vast and complex in nature, were really quite limited in scope. It was within this system that they were forced to work out their own personal strategies for survival or to suffer the consequences. And so they used the system, but in quite different ways than perhaps had been intended. For if nineteenth-century social welfare was a question of manipulation, it is difficult to ascertain exactly who was manipulating whom. [19]

The dependent poor of the last century did not constitute a degraded class of paupers, passive and apathetic in outlook and expectations. Perched as they were on the edge of poverty, even destitution, the laboring classes of the last century created parallel networks of safety valves for themselves and their compatriots. They were not acted upon but often acted in concert to improve their lot. Within immigrant communities all across the country, for instance, extended kinship ties formed the basis of social security and assistance in times of crisis. Whenever individuals had kin available and nearby their first impulse was to look to family rather than to strangers for assistance.

Kinship networks were not just local in nature but extended over several communities and even back to the small towns and villages of the Old World. As circumstances allowed, family and relatives acted as migration agents, labor brokers, welfare providers, and more. Crowded immigrant neighborhoods also seemed somehow to generate associations of comradeship, mutual assistance, and financial aid spontaneously. Fraternal organizations, mutual aid societies, and trade organizations, based on ties of ethnicity, occupation, or religious tradition provided aid and insurance to members in time of unemployment, illness, or death.[20]

Often, however, the poor simply did not have the resources necessary to help themselves or one another. At those times they turned to the only alternatives open to them and shifted their strategies as the winds of welfare reform so shifted. Public outdoor relief is a case in point. In the late 1870s and early 1880s fierce attacks by wealthy professionals and would-be reformers led to the complete abolishment of outdoor relief in some cities and to severe reductions in others. Opponents claimed that they wished simply to check abuses and reduce costs, but mostly they feared that handouts of food, fuel, and cash, no matter how meager or restrictive, would lead to the spread of idleness and the loss of the will to work. There were those deserving of relief—children, widows, and the elderly—but the ablebodied must be purged from the rolls.

Throughout the first three quarters of the nineteenth century thousands of people in every state received outdoor relief, far more than were relieved "indoors," in public institutions. By the end of the century that trend had been reversed. With outdoor relief dropping precipitously, the cost of the almshouse skyrocketed. Likewise an array of other public welfare institutions grew in magnitude, most particularly the number and relative size of orphan asylums. Other factors certainly contributed, such as various state laws ordering children out of poorhouses. But the explosive growth of the orphan asylum in the last quarter of the nineteenth century strongly suggests that poor parents began in these years to cope with the abolition of outdoor relief by breaking up their families and finding substitute care for their young.[21] New York State alone saw the total number of children supported each year in orphan asylums triple, from just under eighteen thousand in 1870 to nearly fifty-four thousand twenty years later. By 1895, upward of sixty-five thousand children passed through the state's orphan asylums and homes for children each year. As outdoor relief declined, the poor became increasingly purposeful in their use of the state's system of institutionalized social welfare; although by the end of the century the architects of the system had begun to despair of it, the poor had found refuge in it.[22]

## Institutional Choices: The Place of the Orphan Asylum

As with other welfare institutions of the nineteenth century, the orphan asylum may have started out as a tool of social control, but it did not end up that way. Families caught in a temporary or chronic state of crisis tended more and more throughout the century to look to it as a major source of relief. It was no easy choice, but a necessary one. Families were torn apart, sometimes for the short term, sometimes permanently. Yet, as far as many child-care reformers were concerned, what better way was there to abolish pauperism than by removing the child from the degrading influences of community, family, and friend. To many, the asylum remained nothing short of a stroke of genius. Some of the staunchest control advocates felt perfectly exhilarated at prospects for the future. Separating members of poor families, though perhaps not always explicitly stated, was for many an underlying objective. In the asylum, they boasted, "we can control the influences that make up the child's life. We can control what he thinks about, from the time when he gets up in the morning till he goes to bed at night. We can select his teachers. He never will play truant. He never will be absent from school. He never will run with the gang. He never will be out nights. We can control absolutely his physical conditions."[23]

Some reformers believed that ordinary working-class mothers were largely unfit to bring up a child anyway, because of their ignorance of the principles of child study, child culture, and child nurture. A few very radical thinkers hoped eventually to build "the greatest home for girls that was ever seen." It would provide for five thousand inmates at any one time and would employ the choicest selection of women ever assembled for matrons, teachers, nurses, and caretakers. Together they would bring up a "new race of women to become the mothers of the next generation."[24]

The idealists' grand schemes of social engineering had come to little by the end of the century, however. Rather than engineering the perfect social environment from which would emerge a new breed of flawless child, the orphan asylum was just another in a series of failed institutional experiments. Or so it seemed; but social engineering was not the asylum's only purpose and certainly not its only function. Rather, the orphan asylum was nothing more nor nothing less than the late-nineteenth-century response to the plight of children in poverty.[25] Most children brought to the Albany Orphan Asylum in the last two decades of the nineteenth century, for instance, were neither orphans nor severely neglected waifs dragged forcibly to the institution by poor law authorities or charity investigators. Nearly 45 percent of children admitted to the Albany home during that period came from two-parent households, and a nearly equal proportion were classified as "half orphans," those who had at least one surviving parent. Of perhaps greater importance, however, was the fact that institutional commitment of children by county magistrates often reflected nothing more than a matter of practicality.[26]

Most parents could little afford to pay board for the keep of their children. Many tried, but most could only secure a place at the asylum by first handing the child over to county poor law authorities, who in turn would place the child in an appropriate institution where they would be maintained at county expense.[27] New York State's local magistrates demanded no official surrender of the child, nor did the trustees of the Albany asylum. With two weeks written notice a child could be discharged to the care of a parent or guardian, provided there were no extenuating circumstances such as known abuse, neglect, incompetence, or immoral influences. Most children, in fact, were expected to return to friends and family upon discharge, and this proved to be the case for more than two-thirds of nonorphaned children admitted to the Albany home in the last two decades of the nineteenth century.[28]

The evidence suggests that the children of the Albany Orphan Asylum were neither mercilessly forsaken by their parents nor irrevocably separated from their families by avid child-care reformers. Rather, most children came to the Albany asylum at the behest of their parents for reasons of sickness, death, or simple poverty, and most returned to their own homes in the course of time. Although neglect, abuse, and abandonment were not uncommon, children came to the asylum in large measure for temporary refuge during times of destitution and family distress. Quite unintentionally perhaps, some states actually paved the way for this increasingly common practice. With the passage of New York State's Children's Law of 1875, for instance, per capita state subsidies that passed through county administrators to children's institutions created a mechanism whereby families could utilize the asylum in times of need and use it largely without fear of recrimination, personal disgrace, or loss of parental control. Parents who would never have tolerated the stigma of sending their children to the poorhouse now found a palatable alternative in the asylum. They distanced themselves from the personal shame of public relief by relying on the asylum rather than the dole. When the Children's Law stipulated further that care of dependent children be provided in homes or asylums of the same religious faith as that of the parents, the floodgates opened.[29]

By 1894 it was estimated that one child of every hundred in the whole state, and one child of every thirty-five in New York City, was being reared for some or all of his or her young life within the confines of an institution. Critics of the subsidy, or "private asylum system," blamed the system itself for this explosive growth. A greedy competition for state subsidies by asylum administrators greatly increased the number and size of private institutions throughout the state, they claimed. In turn, "the influence of fine and numerous institutions in seducing weak and unfortunate parents from their loyalty to their offspring" could not be underestimated.[30] It was the subsidy system itself, however, that provided one of the few welfare safety nets available to the laboring classes in New York State before the early twentieth century. Many poor parents who sent their children to the Albany Orphan Asylum viewed it that way and used it that way. Ironically, they often perceived the asylum as a means whereby they could keep their families intact, despite the separation. They depended on the asylum in times of economic, personal, and physical crisis and expected that their rights as parents would not be abrogated. They wanted their children to look forward to an easier life than they had known thus far and many times the asylum seemed the best and sometimes the only means for making that happen.

As the following series of letters reveals, the late nineteenth century orphan asylum became the poor man's boarding school. With that image foremost, some parents felt justified in placing stringent demands on asylum personnel for the best possible care and schooling of their children. At its most realistic, the asylum was viewed by parents as a place run by kind and compassionate individuals, a home that would provide the level of care that their poverty simply would not allow. Poor families found a refuge in the orphan asylum, a "haven in a heartless world" of struggle, disappointment, deprivation, and illness. Continually thwarted by economic circumstances from achieving and maintaining a stable home life, the asylum became a means whereby the poor, in a sense, could participate in the "cult of domesticity" that so thoroughly pervaded nineteenth-century middle- and upper-class private life.

The poor consciously used the asylum for their immediate and long-term goals. It became an integral part of their struggle for survival in late-nineteenth-century society. They came to depend on it, but rarely took it for granted. The reform-minded upper classes, however, saw things otherwise. The poor, they claimed, blatantly misused the public trust and used the asylum as nothing more than a personal convenience. Illustrations of abusive practices by self-indulgent parents added color to many national charity conference proceedings throughout the nineteenth century. One former Commissioner of Public Charities in New York City, whose informants, he claimed, exhibited unquestionable veracity, told a story to the New York State Conference of Charities and Correction in 1900 of an Italian family that "having come to America and saved up some money, desired to go back to Italy for a holiday, but considered it too expensive to take the children. Therefore, they placed the children in an institution, went off to their native country, spent the summer, came back, took their children out of the institution and resumed the felicity of the domestic circle."[31]

This same commissioner found himself confronted daily with requests to put children into asylums from parents motivated, he said, by nothing more than greed, laziness, or simple self-interest. "It is only a little while ago a man came to me," he reported, "who is earning $60 a month and wanted me to put away his five children because he said his wife had died, and he thought that was grounds enough for the admission of children into the institution." Even more astonishing, reported the commissioner, was the fact that the superintendent of the asylum in question not only backed up the man's request but begged him to grant it.[32]

Critics believed that with encouragement of this kind from the institutions, the poor would never understand or be held to account for their responsibilities as parents. Yet these commentators clearly failed to come to grips with the fact that there were few options available to poor families in the late nineteenth century; they may have chosen otherwise but could not. With little or no outright cash assistance, with nothing comparable to daycare (affordable or otherwise), with family and kin themselves struggling to subsist, with little if any compensation in times of illness or injury, what options remained? Families with small children were particularly vulnerable. Widows, widowers, unmarried mothers, and those deserted by a spouse carried the heaviest burden. Families split apart by abuse, alcoholism, or simple incompatibility faced a similar impoverishment. "Keeping house" was out of the question, and without a home what was one to do with the children?[33]

As the letters of this volume reveal, the disintegration of the family unit, whether a first or last resort, was emotionally painful and often fraught with extreme anxiety, a draining loneliness, and a sense of frustration that could often lead to despair. Poor parents loved and cherished their children. Rather than being detached, even apathetic, as is often conjectured, they made conscious choices that often involved great personal sacrifice. What many saw as merciless abandonment of the child was nothing less than a selfless act of love. The orphan asylum offered not only immediate refuge in time of severe want; for some, it became the pathway out of poverty, the best means, the only means, for providing a better, more secure life for the child. The sacrifice was in the separation, in the uncertainty of its duration, and in the painful possibility of its permanence.[34]

## The Families and Children of the Albany Orphan Asylum

As it stands, the story of the orphan asylum in American history is a tale only half told. A glimpse of the past reveals a Dickensian portrait full of zealous social reformers, starving homeless children, and tyrannical overseers. Countless scenes from fact and fiction depict the innocent yet morally tainted child plucked, perhaps abducted, from the danger and degeneracy of the streets only to be locked away in the rigid yet purportedly regenerative environment of the asylum. Traditionally, the story of the orphan asylum has been one of institutions rather than people, of expectations rather than circumstances, and of the successes and ultimately the failures of social engineering rather than the human consequences of a single-minded vision of human perfectibility.

Told simply as a narrative of child saving and social reform, the story remains fundamentally incomplete, for when viewed in its entirety it is much more. No longer merely an account of institutions and institution builders, the story of the asylum unfolds as a collective memoir of sorts, a compelling and sobering tale of families in poverty, families in crisis, and families in need. In the letters that follow, the idealist with utopian visions of society, the child-care reformer, and the upper-class philanthropist of the last century are superseded by the families of the asylum. It is they who reveal their stories to us.

Those who came to the Albany Orphan Asylum in the late nineteenth century found it an old and venerable institution. The first orphans had been received in 1829 under the guardianship of two fervently Christian ladies. The Society for the Relief of Orphan and Destitute Children of the City of Albany, as it was then called, was incorporated in 1831 and within a year had built a facility on the outskirts of town capable of accommodating 150 children. A half century later a Board of Managers, which counted among its members some of the most influential citizens of Albany, oversaw a flourishing institution with a large physical plant set on five acres of land hemmed in by a bustling urban community. More than forty teachers, attendants, physicians, clerks, and groundskeepers assisted the superintendent in the asylum's daily routine.[35]

During its first few decades of operation the Albany asylum provided refuge on average to about 100 children each year. They came generally from the city and county of Albany and the institution functioned from day to day by way of community-wide appeals, donations of goods or cash, and special endowments. Through the period of the late nineteenth century, a growing urban population and changing economic conditions placed increased demands upon the home as the population of children rose steadily from a year-end total of 149 in 1875 to more than 500 children per year by 1895. Perhaps less than the economic vacillations of the times, however, it was New York State's Children's Law of 1875 that had the most decided impact on the size and direction of the Albany asylum before the turn of the century.

At the time of the passage of the law, which ordered children out of county poorhouses, few orphanages existed outside of the state's larger cities. Most of the counties had none. Prodded by a number of overburdened county overseers of the poor, who were now mandated by law to place dependent children with substitute families or in orphan asylums or other appropriate charitable or reformatory institutions, managers of the Albany Orphan Asylum voted to open its doors to all who were in need "without regard to the location from which they came." Unable to accommodate a larger population of children, the decision necessitated enlargement of the facility and improvements to existing asylum buildings.[36] A risky and expensive venture, the asylum's move to expand its radius proved successful at least from a fiscal standpoint. No longer a "public beggar" dependent on the charitable graces of generous donors, the Albany home soon evolved into an efficient business enterprise of sorts, functioning according to certain economies of scale. Continued solvency meant competition for limited public funds, however, and the competition intensified in the late nineteenth century with an expanding regional network of orphan asylums, each vying for the same pool of per capita state subsidies.

To remain competitive, the asylums had to keep their own per capita fees as low as possible without affecting basic services. In order to achieve this delicate balance, the Albany asylum continued to stretch its benevolent arm beyond the city of Albany and surrounding counties outward to an area that ultimately encompassed all of New York State. By the 1890s the asylum was receiving dependent children from a twenty-three-county area extending south throughout the lower Hudson Valley region and into northern, central, and western New York. Not wishing to interfere with the work of its "charitable competitors," managers of the Albany asylum nevertheless continued to solicit county supervisors and poor law authorities statewide for "placeable" children. They justified the action as a necessary business decision. Superintendent Albert Fuller stated it succinctly: "until our endowment is materially enlarged, it is absolutely necessary in order to secure sufficient income to properly feed, clothe, and care for our children, to run to our full capacity.

In this way our pro rata of expense is brought to its lowest point. With the new institutions coming on our ground, it is necessary to cover more surface in order to keep our numbers good."[37]

The families represented in the following letters, then, came not only from the city and county of Albany but resided within a broad geographic area of New York State on farms, in small towns, and in larger cities. The parents themselves, dependent on the orphan asylum by force of circumstances or force of law, were by no means sedentary, however. They seemed always on the move, tramping from town to town or moving from one residence to another. Included among their numbers were struggling skilled workers, farm laborers, domestic servants, unmarried mothers, widows and widowers, abused wives, and deserted husbands. There were also inmates of poorhouses, insane asylums, and prisons and those branded as alcoholics, prostitutes, and members of so-called pauper "clans."

As evidenced in their correspondence, some parents were clearly educated, others, probably most, were simply literate, with little knowledge of grammar, spelling, or punctuation. Still others wrote phonetically or were illiterate and depended on neighbors, friends, or relatives to convey their message. For those who were able, writing must have been difficult and time-consuming as they labored over each phrase and each sentence, hoping by their words to elicit some response.

Nearly 85 percent of children admitted to the Albany asylum in the last two decades of the nineteenth century came from homes with at least one surviving parent. About half the fathers for whom occupation was reported worked in skilled or semiskilled trades with slightly more than one-third employed as laborers (many of them farm laborers) and a smattering of clerks, bookkeepers, business proprietors, and others in "white collar" professions of the day. Parental nativity favored American birth, although immigrants accounted for more than one third of all parents. The Albany asylum catered to those of the various Protestant faiths but there were Catholics found among the registrants as well, and, although there are no precise figures, poor blacks were counted among its charges in the closing decades of the nineteenth century.[38]

Statistics are revealing of course, but fail to underscore the fundamental point that the families of the Albany asylum shared first and foremost the single characteristic of a grinding and persistent poverty, a poverty exacerbated by the predominance of single parenting due to illness, desertion, separation, and death. The children of these poor families might remain at the Albany asylum a few days, a few months, or several years, but on average they stayed about two and one-half years. If the asylum retained them longer, there was usually good reason. One young girl, for instance, resided at the asylum for more than five years on account of physical ailments. She exhibited a very "strumous" constitution and had frequent scrofulous (tubercular) abscesses in the glands of her neck and also an impediment in her speech. Another had a mother who was a common prostitute who was raising an older daughter, not yet sixteen years old, in her own profession.[39]

At the time of their admission to the Albany home the majority of children ranged in age from five to twelve years. Older children were accepted when the need arose, however, and after 1890 infants were cared for at the asylum's recently endowed Lathrop Memorial, a nursery located off site in a nearby townhouse. Nearly two-thirds of the children arriving at the Albany asylum in the 1880s and 1890s came with brothers and sisters, although other siblings were often left behind with parents, relatives, or friends. Of those in residence, boys tended to outnumber girls, but that was largely because of the high demand for "indenturable" young girls as domestic servants. Some were bound out from the asylum at the tender age of eight or nine, but most were probably older. Although most children, boys as well as girls, returned to their families upon discharge, there was still that large element within the asylum who by the age of twelve to fourteen were placed out with substitute or foster families, some never having known their true parents, some desperate to return to their own families, some hoping never to see them again.

Child placement or the increasingly anachronistic practice of indenture remained the preferred child-care alternative within the welfare reform circles of the late nineteenth century. Orphan asylums were routinely criticized for retaining their charges too long and propagating a race of "institutionized children," those whose very spirit and intellect were crushed by the rigid and mechanical environment of congregate care.[40] Home placement often proved as controversial as the asylum, however. Critics of child placement argued simply that a good institution was in many ways better than a bad foster home. The sad truth was that although some foster parents wished only the companionship of a child, others clearly desired their labor.

During his tenure as superintendent of the Albany asylum, Albert Fuller noted on more than one occasion that oftentimes very "peculiar people" made application for children, many who ought never to have had them. As a protective maneuver, asylum managers agreed that in the majority of cases it was better for the child's good that he or she be kept in the institution until somewhat matured before placing out. This policy agitated the more passionate advocates of child placement, but trustees held steadfast to the practice of retaining children until "old enough and strong enough to begin considerable work without injury and have mental capacity to protect themselves to a certain extent if their home does not prove to be such as supposed."[41]

## The Asylum and Its Superintendent

Albert Fuller served as superintendent of the Albany Orphan Asylum from 1879 until 1893. In that capacity he carried on a prolific daily correspondence with families of incarcerated children, with many of the children after they left the institution, mostly those placed out on indenture, and with the children's substitute families or foster-care providers. Authors of Fuller's obituary reported that during his tenure as superintendent, he sustained a correspondence of at least 125 letters daily![42] As far as can be determined, he answered most letters personally. Although the magnitude of his communications seems incredible even by today's standards, it may have been possible in part because of his use of a typewriter, his dependence on a clerk who often took dictation, and his frequent, though not exclusive, use of standard replies and phrases. Letter after letter in response to concerned parents, for instance, might say little more than "Your children are well and getting along first rate. They are standing at my side as I write to you and they send ever so much love." Yet most letters included also a phrase or a sentence or two of a personal nature regarding the individual child—his or her health, schooling, behavior, emotional adjustment, or joy over the receipt of a gift from a parent.

This voluminous correspondence certainly stands out in an era before electronic communications. What is particularly fortunate for present historians in the case of the Albany materials, however, is that Fuller seems to have saved every bit of correspondence that was not passed on to the children. He also made carbon copies of all his personal correspondence whether handwritten or typed. And he hand-copied dozens of letters from children and foster parents into bound "Indenture Books" as a way of keeping track of the progress of his former charges. Fuller's wife, Helen, who served as matron of the Albany asylum, took up the task of correspondence after his death and maintained regular, though less frequent, contact with asylum families at least through 1897.

In many respects the Albany collection is unique not simply because of the sheer volume of extant correspondence but also largely because of the nature of Albert Fuller himself. Many asylum superintendents of the late nineteenth century strived to manage their institutions as they might a large family. This was particularly true in the years up to the mid-1870s when asylum populations remained relatively low. But as the number of dependent children under institutional care began to increase dramatically through the end of the nineteenth century, reality most often supplanted ideals. Adherence to family models began to fade as more needy children poured into the nation's asylums in the 1880s and 1890s. In New York State especially, institutions for the care of dependent and neglected children attained a "luxuriant growth" never before seen. A facility containing only two or three hundred children seemed of very moderate size compared to those containing "five hundred children, a thousand, fifteen hundred, eighteen hundred, two thousand, twenty-five hundred."[43]

In these huge congregate-care institutions, managing the orphans grew more difficult and discipline problems increased. Asylum superintendents began to place greater dependence on strict routine, regimentation, and a variety of coercive techniques. In their quest for absolute control, many asylum administrators went so far as to attempt to sever all ties to parent and family or at least to diminish parental influence over the child as much as possible.[44] Perhaps untypically, Albert Fuller clung to the notion of the family ideal while operating under the increasingly rigorous demands of congregate life as the asylum's population increased fivefold under his tenure. He held tenaciously to those ideals, even to the detriment of his own health. However, more than his persistent attachment to the idea of family within his own institution, it was Fuller's efforts to retain the bonds of family and kinship among the poor that at times seems nothing short of remarkable.[45]

Fuller was a friend to the parents of the asylum child, or so he was perceived. In many respects he served as a family intermediary in times of distress. At the least, his willingness to correspond frequently with concerned and anxious parents allowed many to believe that although their parental functions had been severely diminished by the realities of separation, their parental rights and responsibilities were by no means relinquished. It is that illusion, or reality, however we wish to see it, that has given us these first-hand accounts.

Many will ask the question of whether or not Albert Fuller was something of an aberration. In many respects the answer is yes. Certainly his dedication and sensitive nature seem untypical, if not exceptional. He in fact spent much of his adolescence in the Albany asylum working side by side with his parents, who had come to Albany from Rochester, New York, in 1866 to operate the Albany home. As he grew to adulthood, Fuller mingled with the asylum children as siblings and friends, sharing their joys and sorrows and forming many lifelong acquaintances. In 1879, on his twenty-ninth birthday, he succeeded his father as superintendent of the Albany home, coming to the position with far more valuable experience than most men might have acquired in a lifetime.

Not simply an overseer, disciplinarian, or caretaker, Fuller remained friend and confidant to his charges. He had lived so long among them that some of his contemporaries said his own spirit was childlike. Those who memorialized Superintendent Fuller after his death referred to him as a simple, natural, and modest individual disposed always to think and speak humbly of his work and its worth. They recounted that he had a child's joy in life and yet a father's tender mercy. He loved the children as if they were his own and could call each one of several hundred by name. To many of them he gave the only pet names they ever knew and the children instinctively recognized him as their fatherly friend.[46]

Albert Fuller took his "calling" to heart. Reporting to the asylum Board of Managers in 1889 his role was clear, as were its consequences:

> Persons unacquainted with the details of a work of this nature have no realization of the high strung tension at which a person in charge is kept. I have made it a rule to be at all times accessible to the children, to hear their requests and remedy all their complaints. Perhaps you can imagine with a family of 450 children, what that means. . . . The night nurse, Attendants, and Watchman have strict orders to call me at any hour of the night in case of illness with any child or the happening of any unusual occurrence.[47]

Four years later, with a "family" of more than six hundred children, Albert Fuller was dead of heart failure at the age of forty-three. Regardless of the issue of uniqueness, it is through the dedication and sensitive nature of this man as correspondent, confidant, friend, and ultimately as recordkeeper that we are allowed a glimpse of the past, a window into the lives of the poor of the late nineteenth century and the institutions that served them.

Taken as a whole, the letters of the Albany Orphan Asylum weave together a remarkable story that reveals something of the values, attitudes, and outlooks of both family and institution in an exceptional, informative, and compelling way. In a sense, the collection offers a multidimensional picture of the lower-class family of the last century. Family life among the poor was no isolated affair. Asylum superintendents, poor law officials, charity workers, and foster parents distended the family circle to fit those who, by force or by fate, were to take part in a shared parenting of the dependent child.

Beyond this, the letters themselves open a window into the subjective and emotional lives of the lower-class family of the last century. We know so little of that critical dimension of lower-class life, little more in fact than what the upper classes have passed on to us in their writing. So much involves inference, suggestion, and conjecture. Perhaps most hidden is the internal dynamics of lower-class families, relationships concealed from view by a veil of illiteracy, poverty, and a subsistence life style. The image of the lower-class family circle is projected back to us either too faint to clearly discern or too distorted by upper-class claims to have much basis in reality. The relationship of the poor to the system of social welfare that in many ways sustained them is often equally distorted by a singular, class-biased point of view.

In the letters that follow, there are obvious and striking similarities. The sheer frequency of repetition in presentation, phraseology, expression, and content cannot be denied. Albert Fuller's responsiveness to parents, his uncanny talent for humanizing the asylum experience, and especially the very standard format of his letters may have influenced the shape and content of most parental correspondence. Yet explanations may be grounded as well in the fact of shared attitudes, values, and aspirations among the laboring poor of the last century with regard to family life and the parent-child bond.

Perhaps most common in the parental correspondence is a clearly deferential tone. It is difficult to ascertain, however, if it is a deference based on simple self-interest, on the awe of authority on the part of the laboring poor, or on the successes of late-nineteenth-century reformers in reviving social-class relations based on mutual respect.[48] It is likely a combination of all these factors. Certainly the parents whose letters are presented in this volume were self-interested on their children's behalf and they were often effusive in their expressions of gratitude for the care and attention given their children. They frequently deferred to the wisdom and practical knowledge of the superintendent and they were quick to offer apologies when they felt they had gone too far in asserting their demands. They asked for kindness, patience, and mercy, and were not denied.

As asylum superintendent, Albert Fuller was compassionate, responsive, tolerant, and respectful to parents of all social conditions. He did not hesitate to reprimand or correct an errant mother or father but he did so not as one with absolute authority but as one with authority based on mutual obligations. The sense of the relationship between poor parent and asylum administrator derived from this correspondence is one of partnership rather than servility. As the letters reveal, it proved to be a somewhat successful reciprocity in which Albert Fuller maintained his position of authority, even honor, while parents were left with their self-respect, with their parental rights intact (perceived or actual), and with their children receiving adequate, if not merciful care.

As will be seen in the following correspondence, letters from foster parents regarding indentured children also follow recurrent patterns of comment and response. In general these letters focus on the problem child. It is the striking repetition of complaints and charges against these children that more than anything else strongly suggests the existence of a subpopulation of abused and severely neglected youth within the asylum. In contrast, the numerous similarities found in the children's letters to the superintendent boldly illustrate the strength and persistence of bonds formed within the asylum, flatly contradicting any suggestion of the subordination of the child's personality to a rigid authoritarianism within the institution.

These are, of course, letters from only one institution but they offer a new perspective. In the first-person accounts we hear the clearly articulated voices of the poor. In simple, modest, and unaffected language they speak for themselves and for one another and have much to tell about their lives, their losses, their struggles, and their joys. We perceive them as they perceive themselves and see them as they wish to be. It is through their own words and their own expectations about the future that we can begin to balance the story of the orphan asylum and to sharpen our vision of the past.

# Parents and Children

*Dear Sir will you kindly Inform me how my little pets spent this cristmess. oh god only nows how I suffer the absents of them. if thay dont cry after thir mother or me plese tell me. . . .*

*Dear Sir . . . am doing my utmost to get started again to House-keeping. Owing to poor health and scarcity of work during the winter months am unable yet. Will try to be within 2 or 3 months at the farthest . . .*

*Dear Boys . . . papa writes to you with love and respects for you as his children and hopes you are well and learning fast. Someday I hope to give you a good home and make you happy and hope you boys will make papa happy in his old age. . . .*

*Dear Sir Wont you please write and tell me about the children. Oh Mr. Fuller if you could only know how a poor mothers heart ached and longed to hear from her little babies. . . . please write . . . something more about them than just (you children are well and . . . send their love to you). That is so unsatisfactory. some how it doesent fill the great aching void at all. . . .*

The "cult of domesticity" stands as perhaps the most popular theoretical model for the study of the American family throughout the entire period of the 1800s. In a phrase, this term describes the nineteenth-century culmination of the ideology of the companionate family that first emerged in the latter half of the eighteenth century. Simple in formula, the cult of domesticity has been vast in its implications for social change. The landscape of human emotions and human relations has undergone an exceptional transformation. The changing family dynamic, in turn, has produced a wave of demographic and psychological repercussions that are being felt as yet today. The cult of domesticity was largely a middle-class phenomenon, however. It is not known for certain if or how the working classes, the poor, and the various ethnic groups participated. Nevertheless, it remains the prototype for the study of all family relations in the context of nineteenth-century American society and an "ideal" against which families in the past are said to have conformed or deviated.[1]

Theory tells us that the rise of companionate marriage in the late eighteenth century and the separation of work and home in the early nineteenth century led to a number of changes within the family circle. Patriarchy declined, romantic sentiments came to predominate, psychological equality characterized new relationships between husbands and wives, and homes became distinctly child-centered. Most changes were premised on the assumption that the household was no longer the primary place of production. As fathers spent more and more time as wage earners away from home, child rearing increasingly became the province of motherhood, a role now infused with a high moral, even political, purpose.

Mothers essentially became society's moral guardians. They were to be the architects of a new social order, as it were, that would be preserved from generation to generation by way of the children. No longer morally depraved at birth, new religious precepts now portrayed the child as an innocent and malleable creature of God, but one requiring an intense maternal vigilance. To ensure a successful adult outcome, every aspect of the child's behavior needed monitoring by the ever-attentive mother—feeding, diet, attire, play, prayer, and schooling. Gentle reprisals, affectionate persuasion, and emotional withdrawal replaced rigid discipline and will-breaking. Conscience, rather than community oversight, would guide the child. A kind of "portable parent" would assure a necessary measure of self-control and implant in the child's personality those most laudable of nineteenth-century middle-class traits: honesty, industry, frugality, and temperance.[2]

Although considered morally inferior, fathers, as well, were to share in the raising and nurture of the young. Declining patriarchy did not mean loss of function within the domestic circle. Fathers wanted friendly relations with their children and expected close and loving bonds based on mutual respect and affection. Perhaps it was not instinctual, as a mother's love, but fatherly affections were to become a well-learned behavior within the context of the nineteenth century cult.[3]

In order to attain the ideal homelife as prescribed in the cult of domesticity, the nineteenth-century, middle-class family retreated into a world of quiet, seclusion, and privacy. The "purity" of the environment could be maintained only in isolation. The home, as best represented in the form of the middle-class suburb, became a fortification, a bastion against the dangers and dark temptations of the world at large. Home and homelife not only protected its members but served as a refuge, a "haven in a heartless world," and those mutual obligations and affections that kept it functioning were not just important but infused with a sense of dire urgency. If the family did not, could not, function in expected ways it might come apart. There were no longer any other institutions to back it up.[4]

Thus the image of family as unit of emotional and moral support as distinct from its purely economic function came to prevail. But who, in fact, achieved this "ideal?" Certainly not the poor, who could little afford the luxury of separate spheres or physical isolation from the ravages of society. At a minimum, one had to have a place, a shelter, a homebase to serve as refuge.

Many of the poor parents who appear in the following selection of letters were homeless or transient, living as lodgers in "bachelor" quarters, in servants' lofts, or in poorhouses. "Keeping house" was a literal as well as a figurative term. Food, shelter, a few furnishings, and someone to watch over the little ones were the immediate and compelling concerns. The poor were probably intimately familiar with the cult of domesticity, but caught up as they were in the day to day struggle for survival they could hope at best to achieve only some dim version of it. Torn apart by circumstances, their only refuge at times became the orphan asylum. Here, the children at least would be safe, protected, nurtured, even loved.

## Albert Cowan

Most children at the Albany Orphan Asylum arrived rather young and left long before coming of age. Albert Cowan was one such child. His mother had died from "dropsy of the heart" in July, 1885, when the boy was just six years old. Albert's father, William, worked as a blacksmith for a carriage manufacturer in Catskill, New York. Anxious to find a good home for the boy, William hoped that the arrangement would be temporary—two years, no more. He doted over his young son, an only child, seeming to respond to his every whim. Clearly duty-bound to the boy, William in no way wished to be perceived by the asylum personnel as neglecting the child.

As with many single fathers who used the asylum, William placed primary emphasis on the boy's schooling and struggled to make monthly board payments for the privilege of keeping the child where he would be educated. Some of the early correspondence between Cowan and the superintendent in fact sounds vaguely like that between a devoted father and headmaster of a preparatory school, although the correspondents here are clearly not on an equal social footing. William writes from Catskill for the duration of his correspondence.

July 8, 1885

[Mr Fuller Dear Sir]:

i am a man that has lost my wife and i have a little boy that is six years old. he is smart and lurns well at school. i would like to get a good home for him a year or to. i am willing to pay for him for it. it [is] so that i can not keep him and tend to my work to. so can you take him for i want him ware he can go to school and have good care. if you can take him, in your ancear state the price a week that you will charge and if you cant take him pleese inform mee of a home, but i would like to get him in albany for it is not far a way to come to see him. so pleese oblige.

Wm Cowan

July 8, 1885

Dear Sir:

Your favor of this date is just at hand and contents noted. If your child is healthy we will take it if you desire to send it to us. You can bring him any Thursday. Our regular charges are $1.75 per week but will give you the benefit of our special rate which is $1.50 per week or an average of $6.50 per month payments to be made monthly in advance.

Our institution is very full just now (over three hundred and twenty children) and if you decide to send your child please let us know at once so that we can retain a place for him. Our location is pleasant and also very healthy as is shown by the fact that notwithstanding our large family we have had but one death in over two years. I enclose a print of one of our dormitories which will give you a little idea of the rooms.

Yours respectfully,<br>Albert D. Fuller, Superintendent

July 10, 1885

Dear Sur:

yours of the 8th came duly to hand. my child is healthy and from your [description] i think that he will like it thear for he is all that i have to look for and i [mean] to try to make a man of him. he lurns well. so i will bring him up next Thursday. so if i have to doe any thing, that is bring any papers from this place, you can let mee know by return of male.

yours respectfully,<br>Wm. Cowan

September 5, 1885

Mr. Fuller Der Sur:

i did not have time to twalk to you wen i was up so i will drop a few lines about my boy. he says that he does not get a nuf to eate for he says the kitchen boys brings it out and some of the boys that is biger then him will com and grabe his food and eate it up. i should think [there] would be some one to see to that. he says he does not see you to tell you. i asked him if he was not as hapy as some of the outher little boys. he sed that they most all have brothers thear to take thear part. he is a boy that we have tride to bring up well. . . . his Mother taught him good things and never have i knowd him to tell a lie. he went to sunday school and day school. i do not mind children spats for i know ware so many is they will have them, but his food i think more about and his schooling. i would like to keep him thear any way. i will see wen i come up agane how he liks it. i will write next week and send him a little money so wen school begins have him in it. i gess he has a toof [tooth] that bothers him. it acked the day i war up. so we will see how well he will like it out from this time. if he does not i will have to try to do better by him,

yours truly,
Wm Cowan

September 10, 1885

Dear Sir:

Your letter of the 5th. inst. is at hand and contents noted. Your childs statements in regard to the other boys taking his food is in the main untrue. I have made an investigation in regard to the matter and find that in only one instance has any thing been taken from him and that was a piece of bread by a boy smaller than he who sat next to him. Albert himself admits that this is the only time that any one has taken the least thing from him.

Another statement that he makes is entirely without foundation. You say that he says "that he has no oportunity of seeing me to tell of his troubles." As I am myself present in their dining room at nearly every meal and also have all the children in the institution together at least once and generally twice each day for inspection. You can redily see yourself how much ground there is for this statement.

I have changed his place at the table so that he will be nearer where I stand and where I will know just what he has and all about him. He has an abundance of food now and certainly appears to be more fleshy than the day he came but if his appetite is such that he craves more, he can certainly have it.

The tooth that you speak of I found to be badly ulcerated so much so that it had made his cheek sore as well. I extracted it so that that cause of trouble is entirely gone.

School will commence Monday and your boy will then go with the others.

In regard to any spats that he may have with the others they are not worth mentioning. At each daily inspection I call for any complaints and he as well as the others have the privilege of stating any troubles that they may have and if real they will be rectified. I am rather afraid that your boy is naturally of rather a complaining spirit. If such is the case I dont think that you will be able to find any place that will suit him in all respects.

Your good judgment ought to govern you in the matter and decide the course that you ought to take and if you do not feel satisfied to have him remain here we do not wish to have him stay.

Respectfully yours,
Albert D. Fuller, Superintendent

September 15, 1885

Dear Sur:

yours of the 10 i have recevd in regards of my boy Albart. i thank you very much for the truble you have taking in regards of this matter to find out the truth and i hope you do not disregard mee for writing as i did for i felt that it was my duty to find out the truth and i knows that you would make it right. so do not blame mee for it was doing my duty. i have a moore [satisfied] mind now and i think that wen school begins he will like it better. We will try him and see for i would like to keep him up thear on the acount of school. it is handy for him and i will see how well he does if he get to like it. I know that he will lurn then. that is my most desire. so we will see how well he does from this out. his spats you spoke of i did not mind them for i know what boys is, only Mr Fuller if you will oblige mee that is wen you write about the boy ask him how he liks it and give mee his words. oblige. hear is ten cents for the boy. give him five at a time.

Respectfully yours,
Wm. Cowan

September 17, 1885

Dear Sir:

. . . Your boy remains well. I asked him to day how he was liking it here now. His reply was "good". He is going to school and I am inclined to think will learn well. The money you speak about I found enclosed and Albert will go over to the store and get something with it this morning. . . .

Yours respectfully,
Albert D. Fuller, Superintendent

April 6, 1886

Mr Fuller Sur:

you will find inclosed the amount for Albart board. plese let mee know how he is ageting along and if he got the box that i sent last week and how was he pleesed with it. Mr Fuller will you plese let mee know when the school has its vacation for i would like to have the boy to come down then for 3 or 4 weeks . . . for i think it will do him good. . . . so plese oblige. give my love to the boy.

Respectfully yours,
Wm Cowan

April 8, 1886

Dear Sir:

Your letter is at hand with post office order for your sons board enclosed you will find a receipt for the same. Albert is real well and has been since you were last here. He received the box in good order it would have done you good to have seen him when I opened it for him.

He was very much pleased. Our vacation does not take place until after the fourth of July. I hardly think that it would be best for you to take him out then as it might have a tendency to make him discontented and he would probably feel worse about coming back than as though he staid here right along and then again I might not be able to take him back for the reason that our institution is very full and many are waiting for admission and I might not be able to make room for him if his place were taken by some one else. Albert sends his love to you.

Yours respectfully,
Albert D. Fuller, Superintendent

*Albert Cowan remained at the Albany asylum for more than a year following this letter. His father continued to write frequently but because of the distance and the demands of his job he rarely visited the boy. The asylum discharged Albert to the care of his father on June 4, 1887.*

### The Thompson Children

Poor-law authorities brought Frank Thompson's four children from the Delaware County poorhouse in Delhi, New York, to the Albany Orphan Asylum in June of 1891. His wife, Hattie, had recently been sent to an insane asylum. Thompson was black, and a barber by trade. Unable to find work, he remained at the county poorhouse for several months (possibly a number of years) after his children had been taken away. His correspondence from Delhi spans a decade, beginning with a letter in June of 1891. At the time, his youngest child, Bertha, was just two years old. The others—Hazel, Lillie May, and Earl—ranged in age from four to eight years.

Frank Thompson was clearly destitute and barely literate. His letters reveal some of the fatalism characteristic of extreme poverty, yet he seemed to find strength in a fervent Christianity. Perhaps his greatest fear regarding his children was that they would be taken from the institution on indenture, a common and serious concern among destitute parents of asylum children. "Indenture contracts" legally binding a child to a foster home rarely defined the nature of a birth parent's continued rights. Many felt haunted by the possibility of the permanent loss of their children under such a system. Untypically, Thompson's children escaped outside placement though they remained at the asylum for ten long years.

June 14, 1891

Dear Sir:

as I have not hird froom my chldes since thay came to you plase I should like to hear from them and how thay like thir home aspecly the boy for he was such a [coward]. . . . he will have a h[a]rd time of it. I was a shamd to send sch dirtty children away bot as my Wife has been a way I could not git them token care of so sente them to you. I hope I may hear froom them. I dont now What your rules are inregard to [vi]siting or calling to see childern. i should like to call and see them. . . .

Yourse veary troley,
Frank T. Thompson

July 6, 1891

Dear Sir:

I am veary much [pleased] to hear froam my [children] and that thay are geting a long so well. I dont now as you do such things as to boptise [baptize] childern but little baby [Bertha] . . . and hazle has not been bobtises and it worey me vearry much. We was gon to have them bobtised but my wife was sick so . . . that we never got at it. if you do such thnks plese bobtise mine. plese let me here froam my little pets soon as you can. I should like to now if yir let childern go to other pople. I dont want mine [parted] for thir mother is getting [better] and is liktly to come home soon then I shell call ans get them. plese rite me if thay can be bobtised. . . . please bobtise under the Episk-ball osppsse [Episcopal auspices] as we are all of that desine.

Vearry Truley yors,
F. T. Thompson

July 26, 1891

Dear Sir:

I thak you vearry kindly for the Baptising of my baby and I hope the little ones ar enjoying them selves as god nows thare is no comfert for poor popele aftre thay gro up. I dont wants ask to much of you my dear friend bot my daughter hazle has not been baptised. I want my famly to all be good as I am trying to be in my feeble way. I had the best of a wife and if she dont get better We all Will meet in heaven. god has promas that so I [look] for that day to come. I dont want bu[r]den you With my sorows bot I rite this so you may now that I want my little ones to come up rite. so if thay hafts stay thare [long] you can trane them to love good and after thay get old Enoff to come out thay Will always be troue to god and them selves. . . . plese let me here froam my babys soon and if eney of them get dangersly sick plese informe me rite away. god Will bless you dear sir to teach them to be good and if my [prayers] are answrd you shell be and recived.

Youre Veary Truley,
F. T. Thompson

September 14, 1891

Dear Sir:

It has Been some time since I have hird from my babeys. plese rite and let me [know] how [they is] and if my boy Is a worring much and if thay are being tought in school. the boy was vearry moch broken up abot his mother and sffred hir absents vearry much. plese let me now how he takes it and the rest including the baby. of corse she will not miss the parents vearry much.

Yourse Truley,
F. T. Thompson

February 14, 1892

Dear sir:

parden me for bothern you so much but when you now how much I love and think about my babeys you Will parden me for being so ungrateful asto worrey when thar are in such good hands, of [course] and with god to help watch over them. Oh teach them [to] love god and all that is good for I am a fraid that thay will never have a dear mother car agane and may god bless you in your good work and protect the little [ones] at the home and spechiley mine. give them my love and tell them I shell come and see them soon. I should come rite a way bot I am a fraid that thay would wants come home with me and god nows I should brake down. i could not stand it. plese let me hear froam them soon and tell me if thay are all happy. I sepose they are but exuse me. I trust all is well.

Yourse Truley,
Goodby,
F. T. Thompson

February 16, 1892

Dear Sir:

Your favor of the 14th Inst. at hand. Of course you are anxious about your children and you can write whenever you like. I have children of my own and can understand your feelings.

Am glad to be able to report your little ones as doing well. Expect to see the baby within a few days [at the nursery], the last I heard it was well.

With best wishes, I remain,

Yours respectfully,
Albert D. Fuller, Superintendent

[Undated]

Dear Sir:

It has Been some time sence I have hir froam my babys and I shoold like to hear froam them. do you think thay woold ask to come home if I should come and see them. I shell troy and call on them before long if you dont think thay would cry to come home With me. I coold not stand that. plese let me now if hazle has been babtised. you dlays are dangerous. if my little love should hopento die [without] being baptised I should feel awful bad for the bible sus how [thou] shelnot enter into the kingdom except you be borned agane. [May] god grant that some day I may have my Wife and babies a gane. good By and may god Bless you all and the Home.

Youre Troley,
F. T. Thompson

September 6, 1896

Miss Foller:

Will you [kindly] lit me now how my babey ar giting on. I shell be up to see them a bot the last of Septembr if all goes Well. plese dont let them now. I wanto see if thay Will now me When I com. give them my love. I thak you for caring for them and God Will bless you for your good Work. I Remane,

Yurse,
F. T. Thompson

February 26, 1900

Miss Helen Foller:

I have jost hird something that warres me and I thought I would rite you and ask you do you let eney one have childern who ask for them. thar is a famley as to In Delhi Who I am told are trying to get my girls out of the home. thay are a bad low degrade set. . . . Plese rite me and let me now If you ever let little Girls go to soch plases or send them a way without leting me now. Plese rite soon for I am [worried].

F. T. Thompson

*It is unclear why the county poormaster or Albert Fuller himself never authorized the Thompson children's indenture. Some time in 1901, plans were finally made to place Earl, now eighteen years old, with a doctor's family. Unhappy with the arrangement, Thompson demanded custody of the boy and both Earl and twelve-year-old Bertha subsequently returned to live with the father. As for the other two children, registration books disclose that Lillie May, age seventeen, died in October of 1901, no cause given, followed just three weeks later by her sister Hazel, age fourteen, who suffered from pulmonary tuberculosis.*

## Henry Klein

Lewis Klein, a native-born American of German stock, worked as an engineer, probably in the West Albany rail yards. His wife, Rachel, he claimed, deserted him for another man. Klein brought his twelve-year-old son, Henry, to the Albany Orphan Asylum in the Spring of 1887. Bitter over the separation, he sued his wife hoping to obtain custody of the couple's other children, who appear to have resided with the mother. Finding little work in Albany, Lewis eventually moved to Binghamton, New York where he had relatives and greater hopes of securing a job.

Only two letters survive from Lewis Klein's correspondence. For the most part, it appears that father and son communicated directly with one another and it is probably for that reason that so few letters were retained in asylum files. Klein's simple yet expressive style reveals a depth of affection and paternal guidance that is truly compelling. He was a friend to young Henry and referred to himself as such. Though notable, his clearly defined aspirations and expectations with regard to Henry's education and future life were common expressions voiced by many asylum parents.

June 2, 1887

My Dear Son:

I have bin to work hard all Day & to nite after I got Home I was suprised to get a letter from my dear Boy & i was ofel glad to here from you & to here that you are well & Pa hopes & prays that you will be a good Boy & try & learn, so when you are a man that you wont hafts do hard Laborious work & I will try & send you a small box of thing to Eate some time this wek. i will put some stamps in this letter so you can write to me a gain, for I think perhaps you mite improve in writeing by writing to me. this is the first letter that you have ever written & I think you don well for the first time & Pa was ofel glad to here from you & to here that you like your Teacher So well & my Son rember that your Father loves you & will do all I can to help you along, & will come & see you when I can, & Henry ask your Teacher if she wants you to have your School Books & Slate, & if she does let me no & I will send or Bring them up to you, for you mite just as well have them as not, providing you are in want of them. . . . Henry dont forget to repeat your Eavening Prair before you go to Bed, & be a good Boy, & try to learn all you can & you will never regret what you learn now, for I feel for your well fair, now learn all you can So when pa pa comes to see you that he can see his little Boy is learning ofel fast, & I think you will like it up there better after you get more acquainted. wall Henry, Pa is ofel tired & I gess I will draw to a close by Saying good nite & best wishes. Your Father. Be a good Boy.

Lewis Klein

February 16, 1889

Dear Son:

yours of the 24th is at hand & will hasten to reply. I was glad to here that you are well & hope you are learning. but should of thought you would of told me why you have not writen before. it has bin a long time since I hurd from you. I should of sent you a Slay but I had not the means to do it. if I had, you no I would of sent it. . . . I Sued R[achel] some time a go. She was in Catskill. The Sheraf surved the papers on her there, but she dident dare to stand the Suit. . . . I hope Dear Son you will keep what I have writen to your Self, for I shal go for your Brothers & Sister next. I think & I hope things will turn for the best after a while. O if I could of had the work I should of had every thing stratened before this time. Mr Fuller notified me that you wer well & doing well witch I was very glad to here. you wanted to no if I was coming to Albany this Sumer to work. wall Son that I cant Say. but i had rather work in Albany than I had here [in Binghamton] if I had a job. So I am unable to tell you at present what I shal do, but it is very dull here as yet. Cousin Peters Family are all well at present writeing. we have had some very cold wether here for the past week or so. Pa hopes you will be a good Boy & learn all you can. Trust to your Heavenely Father & he will bring you out all rite. I hope you wont wait so long before you answer this as you did my other letter. . . . I should like to See you & dont think Pa will forget you if you onely try & do rite. wall I will close hoping to here from you Soon as convenant. I remain as ever your frendly Father & best wishes. respects all. The Children join me in Sending love to you. Pa will come & see you as soon as I can. Be a good Boy.

Lewis Klein

*Henry Klein remained at the Albany asylum for four and one-half years, leaving to live with his father at the age of sixteen.*

### Ora and Roy Gilchrest

A. J. Gilchrest never mentioned his wife, but according to asylum records she deserted the family leaving two young sons, Ora, age six, and Roy, age unknown (probably the older child). Gilchrest assumed the role of primary parent during the years 1890 to 1894. He placed his boys in the Albany asylum and paid for their board as circumstances allowed. He advised the superintendent on their health and inquired after them in frequent letters. Gilchrest's correspondence occurred at a time when he was struggling to start a new business as an itinerant salesman. The work took him from the Gloversville–Fort Plain–Amsterdam area in Upstate New York, west to Chicago, east into Massachusetts, and downstate to Albany, Brooklyn, and New York City.

With the demands of an itinerant lifestyle, keeping both boys with him seemed out of the question. His travel consumed most of his money and when times were "dull" he could barely support himself. Gilchrest's self-employment should by all accounts have placed him squarely within the emerging middle-class of the late nineteenth century. Yet, as with laborers and many skilled and semiskilled workers of the period, he was always on the edge, never really able to save or get ahead and ultimately dependent on the county for the support and care of his children.

September 18, 1890

[Dear Sir:]

On my arrival home I . . . drop you a few lines [asking] how my Son Ora is doing. I dont think he will get home sick as he likes excitment. I will be down to see him on the 2nd of October then I will pay you for the month of Oct. Hoping to hear from you.

Respectfully yours,
A. J. Gilchrest

December 5, 1890

Mr Fuller Dear Sir:

The case of Ora is only bad blood. I presume the spot on his head has been sore the same as his hands . . . [and turned] into what is called a ring worm. Give him a blossom tea [and] wash the affected spot with warm rain water every morning with castile soap [and] when dried dip in ammonia . . . with a soft cloth. when the hair commences to grow nicely then you have it cured. The ammonia is the common article. any cleansing soap such as garbolic, sulphor, . . . soaps pure are good for any bad blood that may effect the scalp. . . . I will try and see Ora about Christmas if nothing happens.

Yours Respectfully,
A. J. Gilchrest

December 10, 1890

Dear Sir:

Your valued favor of the 5th Inst. has been received. Glad to hear from you.

Your directions in regard to your little boy are all right and I think they will produce a good effect. He is getting very fleshy and is in good spirits, and has a good color. . . .

With best wishes, I remain,

Yours cordially,
Albert D. Fuller, Superintendent

January 6, 1891

Dear Sir:

I will change my residence from Gloversville to Fort Plain for a short time. My Business is in its infancy and it costs me almost as much as I can make to travel about. I would like the other son to be with you as I think Ora would feel better if he were there with him as Ora expressed a sad feeling to me the day I were there about his brother as he would like to see him. What will you charge me for the boys being togeather. answer [this] return mail & oblige.

Respectfully yours,
A. J. Gilchrest

January 7, 1891

Dear Sir:

Your valued favor of the 6th Inst. is before me. In regard to your other son would say that we would be glad to accommodate you as soon as we can. At the present time our institution is so full that could not conveniently do so. Am expecting quite a number of children this week from Saratoga County, cases that I am obliged to receive, being under contract with that county. Think, however, that we would be able to take your little one about the first of April. . . .

Ora is perfectly well and sends his love. Hoping that you are prospering in your business, I remain,

Yours very respectfully,
Albert D. Fuller, Superintendent

February 17, 1891

Dear sir:

Your kind letter was received at Fort Plain this eve. Will answer. It is understood between [the Superintendent of the Poor] and I that you could make out the papers for both [boys], Ora from first of March and the other first of April. Mr Fuller I have had a dull time since thanksgiven and if I dont do better I will have to get some steady employment other wise. I have told [the superintendent] as soon as I had my Depts Paid and again a start I would pay for thair Board my self. P.S. will write you a few days before I start for Albany.

Yours Respectfully,
A. J. Gilchrest

September 30, 1891

[Dear Sir:]

I will state a few lines. how is Roy's cold. I presume you have given him some oil & clover tea. Please do so as I think he needs it or something for his blood before cold weath[er] sets in.

Very Respectfully,
A. J. Gilchrest

March 6, 1892

Dear Sir:

Arriving in [Chicago] on thursday morning will now give you my address. I could not get located right away. Hoping the boys are well. do they enquire for me. This is a very gloomy city and all mud also very chilly. I will commence worke on Monday. I have met a great many friends from Kansas City. Will close.

A. J. Gilchrest

March 22, 1892

Dear Sir:

Once more at home and am feeling bad from a cold. I think the Gripp has favored me again my back & head are hurting in fact I am ailing all over but must work. I presume th[at] Ora & Roy are well. will be in Albany in a few weeks.

Respectfully,<br>A.J. Gilchrest

January 26, 1893

Dear Sir:

Will say I am at the above named place [Pittsfield, Mass.] and am at home selling my article. New York & Brooklyn are all right but I cant live there and save money. There is one foot of slush & mud to look at and it made me homesick. How are the little [ones] doing. I presume well as usual. How has the ointment done its work for Ora. If Mrs Fuller makes it, stir it well when you add the two last drugs and continue stiring it until it is stiff enough to But[ter].

Respectfully yours,<br>A. J. Gilchrest

January 27, 1893

Dear Sir:

Your favor just at hand. Was somewhat astonished to get a letter from you from Pittsfield, but dont much wonder at your leaving New York city. I was talking with a friend the other day who has been there and they say the streets were in a terrible condition. Your little boys are getting along all right.

Very respectfully,<br>Albert D. Fuller, Superintendent

*Although Ora and Roy's mother received no mention in the correspond-ence, she had obviously been working toward obtaining custody of her children as the following letter indicates.*

*March 20, 1894*

*Dear Sir:*

*There were presented to us this afternoon orders for the discharge of the children Ora and Roy Gilchrest I believe the children are to be taken to the mother.*

*The order was given by the Courts, and therefore we had to obey their demands. . . .*

*We merely notify you so that you may not feel we have done anything dishonorable.*

*Yours respectfully,*
*Helen T. Fuller, Superintendent*

## Willie, George, and Josie Smith

Winter froze the northern waterways. Canal boats, ferries, and steamers came to a standstill. If work did not cease altogether, wages still only reflected the intermittent activity. Joseph Smith worked in New York harbor as an "electrician on a steamer." He struggled from season to season, often facing unemployment for months at a time. In the spring of 1887, his wife was dead or gone and he found himself left with the task of raising his three children alone. Like many poor single parents of the era he used a number of strategies in meeting his parental obligations. Ultimately he remarried in order to make a home again for his children. In the meantime, thirteen-year-old Willie was placed at the Albany Orphan Asylum until old enough to return home to work. His sister Josie boarded with relatives in Albany. The youngest, George, who may have remained with the father for a time, joined his brother in the asylum sometime in 1888. Smith himself lived with relatives in Brooklyn or, more likely, simply slept there, spending most of his time on the boat. Much of Smith's correspondence is addressed from the *Steamer Drew* in New York Harbor.

December 29, 1887

My Son Wiliam:

hoping thies lines will find you in good health as thay leve me hoping you are a good Boy and trying to make a man of yourself for it is for your own good. lurn all you can while you hav the chance. I recived a letter from aunt Sarah in it she stated that [your sister] Josie was well. Willie I hope you hav a good time with your Skates and Enjoy the Book that annie fetched you for Crysmis. hoping you had a Merry Crysmis and Wishing you a Happy new year, likewise Mr Fuller and all Conected with the institution. I hope you will anser this. Mr Fuller will giv you Righting Paper. we hav no Snow but it is verry Cold. Now Willie be a good Boy and god bless you. I dont forgit you and josie. Pleas giv my Respects to Mr Fuler . . . with a goodby.

Your loving Father,<br>Joseph J. Smith

March 1, 1889

Mr Fuller Dier Sir:

Inclosed will find the money for Board hoping to find you well also all of your Charge[s]. as for My Self I ante verry well. hav a bad Cold. your last welcom letter Came to hand. Mr Fuller hoping you will forgiv me in not Sending the Balance on last munth Board. it is hard work for me to make a nuff to Pay my way. Thay Cut my wages down so in the winter time. hoping you will let that Balance go till the Boat gits Runing and Oblige. Pleas giv my love to the Boys.

Yours Very Respectfully,<br>Joseph Smith

March 5, 1889

Dear Sir:

Enclosed please find a receipt for the money enclosed in your letter of the first inst. Am sorry that you are having difficulty in getting along on account of your low wages at this time of the year. I will allow the balance to remain until navigation opens again.

It gives me much pleasure to be able to say that your children are enjoying excellent health. They send much love to you. I remain,

Yours respectfully,<br>Albert D. Fuller, Superintendent

December 15, 1890

Mr Fuller Dr Sir:

I supose you think it verry strange in me in not being more prompt in my paying my Boys board. I am verry Sorry that I could not do as I would liked to but I hav been so that I could not work for the past four months. I am now at work. I will try and Settle with you. Willie is at work.* he is well and sends his Respect to you and all hoping to find Georgie in good helth.

---

*Willie had returned home in the winter of 1889 at the age of fifteen. He lived with his father's family on Fulton Street in Brooklyn and found work operating his own news stand near one of the elevated railroads. George remained at the asylum until his father's remarriage two years later.

Mr Fuller I will now send one months Board and will you Pleas Rite me and State the amount yet due and oblige hoping to find you in good helth also all of your charge[s].

I am yours,
Joseph Smith

April 8, 1891

Mr Fuller Sir:

Inclosed pleas find one months board hoping this will find you and all your Care in good helth. My Self and Willie are well hoping to find George well and a good Boy. Willie will try to Come up and See you this Summer. I think that I will Soon hav a home again for my children. that is I think of giting Maried then I Can hav my Children with me again. . . . My work is night work on the Union Ferry.

I remain,
Joseph Smith

April 10, 1891

Dear Sir:

Your favor at hand. Enclosed you will find a receipt for money sent. Glad to know that Willie is coming to see us. Hope you will get a good wife so that you may have a happy home. With best wishes, I remain

Yours sincerely,
Albert D. Fuller, Superintendent

November 15, 1891

Mr Fuller Dear Sir:

Willie and Georgie got home all Right and we think that George looked good. he is a good boy. he goes to School and he likes it. he often speaks of you and the asylum. Willie was pleased with his trip to Albany. Now Mr Fuller, pleas alow me to thank you and your Instituion for the kindness you hav shone to me and to my two Children. Mr Fuller will you pleas let me know how much I am in your debt. Willie, George, and My Self all join in Sending you our Regards and well wishes. I remain

Yours Respectfully,
Joseph Smith

*Although a single parent, Joseph Smith was apparently not widowed but obviously presented himself as such. As the following correspondence reveals, there was no record of his first wife's death. Getting a home and a mother again for his children appears to have been costly to Joseph's second wife, Ella, who after twenty-five years of marriage may have been denied the full rights of her widowhood.*

*November 20, 1916*

*Dear Sir:*

*I write to you in regards Joseph J. Smith's Children that was put in the asylum at Albany I think it was in the year 1887. their names were William & George Smith. the reason I am asking is this: of course I married their Father Joseph J. Smith and now that he is Dead and I am applying for a Widows pension. when I married I took the chrilden with me and brought them up but I do not know what year their mother died. so I will have to have that. and I thought perhaps it might be up there on the books. so will you kindly look it up when they were put in there and what was the reasn and oblige me very much.*

*Mrs. Ella J. Smith*

*November 21, 1916*

*Dear Madam:*

*Replying to your letter of the 20th inst. I would say that . . . the records do not show that the mother, Louisa Burns Smith, was dead at the time the [boys were] committed. [She] may be living . . . in Brooklyn . . . which was her last address.*

*Very Truly,*
*Superintendent*

### LeRoy and Jesse Miller

Illness and injury plagued the lives of the laboring classes in the nineteenth century. Such occurrences set within the context of major economic depressions could be devastating. Single fathers carried an additional burden and indebtedness in the costs associated with maintaining a housekeeper. William Miller, a widower, brought his two young boys, Jesse and LeRoy, to the Albany asylum at a time when the pressures of single parenting had simply become too great. His story vividly illustrates the personal anguish of those who, like himself, had few options when calamity struck.

At the time of his correspondence, William worked as a moulder for the Union Stone Works in Peekskill, New York. He wanted to raise his children himself, but was frustrated at every turn. Deep bonds of mutual affection were severely strained as months of separation turned into years. William's trail of bad luck began soon after the boys were sent away. An accident on the job left him out of work and nearly lame for several months. He recovered only to find himself facing shop closings, work slowdowns, and severe unemployment brought on by the Panic of 1893.

Illness, "the grippe and malaria," further aggravated an already miserable set of affairs. As the depression intensified through the latter half of 1893 and into 1894 William worked only occasionally, never certain of the hours or the pay. He lived sparsely, looked to family and kin for a loan to see him through, but eventually found it necessary to apply for county assistance in the support of his sons. William's very personal account here reveals a profound frustration, humiliation, and despair. He wanted nothing more than a "fair chance" to provide for himself and his family but, instead, was denied the simple pleasure of seeing his sons, sharing in their daily lives, and watching as they matured toward manhood.

July 19, 1892

Sir:

I will begin by introducing my-self as Wm. Miller. I have been a widower nearly four years have two boys, one eight and the other five years of age. I have been keeping house since my Wifes death and have had a hard struggle and several times have feared I would have to place them in an institution, through not having A house-keeper, two and three months at A time, but with the aid of my Sister-in-law have managed, until I found A woman to take charge. I have none at present and my Sister-in-law, not being a strong woman, is almost sick through the extra work and care and can not possibly do for them much longer. I write for information regarding the institution of which you are Supt. for having tried without avail to find A woman, it seems unless I succeed soon in finding one I must break up [my home]. I have a [much younger] brother Ross who was with you* and knowing through my sister Ida that children were kindly cared for, I would like very much to have mine go there if I must part with them, and it is very hard I assure you, and if you will kindly state as to whether I can put them there, and also the amount per month for each child, including everything you will greatly oblige. Please excuse mistakes.

Yours,<br>Wm. Miller

*The brother mentioned here was probably ten to fifteen years younger than William. His correspondence appears later in this volume under the name Ross Miller.

August 20, 1892

[Dear Sir:]

Please read these few lines to my little boys as soon as you think best, for I think it will comfort them very much, as they have never been away from home A day without me, and it will seem we are near them. Tell Jesse & Roy that Aunt Alice and I reached home all right, and say we are coming to see them very soon, and they must be good boys and mind what is told them, and tell them papa wants them to find out the names of all the little boys and girls, and tell them to him when he comes to see them, and say I will bring their pictures with me as I told them, and we will bring [cousin] Rannie to see them, and tell them Rannie, Auntie and papa send their love to them and please tell me how they got along after we left and greatly oblige.

P.S. Please state what day of month is visiting day and what hours.

Yours, Wm. Miller

August 22, 1892

Dear Sir:

I have your favor of the 20th inst. and will read it to your boys as you request. They are well and doing as well or better than could be expected. Your first visit you better put off as long as you can as it will be better for both the children and yourself. Dont worry we will take good care of them.

Yours Respectfully,

Albert D. Fuller, Superintendent

Oct. 7, 1892

Mr. Fuller:

While we were in the Chapel yesterday, we were speaking with A gentleman sitting near, and he was telling us how you fed and cared for the children, and he said if we sent butter you saved and gave it to them as they wanted it and Jesse hearing him wanted me to send him some, and as he has been used to having it I promised to send it along with A few other things. The book-slate is for Jesse, and the other things are to be divided between him and Roy. I brought them very little as I did not know whether they could have it or not, and trusting you will take no offence, as none is intended and thanking you very much for the kindness and consideration you have shown my children and myself, P.S. Please excuse writing and do not forget Jesse's schooling and my love to both.

I remain yours,

Wm. Miller

October 18, 1892

Mr. Fuller:

Your letter recieved. Glad to know the children are doing well. feel A little concerned about Jesse for he seemed homesick though he tried to hide it. I trust he is or soon will be at his studies as I think it will take [up] his mind and he will not have so much time to think about home. Give them our love and tell Jesse to hurry to write so he can send A little letter to papa. I will enclose order for $16.75 leaving $15.00 monthly up to August 19th, 1893. In case I should fail to send it promptly to date, it will not be long coming.

Yours Respt.,
Wm. Miller

November 22, 1892

Mr. Fuller:

You will excuse my writing with A pencil when I say that I met with an accident Saturday last. I stepped on a piece of iron and it went into my foot a full inch and the doctor says I barely escaped the lock-jaw and am fortunate to have gotten over it and as my feet have to be raised to keep the blood out of it, it is difficult to write hence my reason for using the pencil. I will enclose $15.00 order. Tell the children we all send our love to them and papa & Auntie send lots of kisses and tell them we will send them a box thanksgiving or soon after and oblige.

Yours resptfully,
Wm. Miller

December 23, 1892

Mr. Fuller:

Please read these few lines to my little boys. (I will write on business later) and oblige.

Dear little Jesse and Roy:

Papa thought he would be able to come up and see you at Christmas but my sore foot kept me from coming, but never mind. I hope I can come and see you some time soon. Auntie has gone down street and Rannie is out in the yard with the Dog. Did I tell you Uncle George got another Dog Just like Flash. It had a broken leg and Auntie tended it and it is all well and is as bright and cunning as it can be and it's name is Mischeif. Santa-Claus it seems has not forgotten either of you for he left A box of things for papa to send to his little boys and by the time you get this letter it has reached there, and papa hopes you will have A merry Christmas and A happy New Year and now with lots of love and kisses I will close.

P.S. Auntie and all the folks are out but I know they send Merry Christmas and love to you both, and Jess I want you to be A good boy and hurry and learn to write to me, and that will be almost like talking to me won't it.

From Papa

Mr. Fuller:

I have a sled I made for Jesse last year and he wished me to sen[d] it and if there is A good place to ride without danger of his coming to grief I would like to send it but I leave it to your judgement and I also wish you and all the children A merry Christmas.

Wm. Miller

December 28, 1892

Mr. Fuller:

I suppose you think it about time I wrote on business as I promised. I would have written sooner but was waiting to hear from my brother. I have been out of work nearly six weeks and am about out of money and prefering to get a loan from him rather than ask you to wait I wrote asking him for same. He has been out himself 2/3 of the time and could not possibly share it as he has his own board to pay and he has been trying to get it elsewhere for me but failed so there is nothing left me but to ask you to wait. I am sorry to do so but must, but I would not had I not been out of work so long. I might have had it even at that had it not been for debts contracted by Housekeepers previous to breaking up [the house], as since that time I have paid over $42. I have no wish to bother you with my private affairs, but I tell you this much in order that you may not think I am at fault only through circumstances. My shop shuts down this week for A week and I hope to be to work by the time they start again. I got A piece of leather out of my foot A few days ago and am able to walk on the side of it with the aid of A cane but can not put A shoe on it yet. You see I am forced to depend on your kindness and I trust you know I will send money as soon as possible. When you answer please tell me if the children enjoyed Christmas and oblige. Excuse blunders & writing.

Yours respectfully,<br>Wm. Miller

December 29, 1892

Dear Sir:

Your favor of the 28th Inst. is at hand. We will wait a little for your money until you get to work again. I remain,

Yours Respectfully,
Albert D. Fuller, Superintendent

January 21, 1893

Dear Sir:

Just a line to let you know that Le Roy your youngest child has the croup. He is having the best of care but as the disease is so treacherous thought best to let you know without delay.

Yours Respectfully,
Albert D. Fuller, Superintendent

January 22, 1893

Mr. Fuller:

Recieved your letter. Very sorry to hear bad news of Roy but thank you for letting me know. He had the croup last winter about three days. He was very bad and almost choked. The only thing that helped and in fact cured him was inhaling the steam from lime, and I also gave him A little Skunk's grease and bathed his throat freely with it. The same treatment cured me of the membrane croup at his age after having been given up by the doctors. I hope he is better by the time you recieve this. If he is not please let [me] know as soon as possible.

Gratefully,
Wm. Miller

February 3, 1893

Mr. Fuller:

I trust you will not think me ungrateful in not having written sooner, but I have been unusually busy of late. I was however very much pleased and thankfull to know through your letters that Roy was improving so rapidly, and not having heard from you in some time, have of course concluded he is well. My foot is so much better I am going to work on monday. It has been very slow, but is nearly well at last. When next I write I hope to send some money. Will send every cent I can possibly spare over expences, until we are square. Did you get the sled & also A box and was Jesse pleased with the sled. Tell him to hurry and learn to write, and tell him and Roy I would dearly love to see them again, and will as soon as possible. Give them my love, tell them to be good boys, and oblige.

Excuse writing and mistakes.

Yours respectfully,
Wm. Miller

June 18, 1893

Mr. Fuller:

I received your letter with its ever welcome goodness also the reciept. Please remind Jesse that to-day is his birth-day so I will send [him] and Roy A box with a few things. I intended sending butter to Jesse but as it is rather a poor way of [sending] it in hot weather, I will send A quarter in the box and let [the] boy buy it for [himself if you] do not object. Tell Jesse & Roy papa says he would [love] ever so much to see his little boys, and will try very hard to come, but that he cannot come quite yet because he has been sick quite a good deal, but tell them he never forgets them at all, [and I will] come as soon as possible. Give them my love and lots of kisses. . . .

Yours respectfully,
Wm. Miller

June 23, 1893

Dear Sir:

Yours of the 18th Inst. with box for Jesse and Roy . . . came duly to hand and they thank you for the good things contained therein.

We will have some one purchase the butter for Jesse as you suggest.

We are very sorry to inform you of Mr. Fuller's death which occurred Sunday morning. Heart trouble was the cause of death.

Respectfully Yours,
Helen D. Fuller, Matron

April 17, 1894

Madam:

Your favor recieved also reciept. Was very glad to learn the boys were well. I promised them I would send them 10 [cents] each on visiting day last, but for once I forgot it for which tell Jesse I must beg his pardon. I ought to send their board money but can-not untill I raise it. We are working three days A week, and not A day's pay at that. I am keeping Batchelor's hall and living as cheap as possible in order to do the very best I can which however is very poor and humiliating though it is. There are plenty of good honest men in the same boat, and unless business picks up we will be still worse off. I suppose it is unnecessary to state that I am just about wild over the outlook before me, and the further ahead I look, the more discouraging it seems, (but enough of this.) What I want to know is what can I expect in regard to the boys if things do not change and tell Jesse papa may not be able to send him much, but will do the best I can. give them my love and tell them I never forget them for A day, and oblige.

P.S. Please excuse writing and mistakes.

Yours respectfully,<br>
Wm. Miller

August 29, 1894

Madam:

I write to say that I am working though not as I should like and [am used to]. I will send some money [as soon as] possible. If you can have the patients to wait until business assumes it's old routine I am sure I can catch up. The trouble is it does not look very bright now, but you may depend on my doing my best if only you can wait until I have a fair chance. None of the men employed where I work have A full day's work and as you know it is the same or worse all over. Jesse wished me to send some colored pencils, and I have A box which I have used myself and I will send them by mail, and please tell him Auntie will try and send him the little [ring] he spoke of as soon as possible. Give them my love and oblige. Please excuse mistakes and writing.

Yours,<br>
Wm. Miller

November 1, 1894

Madam:

I recieved your letter glad to know the boys were well hope this finds them the same. You acknolege the recieving the money last sent but forgot to enclose reciept. I have been sick with grippe and malaria three weeks. had money to [send] but spent part for Doctor and medicine and am now working again half time and cannot send it and do not know when I can so if you will kindly give me the address of A Mr. Adams, [Supt. of the Poor], you refered me to some time since I will write him and see what can be done. I want to manage so my children are my own as I can take care of them if I have work, but A man can't be honest and pay his way without work and A fair chance. If I had some one to leave them with when at work I would keep them with me, and get along some way. If times do not pick up mechanic's and laborers will starve to death soon as there are hundreds just like myself. Give my love to the boys and oblige.

P.S. I supose it is unnecessary to say that this is humiliating. It speaks for itself but there is no help for it.

Yours respectfully,
Wm. Miller

June 18, 1896

Madam:

Your favor is at hand, very glad the boys are well. Jesse spoke to me [when I was to see him] about my sending him a pair of white rats he said some of the other boys had them. But if you do not object I will send him & Roy a pair of Rabbits, and as to day is his birthday I trust you will not object as he & Roy would be so pleased with them and if you are willing please write me soon as convenient and I will send them directly I get your letter. give both lot of love from papa and the rest and oblige.

Yours respectfully,
Wm. Miller

*This is the last extant letter from William Miller regarding his sons. Existing correspondence is sparse after the winter of 1894, yet William's long-distance parenting does not appear to have diminished during this time. Although his circumstances slowly improved as the depression weakened, the boys remained in the asylum until May 1900. Having left as young boys, they returned to their former homelife as adolescents.*

## Katy Bertha McCall

Charlotte McCall gave birth to an illegitimate daughter, Katy Bertha, at the Essex County Poorhouse on July 31, 1882. Illegitimate herself and abandoned in infancy, Charlotte was no stranger to the poorhouse. She raised Katy Bertha there for nearly three years, until officials removed the child under provisions of state law and placed her in the Albany Orphan Asylum. Nearly two years passed before Charlotte attempted contact with her daughter. A distance of more than one hundred miles separated them. Communication in many respects seemed fruitless. How could Charlotte, in her poverty, ever find the means of visiting the child or bringing her home? In fact, there was no home.

Several months after Katy Bertha was taken away, Charlotte left the county poorhouse to work as a domestic in a lodging house, but it was still no place to raise a child. Not knowing what to expect, but cautiously hopeful, she wrote to the asylum from Whallonsburgh, New York, in the fall of

1886. The letter marked the beginning of a four-year correspondence from that location. Charlotte may have had others write for her, however, as her letters are composed in at least three different hands.

November 28, 1886

Sir:

I hardly know to whome I am writing but trust to some one with a kind heart. Two years ago the 25 of March next my little girl Katy Bertha McCall was taken from Essex County House to the "home" in Albany. I have heard from her but once and then heard she had been sick with the measels. Now with a Mothers longing love I want to [hear] from her. I was told the keepers name was Fuller but no more and though[t] I would try & see if I could find out by you how she is if still at the home. I want to give her something for a Christmas present but do not know as you would allow me to but know no reason why you should object and if you do not please state what you would rather she would have, that is if you have a choice. I would hate to send her anything the rules of the Home would not allow her to have. Perhaps you would rather I would send you the money and you get her what you think best for her. I would dearly love to see her but know I cant and I well know she is better off where she is than with me but still I cannot give up hearing from her and if you will kindly reply to my letter you will lighten the burden of a poor and lonely mother. I am not at the County house now but have been there to see if I could hear from Bertha but they tell me nothing even if they know and act as if they would rather not be questioned. The Keeper & his wife both avoiding me the last time I called. I will inclose a stamp and hope to hear from her soon.

P.S. Do you allow the parents to visit the children if they wish to.

Yours truly,
Charlotte McCall

December 13, 1886

Dear Madam:

Your letter is before us and contents noted. Your little girl was quite seriously sick last winter with Measles but is in good health for her now.

If you wish to send her a box for Christmas you can do so, I do not care what you send as long as it is nothing that would be harmful to the child.

The [Superintendent of the Poor of Essex County] would no doubt forward the box to me if you would ask him, of course you would have to pay the express charges.

Yours respectfully,
Albert D. Fuller, Superintendent

March 9, 1887

Dear Sir:

As I wanted to hear from my little girl again I thought I would write hoping to hear from her. I am a going to send her a little something to take up her mind, some oranges and peanuts, not noing what would be good to send her. . . . It dont seem like much to send to her. If you have no objections I would like the privilige to send her a little something once in a while. How is she a getting along now. It does me lots of good to hear from her if it hant but a few lines. I would like to ask a favor of you. would you be so kind as to have Bertha's picture taken and send to me. I will send you the money to pay for your troubles. . . . tell Bertha she must divide her oranges & nuts with the rest of the little children. I am going to send her some [advertising] cards and she can divide them around with her play mates. . . . I have been to work out since she went there and havent got much for wages but will try and save so I can come and see her. tell Bertha she must hurry up and learn to write so she can write to me once in a while if her eyes will let her. this is all for this time.

With love to Bertha,
Charlotte McCall

March 17, 1887

Mr. Fuller:

I rec. your kind letter and was very glad to hear from my little girl and to hear that she was well. I am glad to think Bertha has got as good a home as she has for I think it is better than I ever had. ask her if she has any choise of what she has to play with. if she has I will send what ever she would like. . . . I though[t] I would send her a doll if she would like one. when she was with me she liked them to play with. it is 2 years this month since she went away and it seems like 3 long ones. . . . Tell Bertha she will be 5 years old the 31 day of July and if any one asks her how old she is she must try and remember so to tell them. I am going to send a dollar for the picture not knowing how much it will cost. I would like to have her stand up so I can see how big she is. Tell her she must try and see how nice she can behave when she is haven it taken. I would like to have it look natural as it can. now Bertha, you must try and be a good girl and try to do what is right. I think if she has grown since she was there as much as she did when she was with me she must be quite a big girl. this is all. with love to Bertha from,

Charlotte McCall

July 8, 1887

Dear Madam:

Your letter of the 4th inst. has been received. I want to thank you for your good nature and patient waiting for your little girls pictures. * I have so many care[s] on my mind that the matter has been delayed much longer than it ought to have been. I have had great difficulty in getting any picture on account of the childs eyes although I had pictures taken four different times still none of them would answer to send and these that I send in this letter are not at all good but the best that I could get under the circumstances.

I return the money you sent. I am glad that you are doing well and happy to be able to inform you that Bertha is well and getting along all right. She sends much love to you.

Yours respectfully,
Albert D. Fuller

July 24, 1887

Dear Sir:

I am a going to send Bertha a little some thing and thought I would write a few lines. . . . I wanted to ask you a few questions in regards to her eyes. do you think they are any better than they was when she went there. do you think she can see well eneough to learn any at school. I feel anxious to know about it. I hope that she can. her eyes look funny to me in her picture. do you know what made it. was she laughing or crying that made it look so. her picture looks better than I expected to see it on account of her eyes. I would like to have you tell me all about her eyes and herself in regards. † this is all. from,

Charlotte McCall

July 28, 1887

Dear Madam:

Your letter has been received also the package [for your daughter]. She was greatly pleased with what you sent her and thanks you for them. In the picture she was laughing not crying, this adds to the peculiar expression.

Bertha's health is now very good and she is happy and contented, but I

---

*Parents often requested photographs of their children from the asylum. For a small fee, photographs of a child or the institution buildings and grounds were provided.

†The child's problem with her eyes likely came about as a result of her bout with the measles shortly after coming to the asylum.

am afraid that she is not going to be able to learn much from books on account of her exceedingly poor eyesight. She sends much love to you.

Yours respectfully,
Albert D. Fuller, Superintendent

February 5, 1888

Dear Sir:

As it has been quite a while since I have heard from Bertha I thought I would write again and ask you if she has been well this winter. Has she been to school any yet, if so can she learn easy or does it come hard for her. I often think how glad I shall be when she gets so she can write to me. I hope her eyesight is not so poor as to hinder her learning to read. Little did I think three years ago when I bid her good-by it would be so long before I saw her again but it may be all for the best. I wish you would tell her for me to be a good girl and mind what is said to her and not to forget her lonesome Mother so far away for I never go to sleep but what I think of her & hope she is well. If it is convenient, please write just a little to let me know how she is and you will confer a great favor on a lonely woman & have my sincere thanks, please give her my love. good by for this time.

Charlotte McCall

May 28, 1888

Dear Sir:

I have been thinking of answering your kind letter which I received some time ago. I am feeling quite well now but have not been very well most of the time this spring. I wish Bertha could see the trees. they are all in bloom and smell so sweet. I have fixed a box to send to her. I send some stockings as I thought them useful. Is it so that you dress the children all alike and do not let them have the clothes that are sent to them. I have been told so but still I venture to send the stockings but if it is so will you please tell me as I will be sure about it. It was a little [comfort] thinking she wore what I sent but if she does not I blame no one of course but thought I would like to know the truth. I hope she is well and a good girl. please tell her so and give her my love.

Yours truly,
Charlotte McCall

June 6, 1888

Dear Madam:

Your kind letter of the 28 ult. has been received. I am sorry that your health has been so poor this spring, but glad to know that you are now so much better.

I believe that you think a great deal of your little girl, and it therefore gives me much pleasure to send you pleasant tidings in regard to her. She is well and has been since the date of my last letter to you.

The box that you spoke of arrived all right, and Bertha was much pleased with the contents. Of course she can have the stockings herself, and any little article that at any time you may wish to send her will be acceptable. The children dress mostly alike, but that is a point that we do not insist upon; and anything sent to a particular child is always used by them.

Bertha wishes to be remembered to you. Hoping you will write us when ever you [may] feel inclined to do so, I remain

Yours respectfully,
Albert D. Fuller, Superintendent

July 12, 1888

Mr. Fuller:

I have long neglected to write to you but have been very bussy. We have 22 cows but Mr. T. [my employer] has recently bought a new creamer & we have it a little easier. Bertha must not think I have forgotten her but I have so much to do that I have but little time to write. Tell her to be a good girl and not forget me and I will send her a present of some kind her birth-day. I live in a publick house & some days we have a very large family and there is but two of us to do [the work]. Does Berth[a] seem to realise the relation I am to her when you read my letters to her. Tell her she will be six years old the 31 of this month. I hope she is & has been well since you wrote last but if not pleas tell me when you write. I will close now with much love for Bertha and sincere thanks for your kindness in the past. I remain,

Yours Resp.,
Charlotte McCall

July 13, 1888

Dear Madam:

Your letter of the 12 inst. has been received and it gives me pleasure to be able to once more write that your little girl is well and has not been sick at all since my last letter to you.

I think that she still realizes that you are her mother. I try to have her remember you the best I can, and occasionally talk to her about you. She sends much love to you.

I am glad that you have a good situation and hope that you may retain it.

Yours respectfully,
Albert D. Fuller, Superintendent

September 30, 1888

Dear Sir:

I thought I would write to let you know Mrs. T. & I reached home safely but very tired.* Did Bertha make any trouble when she found out I had gone & is she well now. Did she say any thing about me when I was gone or did she for get me as soon as I was away. She asked me if I would come & see her visiting days, but I think I made her understand I lived too far away for that. I would like to so as to keep her memory of me fresh in her mind but I keep thinking now I have seen her it will help her to remember me, as I may [not] be able to see her again before many years. I am going to send her a box soon & I will write as often as I can get time. I often think how she asked me if I liked her. I hope you will tell her I love her dearly and she must be a good little girl to pleas mamma for I was so very lonesome I could hardly set my self at work when I got home but I try to use reason.

Remember me to your Mother please, for I took a great liking to her & know she felt for me in my troubles. . . . I remain

your grateful friend,
Charlotte McCall

November 11, 1888

Dear Sir:

I was glad to get your letter and that it contained good news of Bertha. I hope she continues to be well and that she may be all winter. . . . It seems so different to me now when I think of Bertha, the kind faces of those who care for her come to my mind and I feel so much more reconsiled being parted from her. I try hard not to be lonesome with out her for I know she has better care than I can give her. When you have time please write me and I will be very thankful. give Bertha my love and tell her to be good to please me.

Yours as ever,
Charlotte McCall

December 2, 1888

Dear Sir:

I write a few lines in hopes I can hear good news from Bertha once more before long. . . . I often think how much better off Bertha is than I was at her age and am thankful and live in hopes her whole life will be happier for haveing [such] a good home. I feel thankful to you & yours for all you have done for her and know you will have your reward hereafter, if I can give you

---

*Reference here is to Charlotte's first visit to the asylum, which took place a few days before she wrote this letter.

nothing but thanks. At Berthas age I was left without a mother and have never heard from her but once since and dont know whether she is living or not. I feel sorry to think I did not have more of a talk with you and your wife, but I could not get up courage to talk then. give my love to Bertha and tell her to be a good [girl] to please mamma.

Yours resp.,
Charlotte McCall

*Only a few letters from Charlotte exist after December of 1888. Her correspondence ceases entirely in 1890. A communication from Albert Fuller to a Jane McCall in 1892 suggests that the child's grandmother, Charlotte's mother, may have visited the girl at one time. Untypically, Katy Bertha spent nearly fifteen years at the Albany Orphan Asylum. Six days before her eighteenth birthday the asylum discharged her to the care of the same poorhouse in which she had been born.*

### Robbie Van Allen

Robbie Van Allen hailed from the infamous Van Allen "clan" of paupers in Washington County, New York, and vicinity. Little is known about this extended family aside from claims that they added to the population of the state's orphan asylums, poorhouses, prisons, and reformatories in the closing decades of the nineteenth century. Robbie's mother, Mary, placed the boy at the Albany asylum on her own initiative in January 1884. Two of Mary's teen-aged sisters, Anna and Lottie, resided there at the time. Mary herself was likely quite young, but sickly. She lived in the poorhouse for a time and worked only intermittently. Her first marriage took place in 1885 or 1886, a union which did not welcome the illegitimate infant son Robbie into the new home. Not untypically, poor widows in second marriages or single mothers of illegitimate children often had to leave their first-born behind in orphan asylums or elsewhere because of a stepfather's inability or unwillingness to provide.

Over a period of a decade Mary wrote from various locations including North Adams, Massachusetts; Shushan, New York; Bennington, Vermont; and Keene, New Hampshire. Her moves seem to have been predicated on matters of work or family.

January 8[?], 1884

Dear sir:

. . . . i have got a little boy, of course i spose you no it with out my telling you, and i want to no if you will take him there a while for me. it

takes every cent i can earn to board him and i cant keep him half clothed let
alone my self and not a soul to help me to one pennys worth and i think it is
pretty tough. if you will keep him for a few years till i could get something
ahead and could i get him back again all right. if so i should like very much
to send him. . . . let me hear from you. . . .

Yours etc.,
Mary Van Allen

January 14, 1884

Dear sir:

I, thought I would wright you A Letter to find out how robbie is getting
along. is he well does he act lonesome or is he cheerfull and happy & does
he speak of me atall and does he give much trouble to you. I am his
mother. . . . how About any one that has friends there, are they allowed to
stay over night ever . . . and will it make any diference how often i come to
see robbie or the day of the week. this is all I Can think to wright this time
except to please give this slip of paper to the woman that has the Care of
robbie & oblidge me.

Kind lady:

will you please to watch robbie A little. he has the piles real bad some
times. if you could have the Doctor give you some thing for him his little
body comes down A good deal some times. I suppose you know what the
piles Are. now please dont have him forget that hes got A mother. talk with
him about me. dont let him forget his prayers, the lords prayer & the little
prayer, he knew the most of them. I hope and pray that he will grow up to
be a Christian and to love his mother. May god love and protect him All of
his life. this is all. so good by from robbies mother. tell robbie that ma ma
wants to see him and kiss him for me & may god bless you to take good care
of my little boy. good by.

respectfully yours,
Mary Van Allen

April 24, 1885

Dear sir:

it is over A month since i have heard from robbie & therefore i thought i
would pen A few lines to you to find out how he is getting along. is he well.
oh how i would like to see him, poor little friendless boy, ma mas little angel,
lamb, pride and joy of my heart. this world is but a lonely home for me
without my little man. is he of any trouble to you. does he go to school. does he
learn good. does he know all of his ABCs. does he ever ask for me. i have not
had any work yet. have you heard from Lottie lately. how does anna like robbie.

please send me his length from his belt down. as long as he would want a dress i want to bring one to have his picture taken in when i come to see him. robbie, ma ma sends her love to you & Anna also and i will ever remain

very respectfully yours,
Mary E. Van Allen

August 15, 1885

Dear sir:

I thought i would rite A few lines to you to let you no that i am not very well. i would like to no the reason you dont let anna rite or rite your self & let me no if robbie is dead or Alive & is he contented. does he ever ask for his ma ma or has he for got me entirely. please answer soon. . . . when this reaches you i may be dead but you can Answer it just the same. if you can find me A place i will come, if not i dont know what i will do.* i havent had a days work hardly this summer. this is all.

Yours truly,
Mary E. Van Allen

August 9, 1886

Dear sir:

I was very glad to hear from robbie and know he was well and only wish that he was here with me. has he been to school any yet. does he wear pants or dresses. oh you dont know how lone some it is keeping house and have to be alone all day when my husband is working.† the lady that came to see robbie lives in the same block with me. she is an awfill nice woman. if i had robbie here he would be so much company for me and then i am so sickly all the time he would be so much help to me to bring in a little wood or water and a good many other little chores that he could do. now Mr fuller if you will please to write and let me know all about what i can do about getting him. you told the lady i could get him any time i wanted to come for him. I may not come for him untill next summer. i aint well enogh to ride so far. if he is wearing pants let me no & send me his measure. if i come for him before i will let you no about a week before hand. is annie there yet & how does she get along. is she a good girl & do you no where lottie is. . . . write as soon as you get this. . . . i remain

yours respectfuly,
Mrs. Mary Kierney

*Here Mary is requesting employment at the asylum. Many single mothers solicited Albert Fuller for jobs at the home.

†This is Mary's first reference to her husband. Note the change in name from Van Allen to Kierney.

August 10, 1886

Dear Madam:

Your letter of the 9th inst. is at hand and contents noted. Am sorry to learn that your health is no better. Robbie is well with the exception of one of his eyes which has bothered him more or less for some time but is better just now. I heard from Lottie about two weeks ago, she is well. Annie is still with me and is in good health. I just gave her the little note that you enclosed for her and she seems to be much pleased and will doubtless write to you herself before long. Her health has been good all the time since I last wrote you, that is good for her, she is not naturally as strong as some children. You can have Robbie at any time that it may be convenient for you to come for him, that is on a weeks notice. . . . Annie and Robbie both send much love to you. On receipt of this please be so kind as to drop me a line giving your street and number and some time when I am in North Adams I will call at your place and you can then make all the enquiries about Robbie that you like. I am in North Adams occasionally.

Yours respectfully,
Albert D. Fuller, Superintendent

March 16, 1888

Dear sir:

As i did not get any answer from the letter i sent you some 2 weeks ago, feeling able, i thought i would write a few lines myself to find out. . . . i feel more anxious than ever about him knowing i can have him with me this spring, you said you would send him to me. i am going to move and will send for him as soon as i get straightened around. how is he getting along. i shall be very glad to have him with me for it will take up my mind from the two i have buried since i parted with robbie. my husband is very fond of children and as we have none spared to us i know he will be kind to him. please answer as soon as received. i remain

truly yours,
Mrs. Mary Kierney

January 3, 1889

Dear sir:

i wrote to anna last monday to Come to north adams & to bring robbie if you would let him come. i have got A place of my own & think i can afford to take care of him and he can do little jobs for me & go to school. I want you to send him as though i dident no any thing about it. tell anna when she comes there for him not to tell any one when she gets to north Adams that i sent for him. i want them to think you got tired of keeping him & sent him unbeknowns to me. send word by her you cant keep him any longer, that i will have to take care of him my self. now i would have written before but have been very busy with my boarders & have not been very well. how is robbie. is he well. my place is in bennington Vt. . . . . i will be in north Adams next saturday & sunday that will be day after tomorrow & next day & like enough monday to. now write soon as you get this and oblige. now please dont say no to the favor i have asked about robbie and god will reward you. this is all so good by

ever yours,<br>
Mrs. Mary Kierney

June 9, 1890

Dear sir:

i guess you think it is about time I rote to you. i do anyway. you see i have seen so much trouble sence i rote last that it just about made me crazy, was sick a good deal And had A baby to take care of and my husband and sister anna running together all the time and had to bury my darling baby at the age of 11 months and 3 days old. he was my only comfort what time he lived for. it was right after he was born that anna came here. i thought she was going to be a Christian but she is far from it. she got in trouble at saratoga and left there so not to betray the man as he was a married man with a wife and 1 child.* [she] came right here and broke up her own sisters home. i could have taken robbie if it had not been for her destroying all that i had to lean upon, that was my husband. it just about killed me. he was good as he could be to me till she come here. Well how is my little boy robbie. i hope he is well and a good boy. i am coming there this summer if i live. i am at work. . . . my husband is working at fitch gorge [M]ass. he is A good deal better to me since anna left town than he was when she was her[e]. i will have to close by saying good evening. please ans soon as i want to hear from my boy. please give this to him, read it to him please.

Dear little robbie:

do you no you have got a ma ma. she aint forgot you and never will. she is coming to see you before long. be a good boy and rite to your ma. so good night. robbie you had as good a little brother as ever lived and ma ma had to put him in the ground. your ma wants to see you awfull bad. be good and good night with a kiss to my boy.

---

*Anna had been indentured and was living away from the asylum when this incident occurred. She was probably seventeen or eighteen years old at the time.

Mr fuller was my husband there this last winter. he told me he saw you and said you wanted to see him again, you wanted to tell him somthing.

Mrs. Mary Kierney

October 26, 1890

Dear Sir:

i thought i would write you A few lines to let you know where I am. i am in Keene N.H. at the present time. i am going home on A visit & then we go to keeping house here i guess. i dont know where anna is now & dont want to, if she will only let me & mine alone. well Dear Sir how is little robbie. i hope he is well and grows big i suppose. does he learn well. how i would like to see him but dont know as i ever will. my husband aint very good to give me money to travel with. did he call there last winter he said he did. well my health is not very good any of the time. i burried my little boy last march . . . now i havent any. if my man would let me i would take him. if you would let me have him but i spose i cant have him for i would not like to take him & have my man abuse him but will come and see him if i ever can get money enough to get there. please answer soon i want to hear from him and oblige. please read the little note to robbie and tell him who its from.

Dear little son robbie:

mama thought she rite A few lines to let you no she was well and I hope you are the same. do you go to school and are you a good boy. mama will come to see you some day. I will bid you good morning with a kiss from your mama.

Mrs. Mary E. Kierney

October 31, 1890

Dear Madam:

Your favor of the 26th. inst. is just at hand. I am sorry Anna has been so mean to you; if at any time you find out where she is you let me know.

Robbie is perfectly well, infact I think is enjoying better health than ever before. Your husband called here about a year ago but I have not seen him since. I am sorry that you lost your little boy, you must be very lonely without him.

In regard to Robbie, would be glad to let him go with you but am afraid that your husband would not want it so. If you should change your address be sure and let me know at once so that I could reach you at any time if anything should happen to Robbie.

Yours respectfully,<br>Albert D. Fuller, Superintendent

February 15, 1891

Mr. Fuller:

would [have] sent this before but have been sick abed since it was rote. i now take the oppertunity to pen you a few lines letting you know i am still in Keene. i get along pretty good but not so well as i wish. my health is not as good as it might be. well I will change the subject. how is robbie. i wish i could see him. i spose he is almost a man now. tell him his little playmate georgie . . . he used to play with at north adams, only six months older than he is, boards out and goes to school and does chores for his board. he can milk the cows and harness A horse. he feeds the pigs & all the rest and the little girl he used to call his baby who is 7 now, she had her leg broke last month and was hurt inwardly besides to. these are children of my husband[s] sister. i can not think of anything more to write this time except here is a letter enclosed for robbie. please give it to him and say for me i would like to have him answer it if he can and oblige. PS please write soon. please excuse bad writing and all mistakes for my arm and hand trembles so bad.

yours truly,

Mrs. Mary E. Kierney

March 7, 1891

Dear Madam:

Your letter of Feb. 15th was received a few days since. Your little boy Robert was very much pleased to get the letter you sent him.

He is quite short for his age, but fleshy and quite strong. He is growing up to be a strong boy. I think he has entirely forgotten the children you mention whom he used to play with.

He sends ever so much love to you.

Your friend,

Albert D. Fuller, Superintendent

*Mary Van Allen Kierney's letters stop in the fall of 1892 as do any possible connections between mother and son. She married a second time and in the ensuing years had at least four surviving children. Although the circumstances of Robbie's release are unknown, he was discharged from the Albany Orphan Asylum in May 1898. Alone, he spent years searching for family and friends and was ultimately reunited with his mother, almost by chance, more than twenty five years after their initial separation. The following letter was sent to the superintendent of the Albany asylum from Auburn, New York, some time between 1911 and 1916.*

*[Undated]*

*Dear Sir:*

*Just a line to let you know I am well and happy. I thank you for information you gave me to find my Mother. I was in search of her a number of years and but for you I do not think I would have even found her. I gave her up as dead and gone at one time and went off to sea for eight years. I have found her at last and am living with her. I lived with my Aunt . . . all winter and when Mother saw about the wreck in the Hoosic Tunnel in which one flag man, Mr. Reuben K., was killed with three others, wrote to my aunt and found that I was living with her in North Adams. she wrote for me to come home. . . .*

*My mother isn't in very good health since a year ago when she went through an operation in the Samaritan Hospital in Troy, New York. . . . I have a half brother with us here in Auburn and another half-brother and two half-sisters in care of the state of Mass. I owe to you for my happiness of enjoying a home with a mothers presence and I am truly Sir,*

*Mr. Robert Van Allen*

## Charles and Cora Loveland

Letters and photographs kept parents in contact with their asylum children, but years often passed before they might see one another again. Mary Loveland knew she had waited too long when word came that eleven-year-old Cora was dead. The child had been in the asylum for five years with her older brother, Charles. Mary wrote once or twice every month and sent special notes along to the children. But money, time, distance, and circumstances kept them apart.

Mary's first husband worked as a laborer. He died sometime shortly before Charles and Cora came to the institution. Two other siblings remained behind. Emma, the oldest, was placed out with another family, while young Willie stayed with the mother. During her correspondence with the asylum, Mary moved a number of times, but only short distances in and around the vicinity of Saratoga Springs, New York. She lived for a while at the poorhouse, later resided with her parents, worked out briefly as a domestic, and finally made a home with her second husband, with whom she had another child. Cora and Charles remained excluded from the new family. Mary made no mention of the stepfather's refusal to support them. In fact, her letters made no mention of them coming home at all.

February 15, 1888

Dear Sir:

as it is With pleasure i now Will answer your kind and Welcome letter that i recived in Doe time. i Was happie to heare from the Childern and to heare that thay Was Well. it makes me feel bad When i think that thay are so [far] off from me but i Will have to put up With it. i hoape thay Will not be loney [because] i am. Will you be so kind to have both of thir pictures taken if it Will not be to mutch truble if i send you the money. you can Write and let me no.

yours respectfully,
Mary E. Loveland

February 23, 1888

Dear Madame:

I am very sorry to be obliged to inform you that your little girl Cora is sick. She has membraneous croup. We hope that she will recover. . . . (S)he is having every attention that is possible to give just as good as my own children could have under similar circumstances. The disease however is a treacherous one as you probably know and we can not tell how it may terminate. We will however do every thing that lies in our power for your child and she shall want for nothing and all will be done for her good that can be. Will write you again in the morning. Cora is sleeping quietly now as I write.

Yours respectfully,
Albert D. Fuller, Superintendent

February 24, 1888

Dear Madam:

I drop you this line as I promised in regard to your little girl. After I wrote you last from say nine to twelve o'clock to day she was quite bad much worse than at any time but from twelve until six this evening she was very much better. Since that time she has had two or three times of hard coughing and great difficulty in getting her breath she is more quiet just now and is sleeping fairly well.

The disease as you know is a treacherous one and we can not tell how it may terminate but are doing everything that lies in our power for her and she is having the attention of two good physicians. Will write you again in the morning.

Yours respectfully,
Albert D. Fuller, Superintendent

February 27, 1888

Mr. Fuller Dear Sir:

i have just got your letters and Was veary Sorry to hear that little Cora Was sick as she is but i hoape that i Will hear that She is beter next time. thank you So much for beang So kind to her and me. it makes me feal veary bad to think that she is So far off but i Will trust in you and god for taking care of her.

Dear Children:

i am Well and hoap When i hear from you i Will heare that you are Well. Cora i have just got a letter from [your sister] Emma. She is well. Cora you must be a good girl and do What that thay Want you to do So you can git Well. . . . Well i cant think of eny thing more to Write this time So i Will Close for now. i send My love to you both and Was glad to have you send me your love. good by

from,
your mother

February 28, 1888

Dear Madam:

Just a line to say that Cora is doing nicely since I wrote you this morning. The Doctor was in to see her a short time since and felt very much encouraged in regard to her. I will write you again in the morning.

Yours Respectfully,
Albert D. Fuller, Superintendent

March 7, 1888

Mr. Fuller Dear Sir:

i got your letter and Was So glad to [hear] from the Children and that Cora Was gitten better. i thank you and your Wife so mutch for taking care of Cora. She never Was so Sick in her life before but i am So glad that She is gitten [a]long now.

Yours Respectfully,
Mrs. Loveland

March 20, 1888

Dear Madam:

Your letter to your children was received this morning; they were glad to hear from you and were pleased with the pretty cards that you sent them.

Cora has had a slight relapse since I last wrote you, but is [much better] now, and is doing well. Your boy is in good health, and they both send a great deal of love to you. They are always glad to hear from you and I hope you will write frequently, if only a few lines. . . .

Yours Respectfully,
Albert D. Fuller, Superintendent

May 4, 1888

Dear Sir:

i received your kind and Welcome letter a long time a go and Was glad to heare from the Childern but i Was not Well so i Could not Write. i am So i Set up but i Cant not Work. i am under the Doctere Care yet. i never Was So Sick in my life. did you git the large pictures that i Sent to the Childern. Mr Fuller [someone] Sed that you had Cora age 10 years and She is 7 years old Charley is 9 years old. Well i Close for now hoaping to [hear] from you soon.

Mary Loveland
oblige

May 17, 1888

Dear Madam:

Your letter of yesterday was received this morning. I am glad to know that you are in better health and glad to be able to inform you that both your children are well and have been since I last wrote you.

They are going to school every day and although they do not learn as rapidly as some children, still are doing fairly well. They are well disposed, and I have never yet had to punish them in any way and hope I never shall be obliged to do so.

They are glad to know of your improved health, and send a great deal of love to you; also to their uncle Charlie, and especially to their little brother Willie.

Hoping that the next time I hear from you, you will have recovered your health entirely. I remain,

Yours Respectfully,
Albert D. Fuller, Superintendent

June 11, 1888

Dear Sir:

as it is With pleasure i Will Write a few lines to heare from the Childern. i am trying to W[o]rk out now but i am not veary Well but i [am gaining my health]. Well i Will Say a few Words to Charlie and Cora now. . . .

Dear Childern:

i am to W[o]rk to Saratoga now. i left home Satday. the foaks Was all Well or Common. [Your little brother] Willie Was Well and Erwin Was Well and When i got to Saratoga, Emma i Saw She is Well and i hope that this few lines Will find you boath Well to. Well Charlie and Cora you must be good Childern and try to lern your lesson When you are in School and do as your are told, then you Will not have eny truble to git a long in this Wirld. Well i must Close for to day hoping to heare from you Soon. With love to you both, this is from your kind and loving mother to Charlie and Cora Loveland. good by for Now. Write soon.

Mary E. Loveland

August 23, 1888

Mr. Fuller Dear Sir:

i got you letter in [due time]. Was happie to heare frome the Childern and that thay Ware Well. . . . What doe you think about my Commin to See them. i Would like to See them veary mutch. do you think it Will make them uneasy if i Should Come to See them. So What do you think. doe thay ever Say eny thing about me Comeing. Will you be so kind to tell me What you think about it. it seams to me as though i must Come to See them but i Want to do What is for the best. . . .

From<br>Mrs. Mary E. Loveland

August 29, 1888

Dear Madam:

Your favor of the 23rd. inst. has been received. Cora is not quite as strong as usual but I think will feel stronger as the cooler weather comes on she is not sick at all but not quite as plump as before her sickness and color not so bright but she is happy and does not appear to feel sick at all. Charlie with the exception of a sore throat for a few days has been in excellent health. He is in good spirits has a good color and a splendid appetite.

The children enjoyed [the asylum's summer excursion] to Lake George exceedingly. Charlie and Cora both send a great deal of love to you. I am glad to know that you think of coming to see them this Fall.

Write as often as you wish.

Yours respectfully,<br>Albert D. Fuller, Superintendent

October 23, 1888

Mr. Fuller Dear Sir:

i got your kind and Welcome letter and Was happie to hear from my childern and that thay Was Well and in good health, for that is the mane thing. Well, now i Will Write to Charlie and Cora. Well as i have Changed my name now i have [married again], change from Loveland to Walters. . . .

Dear Charlie and Cora:

i am Well as Common and hoape this Will find you the Same. We ar all Well but your uncle Ned he is not Well. Willie Send[s] his love to you. Well i dont think of mutch to Write this time. i am married to Mr Walters. Write soon, from your mother to Charlie and Cora. now i Will tell you What Willie Says, he Says Willie Loveland is my name, playing [horse ?] is my game, fore years old is my age and in to bisness i Will in gage. love to you.

Mary E. Walters

December 7, 1890

Mr. Fuller Dear Sir:

i read you letter some time ago. Was glad to hear from my Childern and that thay Was Well. i hurd that Charlie Was not thar. is he thar or not. if he is not thar, Will you tell me Whare he is and Who has got him and how far off he is. it makes me feel bad to think of it for it Seems to me that i Will not See them a gain but i hope that i Shall Some time. . . .

Mary E. Walters
Oblige

December 10, 1890

Dear Madam:

. . . I cannot understand why people should wish to alarm or annoy you by telling you that Charlie is not here. He is still here and both he and Cora are both well and have been ever since I last wrote you. . . .

Yours Respectfully,
Albert D. Fuller, Superintendent

October 23, 1892

Mr. Fuller Dear Sir:

i Will [Write] to you a gain to heare from the Childern. it has ben along time sence i have hird from them. now i Will Say a few Wirds to them. . . .

Dear Childern:

. . . We ar all Well now except bad Colds. We have got a nather little girl. She is fore month old. her name is gracey. i Would rote before now but i have had So much to do that i did not git time . . . So i Will try to do better now. . . . With love to you from your mother good night.

Mary E. Walters

December 27, 1892

Dear Madame:

I am very sorry to be obliged to inform you of the death of your daughter Cora which occurred at 9:30 a.m. today. It was entirely unexpected, had been ailing a little for two or three days but was not seriously sick until this morning when she was taken with convulsions and died in one of them. Her remains will be interred in the Albany Rural Cemetery. If at any time in the future you want to have them removed to some other place it can be done. Everything possible was done for the child. With much sympathy I remain,

> Yours sincerely,
> Albert D. Fuller, Superintendent

December 29, 1892

Dear Sir:

i got your Welcome letter of the 27 last [night]. it makes me feel veary Sad to heare that my little girl Cora is ded but i think that she is better off then i am but it seems hard to me be Cause i did not See her. i have Wated to long to See her in this World but i Will try to [?] so i Can meet her in a better World than this. if you Will mark the Place Whare She is [buried] if i live i Will have her Body took up and put beside her father. if her deth is in the paper Will you plese send it to me. i do thank you so much for your [kindness]. Mr. Fuller Will you [be] so kind to send me the address to the place Whair Charlie is [on indenture]. i do feel as if i must here from him. Well i Cant Write to Cora no more. So i Will Close for now With best Whises to you. Plese tell me When she Was Barried and What time, Will you.

> Mrs. Thomas Walters

January 17, 1893

Dear Mr. Spaulding [Overseer of Poor, Saratoga County]:

Your valued favor at hand. Glad to know that you met [Charlie] Loveland and that Mr. L is pleased with him [and the indenture agreement]. I was a little worried about sending [Charlie] on alone from Saratoga but an engagement in Troy prevented my going farther than Saratoga with him. The sister Cora died suddenly in December at this place with convulsions probably of enemic character. I notified the mother and held remains for nearly a week but the Mother was not able to come on and so the remains were interred in the Albany Rural Cemetery. Everything is moving nicely with us just now. Glad to know that yourself & family are well. My own family are in excellent health & among the 610 children of the asylum we have but two in bed and they are not seriously ill.

> With kindest regards,
> Albert D. Fuller, Superintendent

*Mary Loveland's correspondence with Albert Fuller ends with the death of Cora and the indenture of Charlie.*

## Daisy and Emma Evans

A husband's desertion more often than not spelled immediate destitution for poor mothers with small children. The sense of loss and abandonment was certainly no less severe than in the case of the death of a spouse, but circumstances might also include a volatile mix of anger, abuse, and alcoholism. Emily Evans's husband, David, worked as a boss spinner in a wool mill. In the summer of 1883, he left his wife with three small children, all under four years of age. He was said to have been a "moderate drinker" and, though no signs of family violence are apparent, Emily feared his return. Reluctantly, she placed the two older girls in the Albany asylum while she and the baby boarded for a while with her husband's sister in Catskill, New York. Emily eventually moved in search of work (possibly in textile mills) from Catskill in Green County to Pownall, Vermont, and finally to Waterford in Rensselaer County, New York. Emily worked hard and persevered, but the weight of her burden left her weary, distraught, and desperate.

July[?] 29, 1883

Mr. Fuller sir:

as it was Convenient to write a Few lines I thought to write to you and fine out about the Children, if they are well. please write and let me know about them. I am working in Catskill, Green [County]. do the Children Ever ask for me. is daisey walking anny better and gaining strength. if you want anny help, please let me know. I am verry lonny with out them and ansuer this Letter soon please. . . . heare is a pocket Book for Emma. I will come up and see them soon and would like to sent them some monny but I pay my husband Sister 8 dollars a . . . [month] . . . for the baby and my self . . . and my board takes all I Earn. . . . i think some times why it is that I do suffer so mutch in having so mutch trobble but god will be and so [I try] to make the best of it and do the best I can. the mills in pownal [Pownal, Vt.] stop and the work in stottville [Columbia County ?] is slack, so I came heare [to Catskill] to worke. Excuse this letter. I am heart broken and wearry. if the children is well and happy then I am more Contented. i am thankful that they have such a good place and god have put in your mind to see to them. I feel thankful to you. . . . I will close.

from,<br>Emily Evans

December 9, 1883

Mr. Fuller sir:

I reseive your kind and wellcome Letter. how is the Children. are they well. do they Ever speake of home and Cry. if anny one comes after them dont let them see the Children or Have them. dont let Evans see them or have them. please write and Let me know a bout them. How is little daisey. is she awalking anny better. let me know about [her].

from,
Emily Evans

June 9, 1884

Mr. Fuller sir:

I was up to albany last weake to see the Children and please let me know how they are. Emma is not verry well is she. i thought she look as if she was sick. has she Been sick or else she frets fore home. please let me know about her do, for she is all i have. Emma and daisey, may god protect them the little darling[s]. fore I am heart broken fore them and if i had things to keep house with i would take in worke . . . Mrs. Fuller can you make up monny fore me, o kind friend, so i Can take the Children out. i have my self to keep and 8 dollars for the baby Bord and I Cant Earn nothing to keep house with. please help me or i will die brokenhearted. please answer this. i think Emma gets good care but she is home sick and i am sick for her. oh my Darling little Children how i mist them. for the love of god and heaven may some one help me to get them together . . . thy will be done.

Emily Evans

July 7, 1884

Mr. Fuller Dear sir:

I reseive your kind letter in dew time and glad to hear from you. I would like to See the Children but you have a particular day to Come [and] I Cant always come on that day on Thirsday be Cause I Cant get away anny day to leave my work.* my love to the children. please answer this. let me hear from them.

Emily Evans

*Visitation policy at the asylum, one day per month, severely restricted contact between parents and children. Parents many times simply had to forego the monthly visit or make the trip under a certain degree of hardship.

December 8, 1884

Dear Sir:

in Regard to the Children i intend to take them out. i give you a weake notice next tuesday afternoon, aweake from to morrow and I thank you fore your kindness to me and them. is the Children well, Emma and Daisey Evans. please write.

truly yours,
Emily Y. Evans

*Emily's anxiety over the separation from her children seemed her driving force. It was perhaps that emotional intensity that brought her children home within eighteen months despite the fact that Emily's situation had likely improved but little.*

## The Patterson Children

Poor single mothers might make purposeful decisions regarding the use of the orphan asylum in their struggle to survive, but very often the decision would be made for them. Roxy Patterson's husband, a farmer, died in 1893, leaving her the sole support of the family. Montgomery County officials forcibly removed her six dependent children from their home and brought them to the Albany Orphan Asylum in August of that year. The oldest boy, Ira, an epileptic, was subsequently sent to a hospital in Amityville on Long Island. The other children were all under ten years of age. Despite Roxy's vehement protests, the asylum quickly arranged for the indenture or adoption of all the younger children except for five-month-old Lena, who died in infancy. By the language and tenor of her letters, Roxy was a fiercely dedicated, loving, and anxious mother with strong Christian principles. Others, however, branded her unfit to raise her children. Nineteenth-century standards of proper motherhood wrenched many families apart indefinitely and forced single mothers, in particular, to justify or alter their lifestyles, or to suffer the consequences. Roxy Patterson's letters are addressed from Amsterdam, New York.

February 1, 1894

Mr. Alaxander Sir:*

as i have Just found out your address I will rite to you to see if i can hear from my Children. i am the Mother of the Patterson Children that Mr.

---

*Roxy Patterson was writing here to J. H. Alexander, Superintendent of the Poor of Saratoga County. The letter was forwarded to Albert Fuller for his reply.

Charlie W. Spaulding of Greenfield Fetched to the Orphans Asylum last August. the names of the Children is Ira Patterson, Lizzie Patterson, Minnie Patterson, Annie Patterson, and Clarance Patterson but little Lena May, that was my Dear little baby, i heard that she is dead, but she had been dead 2 weeks before i hird of her death and will you please to be So kind as to rite to me and let me know how my Dear children is all getting a long and are they all there. they told me when they took my children a way from me that they would keep them there untill i give them leaf to let them go and i have not given them any leaf to take any of the children away from there only Ira, the boy that haves fits. i gave my consent for him to be taken to the Hospital to see if he could be cured of his fits for he does suffer so much and if he cant be cured I want him brought to me, or if he can be cured, when ever Ira is taken from the Hospitle I forbid them taking him any whare else but bring him to me and will you please to give me the Keeper[s] Addres of the Hospital where Ira is. will you please rite back and let me no how the children is but oh if i could see them and have them with me I would come and see them but oh the thoughts of leaving them again. if i should come up there to see them and they would hate to have me come away and leave them. so i have not been to see them. but there is no rest nor peace on Earth for me now without my children with me. now please rite soon to me for my heart does ake and i do want to hear from the children so bad that i do not know what to do i will rite the directions on the other side. this is from,

Mrs. Roxie S. Patterson

March 17, 1894

Dear Madam:

I now will answer your kind letter which i received some time ago. but as i have had Trouble on my mind and as i have been trying to save my farm so that my Dear Children Could have it left for them I have not been able to rite before as i did expect to come up there and see the children before this time. but as things has turned out i cant come to see them. so i rite to you to find out how the Children are and to let you no that i am as well as usal and i hope those few lines will find you well and enjoying good health and also that the Children are well. . . . wall i have understood that Minnie . . . has been taken away. i hope you will please be so kind as to write and let me know their Full name whare Minnie is. will you write to me the Directions of the Hospital whare Ira is so i can rite and Find out how Ira is for i have not hird from him Since he was taken there and it does seem as though i never should see the Dear child again. please to be sure and rite to me the Mans Full Name whare Minnie is and the day of the Month that they took her there. Lizzie and Annie and little Clarance, they are with you i suppose.

rite and let me know if they are. if not will you rite and let me no whare they are. but i hope you will keep them there with you untill i give you order to let them go, or untill i can come and see my children for i shall come there and see the children as soon as i can get money to come with, if the Lord is Willing and Nothing happens. for my heart does ake to see my Dear Children once more and I do pray God to bless my Dear Children and to Comfort them and that they may take up their cross and Follow our Dear Savior which is in heaven. . . . tell the children to be good and Trust in the Lord and he will take care of them for I am Trusting in the Lord my Saviour for the Lord knoweth my heart as he knoweth all things and he will bless us and help us through this world of sin and sorrow. I will now close for this time. i hope you will not be affended of my riting for i do want to hear from my children so bad. excuse my mistakes and poor riting for this time this is from Mrs. Roxie S. Patterson. . . . I send my love to all the children and to you. good by.

Roxy Patterson

April 17, 1894

Mrs Fuller:

will you please send me the Indenture papers, if that is the right name for them, for Minnie Bell Patterson. Her mother is trying to get her away from me and my lawyer wishes you to send me these papers and also an [authorized] copy of the commital papers. . . . P.S. We like Minnie very much and she thinks everything of us and feels very bad to think that she may have to go with her folks who she does not like. her mother is a very improper [person] to have charge of her which I am going to prove.

Daniel McKenzie

April 21, 1894

Dear Madam:

I desire a copy, authenticated, of the commitment by Superviser Spaulding of Greenfield, Sar. Co., N.Y. of the infant children of Mrs. Roxy Patterson and especially of the child Minnie Bell Patterson now living with Daniel McKenzie of Wilton, Saratoga Co., N.Y. Mrs. Patterson is making an effort through the Supreme court to reclaim the child. . . . The little girl has a good home, is kindly treated, well fed and clothed and carefully watched over night and day. they love her and she loves her adopted parents and her home. Please answer at once. I am,

Truly Yours
Ira D. Roods
Attorney and Counsellor at Law

*Roxy Patterson's poverty made her neither passive nor resigned to an intrusive welfare system. Determined not to lose her parental control, she appears to have carried her case to the highest state courts. Ultimately, the outcome is unknown. Roxy may have been successful in reuniting her family, perhaps even under protest of the children themselves. Certainly her efforts did not cease.*

### Agnes and Mary Rose

Physical abuse often forced women to abandon their children. Sick and "insane" according to her own account, Amelia Rose sent her two young daughters, Agnes and Mary, to the Albany Orphan Asylum while she recuperated in a Burlington, Vermont, hospital. No information exists on this family other than facts culled from the few pieces of correspondence presented here. Amelia's husband, Peter, moved from Ticonderoga, New York, where they had been keeping house together, to Three Rivers, Massachussetts, where he worked and boarded with his brother. Peter Rose requested the return of the children to his care but poor-law authorities denied him custody. He was said to be earning but one dollar per day, not enough to properly support a family. Rose maintained contact with the children over the years, however, and apparently visited them from time to time. The girls' mother eventually made her home in Plattsburgh, New York, where she worked to support herself, but was clearly cognizant of her financial and perhaps her emotional inability to care for her children.

May 14, 1888

Dear sir:

I wish you would write and let me [know] how my tow little girls Agness and Mary rose [are] as thay are in your Care. i am hear to work for my [own living]. the reson i left him is cause he abuse me. i could not stand it. i am allways sick so i could not take Care of the Children my self. so [the Superintendent of the Poor] took them to you. as i herd say there father live[s] in Ticonderoga where we spouse to keep house with him. i would [be] very much pleased if you would rite to me and let me [know] how my Children are as it rite for a mother to [know]. if i had plenty of money i would come and see them and have a long talk with you. my harte longs for to see my little girls. hope thay are well. please grant this favor. no more for present. good day. tell them i am alone.

Mrs. Amelia Rose

December 16, 1888

Mr. Albert D fuller:

please inform me of my Children Dear sir as I have been very sick for all most for one year now. i have been in the hospital in burlington [Vermont] but i have got back in Plattsburgh. i have got back to work. i am riting to you to find out if my Children are well an in good health. as for me i am as well as can be expected. give them my love. i am sorry i cant go to see them. as soon [as] i get able i am commin to see my Children once more. What is the fair. i would have riten before but i have been insane for six month now. trubles is the cause. [oh] how i wish i was with my tow little girls once moor. i could be contented. i love my Children but i cant be with them for am not able to take care of them at present. i now will Close for the present. please rite. give my love to Aggie an Mary.
truly yours,

> good by,
> Mrs. Amelia Rose

December 14, 1888

Dear Sir:

How are my children get along. I received your last and long expected letter a few days since. Will you please write me when I can bring them here with me? I'm at work here in the mill & boarding with my brother and [can] keep them here just as well as not. Now please write me by return mail when I can come for them and I will be there some time next month.

> Yours Most Respectfully,
> Peter Rose, Jr.

January 15, 1889

Dear sir:

[I] write you again in regard to the Rose children. [the father's] friends here say not to let him have the children. his uncle has written there where he is to find out how he is situated. he gets one dollar per day and has to pay his board out of that and the children board would have to be paid out of it and he would soon run under and be in debt. he is in debt here now for his board and theirs. should have written before but have been so bussy had not time.

> verry truly yours,
> J. Woodward
> Overseer of the Poor

January 17, 1889

Dear Sir:

. . . . I agree with you decidedly that it is hardly safe to allow the children to go with the father under the present condition of things. We will endeavor to carry out your suggestion in the matter.

With kind regards, I remain,

Yours very respectfully,
Albert D. Fuller, Superintendent

December 8, 1889

Dear Sir:

Yours recd. of one year ago. I would like to have you write and let me know how the children are and write oftener. Send my love to the children.

Yours respectfully,
Peter Rose

November 26, 1895

Mrs. Fuller:

Can you inform me if my daughter is dead, Mamey [Mary] i mean. You please inform me if so.

Yours,
Peter Rose

*Subsequent correspondence regarding Agnes Rose indicates that at some point the asylum placed her out on indenture. Based on the father's final written inquiry, Mary may have died in the asylum some time in 1895 although asylum records neither confirm nor refute the fact.*

## Charlie Sanders

Many widows and deserted mothers turned to prostitution to survive. Saratoga County officials believed that Susie Sanders was just such a woman. They considered her unfit for motherhood. Asylum registration books reported Susie as a poor widow but added also that she was "a prostitute and unfit to have the bringing up of the boy—is now living with a number of negroes and Italians . . . near the Catholic cemetery."

Susie's husband, a Canadian immigrant and a baker by trade, died of heart disease sometime before 1881. She brought her three-year-old son, Charlie, from their home in Saratoga Springs to the Albany asylum for the first time in December of that year. At the age of seven Charlie was returned to his mother, but after only six months Susie's poor health forced her to seek shelter for the boy once again. Young Charlie was on a train heading home to Saratoga Springs for a second time in June of 1887 when word came that the boy's mother had "misrepresented" herself. Poor-law authorities seized Charlie before she could see him and returned him the next day to the asylum. Shattered by the incident, Susie spent the next five years attempting to prove her worthiness as a parent but never acquired custody of the boy.

October 11, 1886

My Dear little Charlie:

I now write you these few lines to let you know that I am well and hope you are the same. Charlie, Did Harry come to see you this month. the 29 of this month is your birthday and I wish I was there so I could see you. Charlie I am comming down to see you just as quick as possible but I have had the face ache for the last three four days. now Charlie be a good boy and mind Mr Fuller and try and go to school every day. answer this as soon as you can from your mother. *

Mrs. Susie Sanders

January 17, 1887

Dear little Charlie:

I now sit down to pen you a few lines to let you know that I am well and hope when these lines reaces you they may find you the same. Charlie, I want you to be a good little boy and mind your teacher and try to learn your letters. Charlie I am going to move to Albany in the spring. Charlie did Harry come and see you last month. . . . Charlie it snows here every day so it is very bad walking. I will not be down to see you befor spring because it is very hard times up here. this is all I can think of any more from your loving Mother to her dear little son Charlie.

Mrs. Susie Sanders

January 20, 1887

Dear Madam:

Your letter of the 17th inst. is before me and has been read to Charlie as you desired. In reply would say that he is quite well and sends his love to you and the rest of his friends. He says that he is trying to be a good boy, that he knows his letters pretty well and will soon be learning to read. Harry called to

---

*Indications are that Susie Sanders may have been illiterate and had others write for her since this letter and those following are written in a clearly different hand. Harry is a much older brother who worked to support himself.

see him last visiting day. He will be pleased to have you call on him when you come to Albany.

Yours respectfully,
Albert D. Fuller, Superintendent

June 13, 1887

Dear Sir:

Mrs. Susan Sanders, mother of Charles Sanders, a boy 9 years of age, now in your charge . . . wishes to have the child returned to her as she says that she has a good home for him. You will therefore release him to her, if consistent with your rules. . . .

[Respectfully] yours,
A. W. Shepherd
Supervisor [of the Poor, Saratoga County]

June 18, 1887

Superintendent:

The mother of the boy Charles Sanders has, as I have learned from the Police, misrepresented to me her situation, and I have therefore declined to allow her to take the child, and have decided to recommit him to your care. The officer who takes the child will doubtless inform you as to the circumstances.

Yours Respectfully,
A. W. Shepherd
Supervisor [of the Poor, Saratoga County]

June 24, 1887

Sir:

You Sent Charley on the Morning traine and they took him too Fort Edward and then they brought him back too Saratoga and put him in the Balesman[s] Care and they took him too town Hall. I was too meat him on the 3 O' Clock train. Mr Fuller I have A good Home fore him & live way back in the Country. I dont See why they did not let me have him iff I came theire my self. will you let me have him. Mr Fuller I am almost crasy about him. Mr Fuller will you please answer this letter because I am sick in the head over him. . . .

Mrs. Susie Sanders

June 30, 1887

Dear Sir:

I received your kind and Welcome letter and was so glad too hear from Charley. I dont see why they took him Away from me. I am A going too see the Supervisor A gaine, and get Another permite too come after him, because I have A nice home in the Country and every thing nice in the house too live with. I have been sick A bed ever Since they took him Away from me, and I feel real bad about it. Mr. Fuller will you please tell Charley that you have herd from his Mother. Kiss Charley fore me and tell him I will be theire too See him as soon as I can. So this is all.

Good bye.
From,
Mrs Susie Sanders

April 23, 1890

Dear Sir:

Please release Charlie Sandy [sic] and allow his mother Susan Sandy [sic] the bearer to take charge of him and oblige.

Yours Respectfully,
D. Coleman
Supervisor [of the Poor, Saratoga County]

April 25, 1890

Dear Sir:

I am in receipt of your esteemed favor of the 23rd inst., requesting the discharge of Charles Sanders to his mother Susan Sanders.

We desire to honor any order that you may give in the matter and although our rules require two weeks notice in, case of discharge, I have in this matter waived that right and told the mother she could call for the child within three days, that is Monday morning next.

May I ask this favor of you; a few years since I sent the boy home to the mother on the order of one of your predecessors in office. At that time quite a talk was made and I was censured for so doing, as some people said the mother was not a proper character to have charge of him. Will you kindly have a little talk with the Police Justice of your village in regard to the matter? I do not remember now just who the people were who found fault the other time, perhaps he might know. If after talking with him you think that it might be [best] to take a different action in the matter than already arranged for, kindly telegraph me at once at my expense. Please do not misunderstand me. I simply want to carry out your desires in such a way as to avoid any disagreeable features to yourself or us which might arise.

If I do not hear from you will let the mother have the child at time stated. I remain,

Yours respectfully,
Albert D. Fuller, Superintendent

Western Union Telegram
[Undated]
Do not give up Charles Sanders. Will inform the mother.

D. Coleman
Supervisor

October 4, 1892
Dear Sir:
Mr fuller i want you to please Be So kind when Mr Seldon, [Supervisor of the Poor] comes down to inquire a Bout Charley, to please to put in a kind woord for me to git him and i will be ever so mutch oblige to you. if you will pleas to ancer this note and you will oblige me very much.

Mrs. Susie Sanders

*Charlie Sanders was finally released from the Albany asylum at the age of fifteen on July 4, 1893, not to the care of the mother but into the custody of his older brother, Harry, who worked in a glass factory and had a place for the boy.*

## Annie Belle Sunderland

The hard winters of northern New York frightened Mary Rowley. She had lost one husband to consumption and a second to the "crasey house," a victim of sunstroke. Both men had been canallers on the Champlain Canal. Mary was very poor and illiterate. Her only skills were as a domestic, and she put those to use cleaning other peoples houses and working in a boarding house, where she found she could "[earn] a little more than . . . in a privet house." But the work was hard, tiresome, and lonely and left her barely enough time to find someone to write for her every couple of weeks.

Mary's oldest daughter, Annie Belle, was sent to the Albany Orphan asylum from the poorhouse in Whitehall, New York, at the age of eleven. Two younger children by Mary's second marriage remained behind. By Mary's accounts she was a simple but hard working, loving, and responsible parent struggling against impossible odds to reunite her family. Her husband's mental debilitation and her own poverty and ignorance, together with exhausting labor, low and unpredictable wages, harsh winters, and few opportunities left her frustrated at knowing that her best effort was simply not good enough.

September 6, 1887

[Dear Sir]:

I hope you will pardone me for writing you few words in ragard to my lettle gril that I have sand to you by Mr Cook our poor master. I hard last week that you was going to give her away to some boday. of [course] I give you my garil to breng her houp as a good gril for I could [not] see to her my self for I had to work but if you our going to give her to [someone] else I wish you would not for I would rather Pay you some thing and have you ceps her for me ontell nex Spring for now I am laft a lone. my husband [he is] crazey and gone to the crazey house and I have [two] bebys with me, one I give [to] his [folks] and the beby I have with me and I am vary poor and I am not in vary good halth but I have to work and if you will [keep] my gril for me ontell nex spring then she be old anough to takir of the beby and let me work by the day. you know it is hard for a mother to part with her chardren but god sand me the bad lock and I [must find no fault] for he is our master. he [knows] what he doset for.

[Now] will you answer me and tell me what you our going to do with her. if she [is] gone, well I will have to let her go but for my saick dont let her go if she is not gone. I Pray and wish you will not let her go. I can not suport her this winter for I am frad of the winter my self but nex spring I will tray to Pay you all I posibly can and [get] her.

PS well i wish you would sand me her Pectur. I am vary losome of her and it would plaese me vary much.

from,
Mrs Hal Rowley*

September 15, 1887

Dear Madam:

Your letter of the 6th of September was duly received. You need not worry at all about your little girl. She is here with us and in excellent health better than when she came. She appears to be perfectly contented and happy. I have not thought anything about putting her out because she appeared to need schooling for a time. However even if I should do so I would [take] the greatest care in getting a proper home for her one where she could have the privilege of school and church and would be properly care[d] for in all respects. However the girl is right here now and there is no cause for you to feel bad. Anna sends much love to you.

Yours respectfully,
Albert D. Fuller, Superintendent

*Note that Rowley was Mary's surname by her second marriage. Annie Belle kept the name of her birth father, which was Sunderland.

October 3, 1888

My Dear gril:

Pardon me for not answering your letter before and I will tell you the raeson. I have been working avary day clening house for avary boday and I am so offuly tard when I come home that I can not go to have any boday to write for me. but to night our old friend come so She write for me to tell you that me and the babay our well but your Father we hard from him to day and he is not better. if anay thing he is failling fast. So be a good gril and Pray for you Father.

from your Loving Mother,
Mary Rowley

April 7, 1889

Dear Sir:

Yours . . . received and was much pleased to hear my daughter is in good health. I would have answered your letter before but I have moved and have taken the canal drivers to board and do not have much time to write. I will not answer your letters for 2 or 3 weeks after I get them unless Belle is sick because I dont have time. Her little brother and myself send much love to her. I remain,

Yours respectfully,
Mrs Mary A. Rowley

April 22, 1889

Dear Sir:

it is quite a while since I recieved your letter and I am sory I could not answor it. I have been so bissy I could not but I am muched plesed to hear that my girl is improving so well. . . . I wrote you I took the bording house, well . . . I was so bissy I did not think to exsplain to you the way I ment. I am working for the man that took the bording hous and I dont know what I am giting antill pay day.

read this to your self. now do you think I could do any thing with her if I took her home for I am placed now whare I nead her help very much and she would be a grad deal of help to me and if you think I can do any thing with her I would be willing to pay you something for your trouble. answare as you think. if she is taking sick any way be sure and let me know right of[f].

Mrs. Mary Rowley

May 13, 1889

Dear Sir:

since I had a few lesure moments to spare I thought I would use them in writing to you. well I have been pretty buisey since I wrote last. I have been a lone to do my work but I have thought of her all of the time but could not write. . . . since you think I better leave her thare I gess I will for maybe it is better for me and for her both. it was so lonesome for me i thought she would be a great deal of company for me for I am a lone so much [now]. [her brother] and I sends our love. sayes to be a good girl. no more for this time so good by.

frome,<br>
Mary Rowley

July 15, 1889

Dear Sir:

I recieved your wellcome letter and was sorry to hear that my little girl had the [rheumatism ?] but I hope when this reaches her that she will be better. well I am well and her brother is giting better of his [whooping] cough. well I am pretty bissey all the time. Mr Fuller does she ever say any thing about coming home. does she say she would like to or dont she say any thing a bout it. pleas let me know if she does. well if nothing hapens between now and fall I think I shall take her home. whare I am now it aint a proper plase for to bring her . . . and whare I am now I am hear for the porpus of giting her home. I am arning a little more than I would git in a privet house. I am trying to git enough to gether for to keep my famely this winter. no more for this time. love to my little girl. her brother send his love.

from,<br>
Mary Rowley

July 16, 1889

Dear Madam:

Your esteemed favor under date of the 15th inst. is just at hand. I have understood that the place where you were working would not be just where you yourself would like to take your daughter. Am glad to know that you are there only temporarily and that the reason why you are doing as you do is because of lack of funds and that you may have your family together again.

Your daughter speaks about you quite frequently, but has said nothing about going home for a long time. Her health is somewhat better than when I wrote you last and I hope will continue to improve. She sends a great deal of [love] to you and to her brother.

With best wishes, I remain,<br>
Yours respectfully,<br>
Albert D. Fuller, Superintendent

September 3, 1889

Mr. Fuller Sir:

I received your Wellcome letter and Was glad to hear that my Daughter Was Well. I have to Work verry hard every day but I think of her evry day. Mr Fuller I am verry thankful for your kindness to my child and God Will reward you. 1 hope she prises your kindness to her and is a trying to learn and is kind and [obedient]. I onely get 2 fifty per week. . . . I Would take hir myself but I hope you Will keep her for me as long as you can. I try hard to do the best I can. give her a mothers love and tell her to be a good Girl. be kind. hope to hear from her often. you must excuse me for not Writing sooner.

Yours with respets,
Mary Rowley

*There are only a few additional letters in case files from Mary Rowley to her daughter. The disposition of the child is unclear. It appears that she may possibly have been sent to live with an aunt sometime in 1893 at the age of seventeen.*

## Jennie O'Donnell

A poor mother's attachment to her child could often lead to acts of desperation. Although details are sparse, such appears to have been the case with Mary O'Donnell. Following her husband's death sometime in 1893, she and her six-year-old daughter Jennie were forced into the poorhouse. Ten years previous, Mary and Michael had immigrated from Ireland with high expectations for the future. But now, with Michael gone, hopes of a new life turned tragically into a daily struggle for survival. For six months following Jennie's admission to the Albany asylum, Mary did her best to pay board for the child's keep, while traveling from Great Barrington, Vermont, to Pittsfield, Massachusetts, in search of work. Anxiety over the separation turned to desperation, when suddenly and very nearly forcibly she removed Jennie from the asylum in April of 1894. Still unable to support herself or the child, Mary was compelled to return the girl to the home within only a few short months. This time mother and daughter were not to see each another again for many years.

October, 1893

Mrs. Fuller:

Will you Plese let mee no how my little girl Jenny O'Donnell is. I hope she has not taken cold. I will Be thankfull if you Will drop a line and let me no how she is getting on With the children. has she cried for her mama. Will you let mee no. I do feele most ancious about her.

Your obedient servent,
Mary A. O'Donnell

October 27, 1893

Dear Madam:

Your letter enquiring about your little girl, Jennie, has been received and in reply would say that she is well and going to school every day and we find her a very nice little girl. I am in hopes that after a little while she will be able to write to you herself.

She enjoys playing with the little girls very much and I do not think she has cried at all since you left. Of course she was a little homesick at first but that is to be expected. She sends her love to you.

Yours respectfully,
Helen T. Fuller, Acting Superintendent

November 23, 1893

Mrs. Fuller:

Many thanks to you for your letter letting mee no about Jenny. I am thankfull that she is getting on Well and [that] she is in good health. Mrs. Fuller Will you Plese let Mee no or [will] you plese see if she needs any little thing that she is not allowed at school. I do not no but if she doese, if you let her unkle Tom no. I asked them to go to see her. . . . Mrs. Fuller, Will you plese let mee no, [have] they called.* Will you give her my love and tell her I think of her all the time. Mrs. Fuller, it is awfull hard to be Without her, the dear little girl. she is so [affectionate] and did so many little things for her Mama. I enclose 4.00 dollars for her Bord. hope to here from you soone.

Yours,
Mary O'Donnell

April 13, 1894

Dear Sir:†

The bearer of this note Mrs. O'Donnell came to our place twice yesterday to see her little daughter. We allowed her to see her child for nearly two hours. She came back again this morning and stated that she wished to take her child. We informed her that the girl had Whooping cough and ought not

---

*Mary refers here to her husband's brother Thomas O'Donnell and his wife, who resided in the city of Albany.

†This letter is addressed to Mr. Thomas O'Donnell.

go out of doors. The woman insisted upon it until we finally said that if she would take the child it would be at her own risk and that we would not receive her back again except upon an order of some official.

Yours respectfully,<br>
Helen T. Fuller, Acting Superintendent

May 16*

My Dear Mrs. Fuller:

it is With Regret and sorrow that I write to you, for the Lord sake Will you come down here for mee. I am heart Broken to be in such a place as this is. Will you P[l]ese for god sake to come for me. I have not Been sick. I am afraid that these strangers has robed mee. What on Earth happend to Mrs. O'Donnell to let mee come down here With a strange[r]. You no I did not entend to remain. Will you for the Lord sake come and Bring Jenny With you. My Jenny. I have not been appointed in any Way. I hold no Position. For the Lord sake What is Jenny and all of us to do and you no Well I have a very fare house and all my things packed up. it is . . . awful. . . . Believe mee.

Yours,<br>
Mrs. Michael O'Donnell

August 16

My Dear Mrs. Fuller:

Will you Plese Write or send for mee as soone as you possibly can. I am not atall Improved. I feele as the[y] have [deceived] mee in coming here. the[y] told mee that the[y] Were gong to give mee a Position and the[y] have not don so. the Doctor sent a message for mee and unstead of giving mee a position, the[y] locked mee up. it is to Bad that I did not see you Before I came here. I think it is an aufull thing to do to shut mee up in such a place as this is. it is a most aufull place . . . you do not no What I am suffring. I do feele most aufull. I no it is to Bad that the[y] have don such a thing as to shut mee up here. the[y] have [injured] mee for life. . . . What is my child to do. Mrs Fuller Will you Plese ask the O'Donnell's to come for mee. I hope you Will do What you can for mee. could you send youre dauter for mee as I am [nearly] dead. Plese Mrs fuller do send youre dauter or could you send Mrs Harding for mee. . . . ¹ I am nerely dead and it grieves mee verry much

---

*The following two letters from Mary O'Donnell were probably written in 1895 but no year appears on the correspondence. The letters were written from the Poughkeepsie Hospital for the Insane (Hudson River State Hospital).

¹Helen Fuller has only young children at this time. Mary may have been referring to Albert Fuller's sister, Charlotte, who assisted in the operation of the Albany asylum. Mrs. Harding was an attendant there.

about Jenny. I have Written several times and I do not no What the matter is. My Dear little girl What is she to [do] if I am not able to get out. I do hope you Will do What you can for mee. . . . give my love to my Dear child and . . . plese take care of her.

Yours,<br>
Mary O'Donnell

September 6, 1895

My dear Miss Fuller:

Mrs. O'Donnell, a patient in our hospital, has asked me to write to you for information about her little daughter, Jennie O'Donnell. She says she will feel ten years younger if she can hear that Jennie is well and trying to be a good girl. Will you kindly write Mrs. O'Donnell and oblige.

Yours very truly,<br>
Henrietta Lutz

September 23, 1895

Dear Sir:

We have received several letters from Mrs. Mary O'Donnell, an inmate of your institution, and also one from some friend there by the name of [Henrietta Lutz], inquiring after her little girl who is with us.

We have answered a number of these letters, and each time she writes as though she had never heard anything from her daughter.

We thought best to write you that you might inform her that her little girl is enjoying the very best of health, and seems to be perfectly happy.

Yours respectfully,<br>
Helen T. Fuller, Superintendent

*Jennie O'Donnell eventually left the asylum to live with her uncle Tom O'Donnell in the city of Albany. The child's future relationship with her mother is revealed in the following letters. Jennie was to mature to adulthood, but Mary's reality was forever to be the struggle of those early years following her husband's death and the repeated, yet vain, attempt to bring her child home.*

*May 23, 1908*

*Dear Sir:*

*We have received recently, two letters addressed to Miss Jennie O'Donnell written by her mother Mrs. Michael O'Donnell. The girl was discharged from this institution in 1897, and her present address is unknown to us. I am therefore unable to forward the letters and they are still in this office.*

*Sincerely yours,*

*Charles H. Johnson, Superintendent*

*May 28, 1908*

*Dear Sir:*

*I have received your letter of May 23rd in reference to two letters addressed to Miss Jennie O'Donnell at your institution.*

*Her mother, Mrs. Mary O'Donnell, has a delusion that her daughter is still an inmate of your orphan asylum. She imagines that she is still a young child and when her daughter visited her about a year ago she would not recognize her. As she insists upon addressing the letters to your institution she has been allowed to do so but as a rule the letters are readdressed before being mailed. Miss Jane A. O'Donnell's address is now . . . Albany, New York, c/o Mrs. Thomas O'Donnell.*

*If you will kindly readdress the letters, I will be obliged to you.*

*Very truly yours,*

*Charles W. Pilgrim, Superintendent Hudson River State Hospital*

## Willie McCauley

Though many poor parents considered the orphan asylum a place of safety and refuge for their children, others could become confused and frightened by the huge impersonal nature of the institution. Suspicion, even paranoia, perhaps best characterizes Richard McCauley's perception of the asylum. According to McCauley, his family fell victim to a vicious act of revenge by the local political bosses of Little Falls, New York. He refused to sell his vote, he said, so they burned down his home, forced him into the poorhouse, branded him and his wife as "shiftless," and sent their five-year-old son Willie off to the orphan asylum. McCauley believed that the superintendent of the poor of Herkimer County had orchestrated the entire affair and that in some way the asylum was part of a grand scheme to destroy his family. Looking for justice from someone, from anyone, he pleaded his case to local residents and local officials and ultimately to the governor of New York State who, remarkably, were all persuaded by this poor, illiterate man to speak on his behalf.* McCauley's letters are addressed at first from the poorhouse in Middleville, New York, and later from Little Falls.

---

*Richard McCauley may have had his wife or others write for him since the diction, grammar, and handwriting of his letters vary to a considerable extent. They are at one time written almost phonetically and at other times well-composed.

March 5, 1891

Dear Sir:

I write you wishing to hear from my son Willie McCauley who was sent from Herkimer Co. . . . I wish to know how he is getting along. is he contented but I supose he is as he has playmates of his own age and a child soon forgets. They have none of the anxiety of a Parent but I have no fears but he will be taken care of but I would like to hear from him but do not expect you to spend much time for that purpose but if you will favor me this time you will oblige me very much. love to Willie. tell him his Father & Mother thinks of him often. tell him to be a good boy and learn to read and write, then he can write to me himself. hoping to hear from you soon. I remain.

Yours,
Mrs. Richard McCauley

May 18, 1891

My dear boy:

I now set down to rite you a few lines to let ya no that I am well and hope to find you the saim and your mother is well to and she sends a kiss to you and me also. I am back to little falls and fond my house all bornt down to the grown and things to. I think of you night and day. and be a good boy for me. as [quick] as I get a home you have got to come back. . . . I dont [k]now [when] I will be after you. When you see me you will no that I am after you. Your mother cry night and day as well as I do. . . . tell Mr fooler that I am going to send him some dimens [Little Falls diamonds] for your clas in school. . . . I will say good by for this time. good by. ancer soon . . . in hast,

Mr Resced McCauley

July 28, 1891

Dear Sir:

Could I get one of Willie's photos also one of his teacher? Please let me no if it would be posable to get them and how much it would cost me and I will send you the money. I am very glad Willie is well and hope he will continue in good health. Thanking you for past favors. I remain,

Yours Sincerely,
Richard McCauley

August 11, 1891

Sir Mr. Fuller:

As Mr Ritchard McCauley has come to me . . . this morning his heart is broken for his son Willie that is in that place. he would like his chld with him. as i am a mother myself i symphasize with him. he wants me to ask you if he comes for his child if you will let him fetch the child home. i am no way enterested in him eny more than i feel for eny one tha[t] has been treated wrongfully as Mr McCauley & wife certanly has been just because the[y] are poor and his wife was sick. she is well at present. still it is very sad to hear them greave for their child. will you pleas to rite to me by return mail and would it do Mr Fletcher eny good to come for his son and oblige. I write this to you as a favor for a poor father & mother that i do feel very sad for them. I know postively at the time their home was broken up it was did all through revenge. the man that was oversere at the time was mad at Mr McCauley. I ask for pardon if i did wrong in writing this for him.

H. Nemetz

August 13, 1891

My Dear Sir:

You have in your custuday the son of Mr & Mrs Richard McCauley, residents of Little Falls County of Herkimer & State of N.Y. now they are living here togather and taking care of themselves are no county or Town charge and they want their son William McCauley and I demand the same to be delivered to his father Richard McCauley on his arrival at your office corner Western Ave & Robin St. Albany N.Y. please Inform me by Ret mail if you will deliver their son Wiliam to them with out further trouble & oblige.

Yours Very Truly,<br>Capt. Joseph H. Heath<br>U.S. Pension Attny

September 8, 1891

[Governor Hill] Kind Sir:*

will you please grant me a favor by releasing my child from Albany Orphan Asylum. he was taken away from me with[out] cause. he is five years old last march. thay took my child away and burnt my house down and sent me to the poor house because I would not [vote] the way they wanted me to. George C. offered me 20 dollers but I would not except of it and he said he would have revenge so that is the way he took it and I have a home now and a nough to eat and I wish you would grant me this much. answer and let me know what I can do. This orphan asylum is cor Western ave and Robin St Albany N Y. the mans name is Albert D. Fuller. Yours and oblige.

Mr Richard McCauley

*This letter from Richard McCauley to New York governor David Hill was forwarded to Albert Fuller with a cover letter asking Fuller for an explanation of the matter.

September 24, 1891

[Governor Hill] Dear Sir:

Your favor of the 17th Inst. by your private secretary has been received enclosing a letter from Richard McCauley asking for the custody of his child.

Said child William McCauley aged five years was admitted to this institution February 19, 1891 upon the order of Charles A. Snyder Supt. of the Poor of Herkimer county. The parents of this child were then inmates of the Herkimer county Alms House and represented to be shiftless characters.

I have received a number of letters from Mr. McCauley within the last six weeks; in one or two of them he asked for the discharge of the boy. I wrote that we had no objection and all that would be necessary for him to do would be to get an order of discharge from the committing officer and mail it to me. His letters have been so incoherent at times as to raise doubts in my mind as to his sanity. I therefore did not wish to take the responsibility of sending the boy to him without knowing that he was in fit condition to give it proper care. . . . In some of his letters he would write as though he wanted the boy at once and in a few hours I would get another letter in which no mention would be made of the matter.

I will go to Little Falls my self within a short time and try to find out all about the man and the home to which he wishes to take the child. We have [no] desire except to do what is right in the matter and give the child proper protection. I am,

Yours very respectfully,
Albert D. Fuller, Superintendent

September 29, 1891

[Mr. Harris Sir]:*

Just a line to say that I had an interview with McCauley after I saw you which appeared to make him feel considerably better. I also promised to go out to his place and see his wife within a few days and to send them their little boys picture.

I send you in another enclosure a few pictures which will give you a little idea of the work we are engaged in.

I would be glad to have you call and see us at any time that you may be in Albany.

Yours respectfully,
Albert D. Fuller, Superintendent

*This letter was addressed to the chief of police in Little Falls, New York, following Fuller's visit to the McCauley family.

*Willie McCauley subsequently was returned to his parents as this final correspondence from Albert Fuller to the poormaster of Herkimer County indicates.*

November 7, 1891

[Mr. Curry], Dear Sir:

Just a line to acknowledge the receipt of your favor of the 4th Inst. in regard to discharge of [the] McCauley boy. We delivered him to the father as requested. Are glad the family can be united once more.

Would be pleased to have you call any time you may be in Albany, would be glad to make your acquaintance.

Yours cordially,
Albert D. Fuller, Superintendent

## The Lawson Children

Many children came to the Albany Orphan Asylum from supposedly "intact" families, households with two surviving parents. Chronic poverty split many of these families apart but abuse, alcoholism, infidelity, and simple incompatibility shattered many homes already on the brink. Many children were left with no clear understanding of who would care for them. In many cases, parents would not hesitate to place blame on an errant spouse and they looked to the asylum superintendent as an arbiter of last resort.

The two years preceding young George Lawson's death proved difficult and stressful ones for the family. Alcoholism, separation, custody battles, and a series of failed reconciliations left the child's parents, Hattie and George, Sr., angry and full of contempt for one another. George worked as a laborer and was in jail at the time Hattie admitted their four children to the Albany Orphan Asylum.* Upon his release, Hattie refused to subject herself to his drinking and verbal abuse any longer. She considered him fickle and irresponsible and feared that he might leave her at any time without the means to care for the children. Unable to find steady work herself, she depended on her own parents for a time. Even when Hattie and George seemed near reconciliation, they talked past one another and the results proved painful for all concerned. During their three year correspondence both mother and father lived in and around the nearby city of Troy, New York.

---

*The Lawsons had three daughters and a son: Annie, age ten, Lizzie, age eight, George, age five, and Hattie, age three.

April 15, 1890

Mr. Fuller sir:

Has the father of the little Lawson children been to see them. Could he come and take the children from the Asylum with out my consent. I will be down to see the children on visiting day. as he is coming He said in the afternoon I wish I could see them in the morning as I do not care to meet Him there. I wish you would be kind enough to answer this as I feel very [anxious] to know a bout the children as it is my wish for them to stay there.

Respectfully,

Mrs. Hattie Lawson

April 21, 1890

Dear Madam:

Your letters . . . have both been received.

I will not deliver your children to your husband without f[irst] notifying you so that you can put in a counter claim.

You may see them in the morning of visiting day as you request.

Yours respectfully,

Albert D. Fuller, Superintendent

September 15, 1890

Mr. Fuller Sir:

I have neglected writeing and sending what money I could spare for the childrin. I have had but little work and could not earn much. tell them their grandpa and grandma . . . have come back to troy to live and I came back with them. So I will remain in troy with them still. I expected to have been able to get there last month but did not get here in time to see them on visiting day. but tell them to be ready for a good time with me this comeing visiting day. their uncle Willie and their grandma will probily come with me. I know the childrin would like to see them. I send a little change, all I can spare. Will bring all I can when I come. the dear childrin are always on my mind night and day. I am very lonely without them. it makes me feel very bad to see them and not be able to have a home for them. although I know they are perfectly safe in your hands, but it is a mothers love to long for a home for her childrin. I hope I do not have to meet thier father there when I come as it takes a way the enjoyment I want to have with the childrin. give my best love to them. I hope they are good children. . . . I remain,

respecfully,

Mrs. Hattie Lawson

October 16, 1890

Mr. Fuller sir:

I recieved your letter in answer to the one I sent. I did not send the Box, as my Husband called to see me hearing I was sick. We had a good understanding and we find things satisfactory for both and he is preparing a home for the children wich pleases me to think of having the childrin with us again. We Will be down to gether visiting day and explain things to you. give my love to the childrin and tell them We are comeing to take them home soon as I know they Will be pleased to hear it. I thought I would bring what I have when I come. I remain,

Respectfully,
Mrs. Hattie Lawson

November 24, 1890

Mr. Fuller sir:

Will you please inform me how it is that my husband has taken the oldest child out of the institute. I cannot make it out. he has no home yet for them and I have not decided to go Back with him yet. he brought her to see me this morning. it is the first I have seen him for a week. he says he has had her for a week. as I have not heard from you, I think it strange. Will you pleas answer by next mail. I remain,

Respectfully yours,
Mrs. Hattie Lawson

November 26, 1890

Dear Madam:

Your favor of the 24th Inst. just at hand. I think I am fully as much surprised to hear the news as you were under the circumstances to see your oldest child with your husband.

Last visiting day yourself and husband were both here together to see the children, and he told me at that time in your presence and hearing that you made up and were going to live together again and would take the children just as soon as possible. He said also at the same time that he would come for the older girl the fore part of the week following. At that time you said nothing to indicate that you did not agree with him in what he said, if you had done so I certainly would not have allowed him to take the child. He came to me a little over a week ago and said that everything was all right, and believing him on account of your being here together and of your assenting by your silence at what he said in your presence, I allowed him to take your oldest child.

I certainly would not have done so if I had . . . supposed that there was still estrangement between you.

I will hold the other children and will not discharge them unless you come with him, and the older girl can be returned at any time if things are not all right. I remain,

Yours respectfully,
Albert D. Fuller, Superintendent

November 29, 1890

Mr. Fuller Sir:

I recieved your letter of the twenty seventh and in reply would say I was unconcious of the effect of the conversation between yourself and Mr Lawson at the time we were there together but I would say we have come to no conclusions and probly will not for some time if at all. Mr Lawson will at one time say he is going to get a place and furnish it and contradicts what he had said at another time. this has occurred several times and I cannot safely depend on such a fickle mind as he might leave me at any time with the children on my hands to support. Which I could not do while they are so young. Further more, such insinuations, sarcasms & insults as he casts at me would seem to indicate that there is not much affections existing between us. I would sacrifice most any thing for our children but I must say that my judgment tells me to be carefull as I may make there condition worse. feeling assured to our chidrens welfare with you I remain,

Respectfully yours,
Mrs. Hattie Lawson

February 10, 1891

Mr. Fuller Sir:

I could not come conviently to see the Children as we have had sickness here but I should like to hear how the children are. I feel more content after hearing to wait another month. I should like to send some money for them but am not prepared to do so as my work has been very dull on account of the collar strike. Has their Father been to see them. I do not hear any thing of him or the child. if he has not been to see the other children I think I will send some one to see if Annie is with any of his folks. I think it is strange that a man should keep a child from seeing her mother. I do not want any more trouble with him. I hardly know what is best to do. I am anxious about her as I know she must wish to see me. did Mr Lawson pay you ten dollars when he took [her] out or paid you any at any other time. that is what he said when he brought her to see me the next week after he took her out. He keeps her a way for some purpose wich I want to find out. With much love for the children. I remain,

Respectfully,
Mrs. Hattie Lawson

February 11, 1891

Dear Madam:

Your letter has been received. Your children are well and getting along all right.

Your husband did not hand me the $10 when he took the girl away. I find on referring to my books that it was $5 which was placed to his credit at that time. That is the only amount that he ever paid.

I cannot imagine why he wants to keep your child from you. I think he was here and had the little girl with him last visiting day. The little ones [send] much love to you. I remain,

Yours respectfully,
Albert D. Fuller, Superintendent

December 19, 1892

Dear Madam:

Just a line to let you know that your son George is not well, has dysentery. We expect that he will recover but as the disease is sometimes treacherous thought best to let you know so that you could come and see him. He is having the best of care.

Yours respectfully,
Albert D. Fuller, Superintendent

December 23, 1892

Dear Madam:

I am very sorry to be obliged to notify you of the death of your son George which occurred a few moments ago at 4 o'clock. You have my sympathy. The little fellow has had good care—the very best, I could have given my own no better. I have telephoned to Mrs. T., she promised to send you word. Unless notified to the contrary the remains will be interred in the asylum lot in the Albany Rural Cemetery.

Respectfully yours,
Albert D. Fuller, Superintendent

December 27, 1892

Mr. Fuller sir:

All though i am unprepared to write, since i have met with such a great loss, but i feel very anxious to know how Lizzie and Hattie are. they will feel very lonesome with out their dear little brother. it is so hard to bear the loss of a child. it greaves me more to think I was not with him till the last. i am so sory that i did not ask you to let me remain with him, but i did not think the end was so near. i was all prepared to come early Saturday morning and was geting ready to telephone at five o'clock and then thought i would a gain at eight so to know what the changes were as I was so worried. it relieved me some after i telephoned in the morning as i thought if there was a change it would likely be for the better. * the lady that was with him while i was there gave me so much incouragement. she thought he would get better on account of drinking so much milk and she thought a rest would improve him, and i felt that he would certenly be better when i would be there saturday. but if i could only been there and saw him breath his last in my arms how much more of a comfort it would have been to me, but—thank you very much for your kindness to the little fellow and for your sympathy. we laid the little fellow a way to rest in the new mount ida cemetery Christmas day. his funeral took place at three o'clock in the afternoon. he looked very peacefull and happy. i should like to have had Lizzie and Hattie to have seen him and should also have liked to had you see him but thought you would be so buisy that you would not be able to come. please tell the children that i shall be to visit them on visiting day and bring them something. please give them my love. please excuse mistakes.

I remain respectfully,
Mrs. Hattie Lawson

December 29, 1892

Dear Madam:

Your letter of the 27th Inst. was duly received. I have much sympathy for you in your trouble. The day you were here we all had good reason for being quite hopeful that your little boy would recover, in fact, we did not give up hope until within a very short time of his death.

I wish it had been possible for me to be present at the funeral, but [you] can doubtless realize how busy I was. Lizzie and Hattie are real well, in fact, we have not a single child in bed out of our entire number of 610 children. With kind regards, I remain,

Yours Sincerely,
Albert D. Fuller, Superintendent

---

*This was a rare instance of a parent's use of this still very new technology in communicating with the asylum.

December 29, 1892

Dear Sir:

i am satisfied that you done all in your power to save my little boy. i am very much oblige to you for so doing. i had him Buried from his mother['s] house in a decent way and he lays in mount ida Cemetry. i would be oblige to you to tell Lizzie and all his school mates that he looked very happy in his Cofin and tell her not to fret as he is better off and out of all trouble. i have not felt very well ever cence the affair hapened. the mother and i will be to see them next visiting day. he was Buried Sunday, Dec. 25 at 3:30 o clock. tell Lizzie that Annie goes to see his grave ever[y] day. it is but a little ways from our house. you will oblige me in letting me no how the other two ar geting a long.

Very respectfully Yours,
George W. Lawson

Sunday, September 9, 1893

Mrs. Fuller:

I thought I would write a few lines to you as I have not been able to get to the institute to see the children which I am very sory for. but I have been sick most two months. I have not been out only to go to the doctors which is only about three blocks from where my home is. I have been [too] week to undertake to go to visit the childrin. one of my greatest trouble[s] is nervious weekness. the doctor says with the medicine that he has perscribed and if I take care of my self and try and have a change for a while I shall get better. my body and mind has been over taxed and I must have rest and a change. I hope to be able to go out far enough in a couple of weeks to be able to get down to see the children, at any rate to bring some things that I have for them. I hope they are well. I think of them so much. I am so much pleased with them since they have been in your care. Lizzie is learning so fast. I feel very much pleasure with her and hope she apprecieates your kindness by giveing her atention. . . . please give my love to them and tell them I am thinking of them. Hopeing to see them soon. i remain,

truly,
Mrs. Hattie Lawson

*The death of young George and the strain of more than three years of separation and marital conflict left Hattie Lawson emotionally drained as her final correspondence discloses. The estrangement from her husband appears to have been permanent. The two daughters remained in the asylum after George's death eventually returning home to the care of their mother in 1895.*

## Johnny, Katie, and Willie Richardson

A child's death might break a marriage completely or it could lead to a spousal reconciliation. The latter proved to be the case with Jane and William Richardson. Little is known of the family aside from what is revealed in their correspondence with Albert Fuller. In the fall of 1884, William Richardson was incarcerated in the Albany Penitentiary, probably on a charge of drunk and disorderly conduct. Homeless and with no other recourse, his wife, Jane, sought shelter in the Saratoga County Poorhouse with one of their daughters, Maggie. The other three children, Johnny, Katie, and Willie (ages unknown) found refuge at the Albany Orphan Asylum, perhaps by order of the Superintendent of the Poor. Jane was very probably illiterate. Her letters appear to be written by others. William, on the other hand, wrote for himself, although with obvious difficulty. His letters divulge a mixture of remorse, anger, and determination. He blamed his wife for their estrangement but eventually took responsibility for the effect of his drinking on the family's circumstances. Both parents corresponded with their children, but William's letters stand out most notably in their extreme sentimentality and in his single-minded goal to make a home for his children with or without the mother. Jane writes from the County Poorhouse in Ballston Spa, New York, and William from the Albany County Penitentiary.

November 2, 1884

Dear Children:

I [sit] down to write you a few lines to let you know that I am well and [hope] that yas are the same. I am glad that you like you knew home. I hope that you will be good children. I hope that you will learn you well. I think of you every night and day. I will be down to see you as soon as I can, for I means to see all again. I can hardly wait for the time to come. Maggie speaks of you When I dont but it not very often that I dont think of you. I have not heard from your Father since you went away. this is all for this time. [write] as soon as you can. I wish that you could write to me your self. well lots of [love] from me and Maggie.

Jane W. Richardson

November 3, 1884

Dear Madam:

Your letter of yesterday just at hand and contents noted. Your children remain well and are getting along all right. Johny says that he is going to try hard to learn to write so that he can write to you himself. Katie says that she likes to be here and would like to have you come to see her when you can.

Willie says tell Mama that I am getting along pretty well. They all send their love to you and Maggie. They are going to school every day and are doing fairly well in their lessons. They want me to tell you that they think of you every day.

Yours respectfully,
Albert D. Fuller, Superintendent

December 26, 1884

Dear Madam:

. . . Am happy to be again able to inform you that your children are perfectly well and happy. They were delighted with your visit and have talked a great deal about it since you were here. I was very sorry that you got away before I had a chance to speak to you again. I wanted to take you through the building into the schoolrooms, sleeping rooms and other rooms of the building.

The children send you and Maggie much love and want me to ask you to write them again before a great while.

Yours respectfully,
Albert D. Fuller, Superintendent

February 1, 1885

My Dear Children Johnny Katie and Willie:

I now take the Pleasure of Riting to yous to let you know I am Well and in good health and I hope thoes lines Will find youes all Enjoying the Same With the help of God. Children, I would of Rote to youes Before only I did not know Whear to Rite to untill last Sunday. I Rote a letter tow months a go to the County house in Ballston to find out Whear you Ware and I did not Reseave any answer to my letter till last Sunday and they Enformed me Whear you Was. So now I though[t] i Would Rite to youes and let you Know I had not forgotten youes Children. Mr Squire, [Superintendent of the Poor] told me in his letter your mother and your little sister maggie is Well. Now When you Rite to me let me know When you have heard from your mother and maggie or if your mother has Ever Rote to you Since you have Been a Way from her. Now Children, I hope you are good Children [and] are obed[i]ent to your teacher and I Would like to hear of you loving your teacher and of her a loving you and When I get my Freedom I Will come and See you and I Will Be Verry glad to hear you are good children. I do Not Know What I Shall do When I get out But no matter What i do i Shall never forgit youes dear little ones. your mother has done Wrong to Both you and me So She can Not Blame me and you children must not Blame me. But When Ever I do get my freedom I Shall do all I can for you children as soon as I can get to Work to Erne any thing. Now Behave your Selfes and I Shall See you Soone. I Will look for an answer to this letter By next Sunday and I Will See you in Six Weeks time if god Spares us all till then and i hope he Will. I Pray for youes Every night and Every day and I aske god to Spare us all to meet a gane. Now I Will Bring my letter to a close for this time By a Bidding you all good Bye till We can meet a gane and god Bless you all and I hope you Will Pray for me. So good Bye. With a Kiss to you all, I Remane,

Your loving Father,<br>Mr. William Richardson

February 9, 1885

Dear Sir:

Your letter of the 1st. inst to your children has been received, at their request I drop you this note to let you know that they are well and are getting along all right in every respect. They have been perfectly well ever since they came here, they are going to school and are doing very well with their studies, their mother writes to them very frequently and was here for a few moments to see them one day. I think that in some way she missed a train in coming so that she had to hurry in order to catch the train that she had promised to return by. Maggie came with her. Your children were each of them very much delighted to hear from you and will expect to see you as soon as [you are] released. They send you much love.

Yours truly,<br>Albert D. Fuller, Superintendent

April 2, 1885

Dear children:

you must Not think I have forgoten you for I am not to Work yet and as Soon as I do get to Work I Shall come and See you. I hope When you reseave this you Will Be all Well. When you Rite let me know if you have heard from your mother Since I Was thear to See you. I Will try and get a house as Soon as i get to Work if you children Wants to come and live With me. I Will Be down next month to See yous for I can Not come this month for i have no money or any Work yet.* So Be good children. god bless you all. good Bye till i can come to see yous. Rite Soon to me.

Your father,<br>William Richardson

*William Richardson was now living in Waterford, New York, a distance of about twelve miles from the city of Albany.

April 17, 1885

[Dear Madam]:

I drop you these few lines as I promised to do in my note of yesterday. Johnie this morning appeared to be somewhat better but to night he is not so well, has quite a high fever and is delirious, we hope that the morning will show a change for the better but are fearful that such will not be the case.[*] He has been a good boy and very patient during his sickness, and we all think a great deal of him and are doing all we can to help him as is his physician who is very kind and good to him and skillful in his profession as well.

We are afraid that John is not going to recover but have a little hope yet. Will drop you a line again in the morning.

Yours with much sympathy,
Albert D. Fuller, Superintendent

April 18, 1885

Dear Madam:

As I promised in my letter to you of last Evening I drop you a few lines in regard to your sick boy. I am sorry to say that we have about given up all hope of his recovery. He was delirious all last night and is still so this morning and does not know any one and seems to be sinking rapidly. We fear that he will not live the day through.[†]

Yours respectfully,
Albert D. Fuller, Superintendent

April 24, 1885

My Dear Children:

It is With Pleasure I now Rite you those few lines to let you know I am Well and in good health and I hope you are all a Enjoying the Same. your mama and maggie Went Back up to the county house and they are a comming out of thear When your Visiting days is and then We Will Be down to See you. I am to Work now Every day. When you Rite let me know if you Would like to come Back to live home agane. tell Mr Fuller that your mama and Papa Would like to know if he Would let them have one of your little Brothers hankercheff for a Rember of him. tell him We are Verry thankfull to

---

[*]Fuller apparently had sent notice of young Johnny's sudden illness in previous correspondence that is not included in the family's case file. He forwarded a similar message to the father the same day.

[†]Johnny subsequently died sometime between the eighteenth and the twenty-fourth of April.

him for his kindnes to your Brother and all So to us. now Be good children till We come down and give our love and Best Wishes to mr Fuller and his famly and We Send our love to you Both. So good Bye and god Bless you till We meet a gane. Please Rite Soon and let me know how you are a getting a long. a Kiss to you Both.

> I Remane your father,
> William Richardson

May 15, 1885

My Dear Children:

It is With Pleasure my Self and your Mother now Rites you thoes few lines to let you know We are Well and in good health and happy together. . . . [We] are living in Waterford and Keeping house together a gane and We Will Try and have you Both home With us Soon a gane So you must keep up good courage for a little While longer. . . . [M]e and your mama Sends our love to you Both . . . so good Bye my Dear children With a kiss from your mama and Papa. Please Rite soon. We Remane your Dear Papa and mama,

> William and Jane Richardson

May 16, 1885

Dear Sir:

I am in receipt of your favor of the 15th. inst. and hasten to reply. In the first place your children remain well and are glad to hear from you and send their love to you. I am very glad that you and Mrs. Richardson are living together and have a home for the children. It will be a better home for you both to have your children with you and although they have been very good children and we shall miss them much here, still it will be best for them now to be with you and I see no reason why I should not let you have them, and unless I should have notice from the Supt. of the Poor, will let you take them most any day next week, come Thursday if you can.

Hoping that you may get along all right now. I remain,

> Respectfully yours,
> Albert D. Fuller, Superintendent

June 7, 1885

My Dear Frend Mr Fuller:

I though[t] i Would Rite you a few lines to Enquire of my children and to know how they are a getting a long. you can tell them the Reson We did Not come down to See them last thursday Was We Was Expecting to hear from you in Regards to Bringing them home. Mr Spaulding [Superintendent of the Poor] told my Wife She could take them home any time She Wished to So She Will Be down this Week a Thursday or Friday after them. the mother Will not Stay hear if they are not Brough[t] home agane. We are a getting a long Verry nicley Now. I havent tuched [any] liquor Since the first day of April and i hope and Pray to the lord i Will never Drink any a gane as long as i live. Please answer this So i can have an answer Before a thursday if you please. give our love to the children and tell them maggie, thear little Sister, is a Wishing they Was home for She is Verry lonsome hear a lone. So We Will close By a Sending our love to the children and our thanks and Best Wishes to you and all conserned in your asylum. Please answer soon [as] you can. Expect my Wife a thursday or Friday Sure.

I remane yours,
Mr. William Richardson

*Katie and Willie Richardson were subsequently discharged to the care of their parents.*

## Cora and Carrie O'Rourke

Fayette and Caroline O'Rourke, both native-born Americans of Irish descent, drank to excess. Caroline was a "hard character" and a woman who could not behave herself, or so her husband claimed. He walked out on her more than once because of it. In March of 1884, during one of their separations, the Humane Society removed the O'Rourke's two young daughters from their family home and placed them in the Albany Orphan Asylum. The loss hit both parents hard and eventually provided the impetus for a long-term reconciliation.

Fayette labored as a sawyer in the lumber mills of northern New York and Carrie worked out as a domestic. Their work habits seemed sporadic, however, heavy drinking likely being the cause. Remorseful over their behavior, Fayette and Caroline resolved to "prove" themselves in order to win back their children. They knew the necessary triad of prerequisites—hard work, industry, and economy—and they spent the better part of three years demonstrating their sincere adherence to these values. The couple's place of residence during the period of their correspondence is unknown, although they appear to have been living in Glens Falls, New York, for a time.

April 25, 1884

Dear Sir:

You Please Write me how My Children are getting along and if they are going to School. O if i had them Back No one Could ever get them again. O

What Comfort i use to take With them. O Mr Fuller do not Let any one have them for i Shall try and get them Some time. Please Write if there is any Hope of me Ever getting them again and what i must do to get them. i am back to Work in the Mills . . . and i Shall try and Come and See them Soon. Enclosed you will Find one dollar to get their pictures taken and Please Send them to me as Soon as you [positively] Can and Will you Please Send me a Lock of their Hair. do they go to Sunday School. . . .

Fayette O'Rourke

May 4, 1884

Mr. Fuller:

Will you please Write how my Children Cora & Carrie are getting along and Please Send me a Lock of their hair. O how i Wish i Could See them. please to Write me if they are going to School and if [they] go to Sundy School. O may the Lord Forgive me for What i have done and if i Could have them Back i Would do Better and i Would Never give them Up again. me and my Husband are keeping house again and Can you not Let us have them and i Will do all i Can to Bring them Up good and take . . . good Care of them. O Mr Fuller Can you not let me have them again. do help me if you can. give them my love and tell them this letter is from their Mother. . . .

> To my dear Children Cora & Carrie: Be good . . . girls and . . . Learn Fast So you Can Write me a Letter. O how i wish i could See you & take care of little Carrie. i send Both my Love. please send me a lock of your Hair. good By darlings. . . .

Caroline O'Rourke

September 8, 1884

[Dear Sir]:

Will you please to Write how my Poor Children are getting along and if they are going to School now. i Wish you Would take a Little Extra Care of Cora for as [you are] aware She is not a Very Strong Child. as For their mother, Well i Will not say much only we are not Living together now. She could not Behave her Self. i am glad that the Children have as good home as they have. please Writ Soon and oblige.

Your Truly,<br>Fayette O'Rourke

November 24, 1884

Mr. Fuller Dear Sir:

Will you please Write me how my Children are and if they are Well and if they go to School now. We are living to Glens Falls now and We are Both of us to Work and We think We are able to take Care of them. We are going to try and get them Back and take care of them our Selves. please Write soon for we are anxious to hear from them. . . .

Fayette O'Rourke

May 25, 1885

Dear Sir:

Will you Please Send me those Pictures of Cora & Carrie as We are Very anxious to See them. Please Send them as Soon as Possible and oblige. We are Both of Us hard to Work hoping By our Industry and Economy to have Our Children returned to us and When We do get them We Will Support and Educate them as they ought to Be. My Wife is Worring about them a great deal. She says if She could only have them Back She Would Be Contented. Will you Please [tell us] what they are required to do . . . that is about their hours of Schooling and Play and if they go to Sunday School. . . .

Fayette O'Rourke

June 18, 1885

Mr. Fuller Dear Sir:

Will you Please Send them Pictures you Promised to Send them Last Week But failed to do So. Some times i do not think they are there at all. Please to Write me the truth about it. But if they are their Please to Write me a good Long Letter all about them. i Should think you Would Let us have them again and i Promis to take good care of them. me and Fayette are both to Work Every day. give my Love to them. Please send me a lock of their Hair. Please write soon.

from,<br>Mrs. Caroline O'Rourke

*Cora and Carrie O'Rourke were discharged to the care of their parents by order of county authorities in October 1887. The O'Rourkes' determination to achieve the societal expectations of good parenting may well have waned over the years, as a final piece of correspondence in 1892 makes reference to continued intervention in their lives by local Humane Society agents.*

## The Reed Children

Parental negligence might be no more than the tragic force of circumstances. In the matter of John and Mary Reed and their nine-year-old daughter, Adelia, the case remains open. By official accounts the parents were intemperant and made the child beg for them. In the winter of 1890, local charitable agents appear to have plucked Adelia off the streets and had county officials place her in the Albany Orphan Asylum. Her brother Henry, eight years of age, arrived ten months later, followed by two other siblings, Lottie and Charlie (ages unknown), sometime between July 1891 and May 1892.

John Reed worked as a farm laborer in the town of Brewster, Putnam County, just north of New York City. His work demanded all his time from sun up to sun down. Both husband and wife expressed themselves with regard to their children in simple terms, yet their letters reveal a deep and sincere parental affection and worry. They understood the significance of sibling bonds and the importance of maintaining those bonds outside the family home. In this case, it appears that the asylum in fact assisted in nurturing those ties by keeping brother and sister in close proximity to one another within the institution. Ultimately these children may have ended up apart, but for the period of their institutionalization, they may well have had the daily affection and support of one another.

November 21, 1890

Dear sir:

I received your last letter and was very glad to hear from my little girl [Adelia] to know how she was getting along. you must excuse me for not riting to her befor as I have not had chance. I wish you would rite to me and let me know if she is contented there and if she likes it. I would like to know how she is acting along the children. . . . Tell her her father is well and sends his love to her. tell her I send my love to her. tell her she must be a good little girl and learn good [letters]. Charlie sends her a kiss. please rite soon to me for I would like to [hear] from [her]. I will close with lots of love to her. I remain the same,

her loving mother,
Mary Reed

December 15, 1890

Dear sir:

I received your welcome litter and was very glad to hear from my little girl. I am glad she is learning so well and glad she likes it so well up there. I wish you would rite and tell me [if my] little Boy is up there with dealie [Adelia] and how he made out getting up there. tell me if he hays seen dealie yet. I wish you would rite and let me know if he is with dealie every day or if he is where he can see her every day. tell them [the other] children is well and their father and sends his love to them. tell them we ar a going to send them up a nice box of candies christmas. We all send our love to them. This is all I have got to say for this time. tell dealie to be a good girl and [Henry] to. I remain the same,

their loving mother,
Mrs. Mary Reed

December 17, 1890

Dear Madam:

Your letter of the 15th Inst. is at hand. Your little boy arrived safely and I sent him the same night to sleep with his sister. They were both delighted to [see] one another.

They are getting along finely and will be on the lookout for the box you propose sending to them Christmas.

They both send much love to you. I remain,

Yours respectfully,
Albert D. Fuller, Superintendent

July 29, 1891

Dear Sir:

i Would Like to hear From the Children an hear that they are Well. tell them that lotty an Charley is Well an Sends thear love to them. tell them that thear Father an Mother is Well and Will see them soon. tell Delia that i am on a Farm an Would Write to her oftner but i Dont have time. Write soon.

Yours Respectfully,
John C. Reed

October 24, 1892

Dear sur:

I Like To Know how the Children is an Want to know how little Charley is. he Was sick Wen i Was up thare An i did not see him. i Was glad to See the Other 3 injoying Good helth. Tell the Children that i Am Coming up thare to see them Fore Long and tell them that We are All Well And Send Our Love to them All. Pleas Wright Soon.

yours truly,
John C. Reed

*Adelia Reed was eventually returned to her parents in 1895. Henry remained in the asylum until 1901 when at the age of nineteen he was placed out on indenture to a foster home. The disposition of Lottie and Charlie is unknown.*

Albert Fuller, Superintendent of the Albany Orphan Asylum.
*Photograph from Henry P. Phelps*, Story of the Albany Orphan Asylum
(*Albany Engraving Company, 1893*).

Helen Fuller, Matron of the Albany Orphan Asylum.
*Courtesy of the New York State Library, Manuscripts and Special Collections Division.*

Albany Orphan Asylum main building.
*Courtesy of the Parsons Child and Family Center, Albany, New York.*

Teachers at the Albany Orphan Asylum.
*Courtesy of the Parsons Child and Family Center, Albany, New York.*

Attendants at the Albany Orphan Asylum.
*Courtesy of the Parsons Child and Family Center, Albany, New York.*

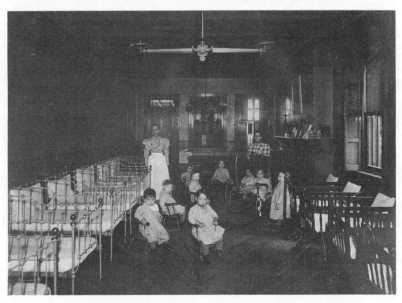

Children in the asylum nursery.
*Courtesy of the Parsons Child and Family Center, Albany, New York.*

Children in the asylum playroom or classroom.
*Courtesy of the McKinney Library, Albany Institute of History and Art.*

Asylum children.
*Courtesy of the McKinney Library, Albany Institute of History and Art.*

Asylum children, Albert Fuller in foreground.
*Courtesy of the Parsons Child and Family Center, Albany, New York.*

Asylum boys.
*Courtesy of the Parsons Child and Family Center, Albany, New York.*

Children of one family after admission to the asylum.
*Courtesy of the Parsons Child and Family Center, Albany, New York.*

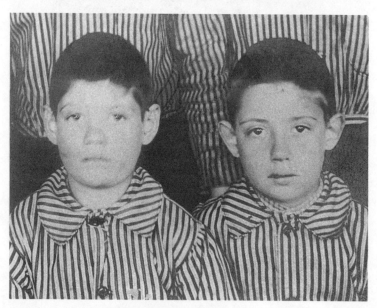

Asylum boys, possibly brothers.
*Courtesy of the New York State Library, Manuscripts and Special Collections Division.*

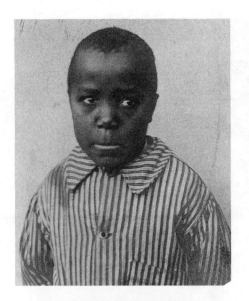

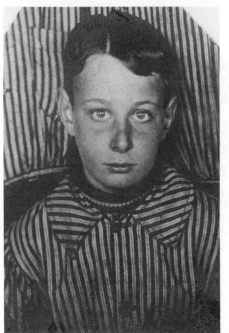

Asylum boys.
*Courtesy of the New York State Library, Manuscripts and Special Collections Division.*

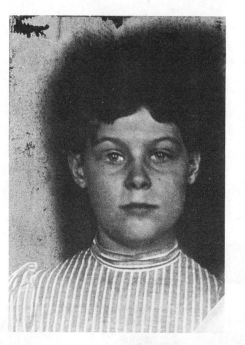

If foreign

Address, i

ad, da

ate

gion,

ver an in

If so, wha

Names an

Asylum girls.
*Courtesy of the New York State Library, Manuscripts and Special Collections Division.*

## MEMORANDA IN REGARD TO THE CHILD.

1. Date of Admission, *May 11" 1887*

2. Date of Birth *Feby 10 " 1881*

3. Orphan or otherwise, *Half Orphan*

4. Permit by *John Mc. Kenna*

5. By whom brought, *Mother*

6. Board Charged to *Albany Co.*

7. Place of birth, *Dublin Ireland G.B.*

8. Last place of residence, *508 Third St. Albany N.Y.*

9. Has it been in other institutions? *No*

10. Date of surrender,

11. By whom given,

12. Physical condition, *healthy*

13. Mental condition, *intelligent*

14. When vaccinated, *has been*

15. Contagious diseases—has had *Whooping Cough*

16. Cause of dependence, &c.

Section from asylum registration book.
*Courtesy of the New York State Library, Manuscripts and Special Collections Division.*

𝕿𝖍𝖎𝖘 𝕬𝖌𝖗𝖊𝖊𝖒𝖊𝖓𝖙, *made this* 2nd of December, 1898 *between the* President *and* Managers *of the* 𝕾𝖔𝖈𝖎𝖊𝖙𝖞 𝖋𝖔𝖗 𝖙𝖍𝖊 𝕽𝖊𝖑𝖎𝖊𝖋 𝖔𝖋 𝕺𝖗𝖕𝖍𝖆𝖓 𝖆𝖓𝖉 𝕯𝖊𝖘𝖙𝖎𝖙𝖚𝖙𝖊 𝕮𝖍𝖎𝖑𝖉𝖗𝖊𝖓 𝖎𝖓 𝖙𝖍𝖊 𝕮𝖎𝖙𝖞 𝖔𝖋 𝕬𝖑𝖇𝖆𝖓𝖞, 𝕹. 𝖄., (*commonly known as the Albany Orphan Asylum*) *of the first part, and* L. D. Harmon *of the second part.*

𝖂𝖎𝖙𝖓𝖊𝖘𝖘𝖊𝖙𝖍; *That the said party of the first part do by these presents hereby put and place* ▓▓▓▓▓▓, born December 8, 1885 *with the said party of the second part until the said* ▓▓▓▓▓▓ *shall attain the age of* 21 *years; and the said* ▓▓▓▓ *shall faithfully serve the said* L. D. Harmon *in the capacity of* Adopted child *until said time. And the said* L. D. Harmon *for himself, his executors and administrators, does agree with the said President and Managers and their successors, that during all the time aforesaid he will provide for and furnish to the said* ▓▓▓▓▓▓▓▓ *suitable food, clothing and all other things necessary for the body in health and sickness. And the said* L. D. Harmon *also agrees to give the said* ▓▓▓▓ *all necessary time and means to acquire a good common school education, and to instruct h im faithfully in* ▓▓▓▓ *and in the moral and religious principles of the Bible, and require h im to attend Sabbath School and public worship on the Sabbath, when not providentially detained; and at the end of said term, the said* L. D. Harmon *shall furnish and give to the said* ▓▓▓▓ *one new suit of clothes suitable for Sabbath and holiday wear and one other suit for every day wear, one new Bible, and One Hundred Dollars in money.*

𝕻𝖗𝖔𝖛𝖎𝖉𝖊𝖉, 𝖍𝖔𝖜𝖊𝖛𝖊𝖗, *that if the said* ▓▓▓▓ *when eighteen years of age, shall prefer to learn some mechanical trade, then the said* L. D. Harmon *shall make proper and suitable provision for the said* ▓▓▓▓ *to learn such a trade as he shall by taste and inclination seem to be adapted to; and the making of such provision shall be an equivalent for the payment of the one hundred dollars.*

𝕴𝖓 𝖂𝖎𝖙𝖓𝖊𝖘𝖘 𝖂𝖍𝖊𝖗𝖊𝖔𝖋, *the parties have hereunto set their hands and seals.*

IN PRESENCE OF

_____ Maurice Vele

For the Party of the First Part.

_____ L. D. Harmon

Indenture agreement.

*Courtesy of the New York State Library, Manuscripts and Special Collections Division.*

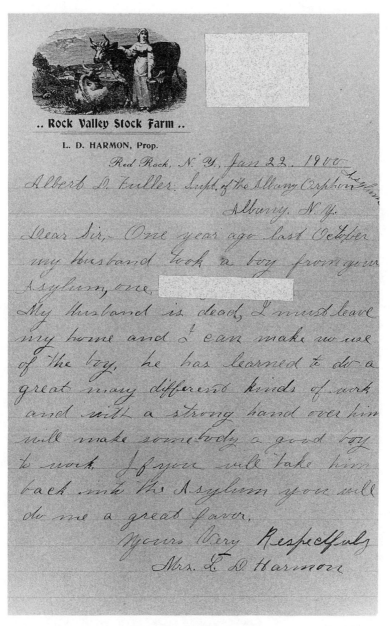

.. **Rock Valley Stock Farm** ..

L. D. HARMON, Prop.

Red Rock, N. Y., Jan 23, 1900

Albert D. Fuller: Supt. of the Albany Orphan Asylum

Albany. N. Y.

Dear Sir, — One year ago last October my husband took a boy from your Asylum, one ▮▮▮▮▮▮▮▮ My husband is dead, I must leave my home and I can make no use of the boy, he has learned to do a great many different kinds of work and with a strong hand over him will make somebody a good boy to work. If you will take him back into the Asylum you will do me a great favor.

Yours Very Respectfully

Mrs. L. D. Harmon

Letter from a foster home.
*Courtesy of the New York State Library, Manuscripts and Special Collections Division.*

# Children Outside the Asylum

*[Dear Sir:] . . . Maggie has ability and can do well, but I am sorry to say that her temper sooner or later seems to get the better of her, and she is also inclined to run rather wild. . . .*

*Dear Sir: I take my pen to address a few lines to you about young Smith. I find in him a very serious defect. . . . He seems to have a weakness either constitutional or acquired which shows itself in wetting the bed nearly every night. If you know of any remidy please tell me. I should not dare to keep a boy of this kind unless he could be cured. . . .*

*Dear [Friend]: I thought I would take the time in writing to you. . . . My mother has been up to see me. . . . She stayed all night and slept with me. . . .*

*Dear Sir: . . . I wish you were with us. . . . I remember when I used to run down stairs and ask for a paper and you used to say get up stairs or I['ll] bite your head off! But now it is all past and I am out in the world trying to be somebody and I shall be someday. For when any body says he shall be somebody and trys to be he never fails. . . .*

*[Dear Friend:] . . . I thank god that there is such a place [as the Albany Orphan Asylum]. what wood become of children if there was [no] place like that for them to go too.*

I n the nineteenth century childhood changed. More precisely, new parental attitudes toward children, evidenced as early as the mid-eighteenth century, coalesced at this time, transforming the whole process and meaning of childhood. For perhaps the first time, families and parents perceived childhood as a distinct stage in the life cycle, a time in which the young would undergo a gradual and painstaking preparation for eventual emergence into adulthood.

No longer miniature adults at age five or six contributing to the family economy, by the mid-nineteenth century America's children had no definable function within the home. No longer considered evil from the moment of birth, they had no wills to break, only innocent minds and hearts to mold. No longer certain of an intergenerational inheritance of land or livelihood, they had no future. No longer primarily producers, but consumers, their numbers within each family dwindled. Fertility declined and child rearing replaced childbearing as a woman's major function within the home.[1]

As a consequence of these changes, children became the centerpiece of the new domestic circle. They stayed at home longer in order to receive the moral guidance, the psychological nurturance, and the education and skills necessary to sustain them in the new industrial marketplace. No longer an asset but a threat to the economic order, young boys attended school instead of going to work, they joined clubs instead of trade unions, and they readied themselves for careers instead of marriage.[2]

Girls' lives changed somewhat less over the course of the century as they found the necessary training and workplace and role models appropriate to their sex simply by staying at home. But they too depended on their families for a prolonged period as they waited to make the shift from the homes of their fathers to those of their husbands. And for girls too, schooling, even advanced education, became increasingly valuable as the "profession" of motherhood took on new dimensions and as wives and mothers appropriated control over the spiritual, emotional, intellectual, and cultural life of the family.[3]

Today, the "new childhood" of the nineteenth century consumes a whole class of historical literature. Historians' interest in children no doubt has been buoyed by twentieth-century advances in the related discipline of developmental psychology.[4] Yet it is not the child, but the child in relation to the parent that lies at the core of scholarship in both fields of inquiry. From a theoretical perspective, the parent-child relationship holds the key to basic human development and successful socialization and is very often perceived as the critical ingredient in resolving society's ills and shortcomings. Infant attachment, the emergence of a sense of autonomy, identity formation, and the ability to meet the developmental tasks of adolescence are all said to hinge precariously on the nature of the parent-child dynamic. The way the child receives treatment at the hands of parents at each stage in the developmental cycle not only determines but can very often predetermine adult behavior, self perception, and general mental health. Parental neglect, abuse, or indifference invariably spawns society's deviants, delinquents, and dropouts.[5]

This perception, based as it is on systematic inquiry in the social sciences, perhaps best explains why nineteenth-century changes in the concept of childhood seem so remarkable, so modern, so essential. How could childhood have been otherwise? But, in fact, it was. Historians tells us that only in recent times, and only within certain (mainly western) cultures, have we achieved a mode of child rearing that can be recognized not only as self-actualizing but as "non-abusive." In the past, society in a sense sanctioned harshness and brutality. Infanticide, abandonment, cruelty, and coercion reigned for centuries before the cult of domesticity emerged to change it all. Only since the late eighteenth century, at the very earliest, have modern cultures reached "a therapeutic stage in which empathy with a child's independent needs is possible," in which love supersedes instrumentality and projective distortion, and in which children reside at the center rather than the periphery of familial relations.[6]

Scholars in a number of disciplines have taken exception to such broad-sweeping theoretical claims.[7] Nevertheless, child abuse existed in the past as it persists today. And if any group of children fell between the cracks of the new domesticity of the nineteenth century, surely it was the children of the asylum. If poor, negligent, even degenerate parents did not crush blossoming childhood, then certainly the asylum keeper and his bevy of cruel attendants would finish the job.

That is the image fixed in our historical consciousness, an image perpetuated as well in fiction and autobiography. That, however, is not the image projected here. Certainly the parents whose correspondence appears in the first series, "Parents and Children," were not demonstrably abusive, but in fact quite the opposite. Abuse may be implicit in the very act of abandonment or separation, however, even when, as in the case of the asylum child, abandonment very often meant survival. In the eyes of the child, prolonged and often repeated separation must at times have been tantamount to the permanent loss of a parent by death. Grieving over such loss surely must have erupted again and again in aggressive episodes or have been turned tragically inward and manifest as depression, indifference, phobias, or physiological complaints.[8]

If the children represented in the following series of letters were in fact angry, frightened, or frustrated, they generally did not express those feelings in their own words. Rare are such comments as those made by a nineteen-year-old boy who had spent five years in the Albany Orphan Asylum. Upon leaving that institution he stated emphatically that he did not want his whereabouts revealed to his mother who, he felt, would surely make trouble if it lay in her power: "Perhaps you can not understand this feeling of a boy to his mother, all I can say is that I feel like this, that a mother's duty does not end in the act of bringing into this world of turmoil children and then leaving them to take care of themselves. She abandoned . . . us when we most needed a mother's care and from her seed of abandonment sown, she must abandonment reap."

For the most part, children of the asylum had neither the schooling nor the opportunity to articulate such ponderous emotions. Yet the question remains: How did young children respond to institutional separation from their parents in the nineteenth century? The answer, quite simply, is that in large measure we do not know. The silence as one sifts through the hundreds of letters written by asylum children is not only disappointing but deafening. Yet, their actions often speak louder than words, especially those children who never returned to their homes but found what home they could in the context of family placement, foster care, or indenture.

As a group, the indentured children seem trusting, grateful, and at times full of joy at their new home life. But oftentimes, once the papers of indenture arrived or as they began to mature toward adolescence, disturbing behavioral patterns repeatedly emerged—lying, stealing, aggressive outbursts, and running away.[9] If the animosity underlying such behavior was directed at parents, these children did not say. Instead, they focused their rage elsewhere, at substitute caretakers, dumb animals, or the self. If they felt abandoned or forsaken, for the most part they did not convey that message. If they agonized over the ambivalent emotions of love and anger, they had neither the psychic capacity nor the literary flourish to reveal such conflict. Yet when they ran away, they ran to their own homes. When they became insolent, rude or disobedient, it was frequently after a visit or letter from a parent, sibling, or relative. If they talked incessantly about anything, it was (however unrealistic) the long-awaited return home.

Sadness, disappointment, and rage often clutched at the very soul of asylum children. Despite such emotions, however, they appear time and again to have had the capacity to love and to forge deep bonds of mutual affection. There were exceptions, of course. But if nothing else emerges from the following series of letters it is this: that the children of the asylum were no pathetic substrata of the maternally deprived. Rather, they exhibited an astonishing resiliency in their readiness and ability to form deep and binding attachments to their temporary guardians within the institution, guardians who very often openly and freely returned the favor.

In order to accomplish a sense of attachment outside the family circle these children must have first had the experience of a secure and trusting attachment at home.[10] But it became those subsequent attachments within the institution that helped so many of these asylum children weather the storm of repeated separation, abandonment, and loss. The asylum became their new home and its keeper their temporary parent and long-term confidant, its teachers and attendants their guides and disciplinarians, its hundreds of children their siblings and friends. It was not a life of joy or childish innocence, but one in which mutual affections tempered the sharp sting of separation and parental loss.

## Daniel and Willie Clemens

Although indenture had fallen into relative disuse by the 1890s, trustees of the Albany Orphan Asylum continued to rely on this ancient practice of labor-in-return-for-care as a means of disposing of older children whose parents could not or would not care for them. The act of indenture did not end a birth parent's involvement with a child, however, although it did very often complicate continued communication. Once a child was legally bound to a foster home, parental rights fell into a tenuous void. Foster parents often demanded that birth ties be severed completely. Parental interference often mixed the children up emotionally and gave them courage to defy the authority of their substitute caretakers. Yet parents continually intervened in the lives of their children, even after indenture, and foster families had little if any legal recourse to prevent it.

Daniel and Willie Clemens, both teenagers, were two of Hattie Clemens's four children. Their father had died of consumption in 1883. Poor and an invalid herself, Hattie turned to the orphan asylum for help. Because of their advanced age, Daniel and Willie were placed out on indenture within a year. A younger brother, George, remained behind at the institution. Their sister (name unknown), previously had been placed out with a family by the mother. Daniel Clemens found a permanent home with his foster care providers. Willie's case proved much less successful. His first "trial" with a farmer in Indian Fields, New York, ended after only six months. A second indenture as a photographer's assistant in Little Falls proved no better. The boy could not be trusted and grew increasingly restless, eventually running away to care for himself.

March 23, 1886

Dear Sir:

Will you please write and let me know in regards to Dannie and where he is and you will oblidge me very much. give my love to the other children. i remain yours with respect.

Mrs. Clemens

March 26, 1886

Dear Madam:

Your letter is at hand. I am happy to be able to inform you that Daniel likes his new home very much so far and the people are pleased with him. I have obtained a home for Willie with a neighbor of the man who has Daniel so that they could be near each other. Willie is also pleased with his home and the people who have him like him also. . . . The persons spoken of are farmers and I think well disposed persons. They came well recommended and I will look after the boys myself so as to see that they are rightly used although I do not anticipate any trouble in that direction. Georgie is well and is so thoroughly acquainted now with the other boys that he does not miss his brothers as he would have done when he first came. . . . . .

Yours respectfully,
Albert D. Fuller, Superintendent

April 30, 1886

Dear Sir:

I received your letter about the boys. many thanks to you. i heard from dannie. they like thair places very much. I would like to know how Georgie[s] health is now as he is not very healthy at the best. please let me know and does he feel homesick after the boys. I remain with respect,

Mrs. Hattie Clemens

December 8, 1886

[Mr. Fuller] Sir:

I send you this in regard to Willie Clemens that we took from your place. As to keeping him . . . and having him do as he does is entirely out of the question, and as to trusting him, you might as well trust a dog with your dinner as to trust him to do what you tell him to after he is out of your sight. and he is so untruthful that he cant hardly speak the truth. . . . He has told lies enough about you and the asylum to sink the whole business. I should like to have a Boy if you will change with me. I will bring him, but I dont want <u>him</u>. I would rather not have any. A good Boy is a great company and can do many little chores if they are trusty. But as for <u>Willie</u> the truth is not in him. When I see you I will tell you more that I do not care to write. Please send me an answer as soon as you get this and tell me what I had better do.

Yours with respect,
Charles H. Conrad

December 29, 1886

Sir:

I suppose you are looking for me to bring Willie back. but I was sick when I recieved your letter . . . and have been nearly every [day] since, part of the time confined to the house and Willie as I told you before has been sore every [day] since he has been here and his feet is so bad at present that he cant wear his shoes. as soon as his feet get well enough and I get able to come I will bring him.

Yours in haste,
Charles H. Conrad

January 3, 1887

Dear Sir:

Your letter of the 29th Dec. at hand in regard to Willie Clemens. You must have misunderstood me.

I have not agreed to take him back; only desire that you bring him here some Thursday so that I may have an opportunity to talk with him. Hope that he is doing better than he was.

Yours respectfully,
Albert D. Fuller, Superintendent

June 6, 1887

Dear Madam:

Your letter of the 2nd. instant has been received. Willie and Georgie are getting along first rate.* Willie is as fat as a pig. They were both delighted to hear from you and send much love. . . .

I am also glad to know that Dannie writes to you and that he is well and happy.

Are you so situated now that you could take Willie. Possibly he might be of help to you. If you can please let me know and I will send him to you. He is a very good boy now and I think would give you very little trouble. His health is also excellent.

Yours hastily,
Albert D. Fuller, Superintendent

---

*As this letter indicates, Willie had been returned to the asylum by Charles Conrad sometime between January and June 1887.

June 19, 1887

Dear Sir:

recived your letter last week. was glad to hear that the children was well. in regards to Willie i am trying to find him a place. i have no home of my own. i work out by the month when i am well enough to for my health is not very good eny of the time. but i will try to get both of the boys a place as soon as i can and very thankfull to you for your kind care of my fatherless children.

respectfully yours,
Hattie Clemens

October 1887

Dear Madam:

Your letter of the 3rd inst. is before me and contents noted. I have found an excellent home for Willie in [Little Falls]. I hope that he will please the man so that he will keep him as I consider the home a good one. . . . Hope the next time that I hear from you that you will be better.

Very respectfully yours,
Albert D. Fuller, Superintendent

November 14, 1887

Dr sir:

I have to inform you this morning of an event that is least looked for by us. the Boy Willie Clemens skiped out yesterday Morning betwene 9 & 10 oclock very suddenly with out having a word of trouble or giving us any warning. I went up to my Gallery to look after things a little and while I was gone and while Mrs Bernard was in another room for a few moments he left on a run. Some of the Neighbors saw him running and told us whitch way he went. This was Sunday Morning and so early that he had not changed his clothes for sunday school and had on his old clothes that he wore when he sifted ashes. If he had wated an hour later he would have been dressed for church. He had about 40 cts that we had given him by little at a time and one dollar that we mised the other day whitch he probably had taken. he steared right for the RR station and has headed to wards Saratoga. he talked a great deal about his mother and probably will fetch up at that place, if he has good luck. Willie done first rate until the papers of addoption [indenture] arived here, then he seamed to turn his actions differently. he began to act as if his restraint was off and act out nature. we caught him in several capers, and on one occasion I gave him a severe lecture and told him that the next time I should punish him but up to the time of his leaving had not laid my hands uppon him. He had grown quite fleshy and not grown 1" in hight in 8 weeks by actual measurement. He had good care and plenty to eat and slept in a nice feather bed. Our Neighbours can testify that he was nicely used but as he has turned out I dont want him back. this has shaken all the confidence I had in him and will not take him back on any terms. No child could be used better than he was, even if he had been our own. He had a new pair of pants that he never had on and left them and went off with an old pair on. This week we was to get him a new suit and over coat and fix him up for winter. He got quite handy in the gallery by assisting in the printing and had went out once with the armature and took quite a good view all alone. Perhaps I pushed him ahead to fast for his judgement and gave him to good an oppinion of him self. The old saying to often proves true, what is born in the Bone remains long in the flesh. I guess he sprung from quite low people. We are sorry to have this happen but as it was, we can do no more.

Yours respectfully,
J. J. Bernard

December 4, 1887

Dear Sir:

I now sit down two write you a few lines. I am going to do my very best and I hope you have forgiven me. . . . I have got a lot of new cloths and I go two Sunday School every Sunday and I will send you the picture to-morrow of the house that I took. please write and tell me how my brother is. Good Bye.*

Willie Clemens

December 16, 1887

Dear Friend:

Your letter of the 4th inst. was duly received. I am very much pleased with it. It is a good letter and I am glad to know of your resolutions. The picture sent, I will keep. I guess you will make a good photographer yet. . . . I will call and see you before long.

Your friend,
Albert Fuller

February 2, 1888

[Dear Mr. Fuller]:

I recieved a letter from you 3 or 4 days ago in regard to the Boy Willie. He is well and is well pleased with his home. He does as well as most boys of

*This letter is written by Willie from Little Falls after his return to the Bernard family. It is unknown if he returned of his own volition or was brought back forcibly.

his class can do. He will tell untruths and that is about the worst failing he has but we have got him partly corrected in that regard. His mother since his trip to Saratoga last fall having got hold of his whare-abouts has written to him 3 or 4 times and posted all the rest of the brothers and sisters and they begin to write to him and when he gets these letters it has a tendency to make him uneasy and consequently keeps him mixed up. his mother writes that when he gets large enough she hopes he and the rest of the family & her will yet all be living to gether. Wall that may seem all right to her but it has a bad influence on the Boy and gives him to understand that we can keep him until such time as he may deem sufficient and then go to his mother. Now Mr Fuller she gave up all claims on her children and put them with you to do by them as you saw fit and if so, what claim will she ever have on them. If it were not for this writing he would be better contented. The boy is willing to do every thing we want him to do and enjoys him self as well as any one Boy out of a thousand and is well fed and clothed and is growing verry fast.

Yours Respectfully,

J. J. Bernard

May 22, 1888

[Dear Mr. Fuller]:

The Boy Willie Clemens has skiped again. He left yesterday. He has developed badly very fast since the snow has gone and cold weather has disapperd. he has watched the river and canal and longed to fish and rove about but we have kept him about his business as well as we could but he has been very Saucy and stuborn and taken to stealing from us. . . . he is a very Bad Boy indeed and he must never come back here again. You will probably find him with his mother . . . or at Saratoga at his Uncle's. he made his brags that his uncle would hide him if he could get there. We kept his clothes locked up quite a while so he could not get them but he got dangerous for only a woman to deal with through the day. He got to be such a notorious liar that we could not place any faith in what he said, would make fuses among the neighbours and finally he got so we could not trust him out of our sight. He would be stoning children or up to some mischies all the time.

Yours respectfully,

J. J. Bernard

P.S. Dont Send Willie here again under no conditions. We cant have a thief and a liar here. All this spring we have had to keep every thing locked and well guarded and will not do it any more atall.

June 27, 1888

Dear Sir:

. . . I wish to ask you if you know where willie is. i recived two very important letters from the folkes he was with and in the last one they say that he has run away from them. if so you would oblidge me very much if you will let me know where he is. i am very sorry if he has done wrong but they had not ought to blame me for i always tried to bring my children up to do what was right and in a Christian way. if you will let me know where he is i will thank you very much indeed for their letters was very unsetling to me and made me feel very bad. here is a stamp for return mail. i remain

yours with respect,
Hattie Clemens.

June 29, 1888

Dear [Mrs. Clemens]:

. . . I am very sorry that Mr. Bernard has written you an unkind letter. There was no necessity for that that I know of. I do not think that you want your children to do wrong or that you have ever encouraged them in so doing.

I am sorry to say that I do not know where Willie is. I supposed that I would get track of him long before this, but have not done so. I have no doubt but that he is well and safe. He is large enough to look out for himself.

I am afraid that he has not been a very good boy for sometime past as I have been informed that he has taken what did not belong to him. I do not know positively as regards the truth of this charge, but to my own knowledge has told a good many falsehoods. I can assure you that Willies wrong conduct has given me a great deal of pain. I like the boy and have always tried to be just and kind to him. Some months since I visited him at his home in Little Falls and had a long talk with him by himself. I found the home where he was staying to be a very pleasant one and Willie told me that he was kindly treated. He appeared to be comfortably clothed and gave evidence as far as I could judge of having the right sort of treatment. I questioned him closely in regard to his condition and as to whether everything was all right in regard to his home. He told me that he was trying very hard to be a good boy and he had no complaints to make in regard to his home.

If I hear from [him] I will inform you at once, and if you find out where he is please let me know without delay.

Yours respectfully,
Albert D. Fuller

*Willie Clemens eventually drifted to Troy, New York, where he supported himself and maintained infrequent correspondence with Albert Fuller at least through 1890. Hattie Clemens was also living in Troy about this time and working out when her health permitted. She arranged to have George returned to her in June 1888. As far as can be determined, Daniel remained with his foster family throughout the course of his indenture.*

## Helen Shagrin

Many children who faced indenture came from abusive or severely negligent circumstances with parents unwilling or incapable of providing care. Such children at times rejected their birth parents as they felt they had been rejected and held fast to the promises of a new home. Ten-year-old Helen Shagrin was sent to the Albany asylum with three sisters in 1884 on complaint of the Humane Society of Saratoga County. The girl had little if any education. Her family was reportedly in deplorable condition, the mother having recently died and the father "a confirmed drunkard." Between May 1884 and June 1886 the asylum placed Helen no less than four times. Each time she returned to the asylum within only a few months, foster parents complaining that she stammered too much or that she was "stupid" and unable to understand or that they simply could not manage her stubborn, willful and disobedient nature. Helen's fifth placement in the rural New York community of Nassau in Rensselaer County, however, proved the charm.

September 17, 1886

Dear Sir:

I will now write you a few lines to let you know that I received Helen Shagrin's certificate [of indenture]. I had meant to have written to you or come & seen you, but it is just as well, for she is as good as any girl of her age, that has not had any parents to bring them up; and I shall try to be a good mother to her, & do the best by her I can. To see her one would think it had always been her home, she is so contented & happy, she sings most of the time. She has only missed one day at Sabbath school since she has been here. She sends her love to you all. This from,

Lydia B. Wilson

February 5, 1888

Dear Sir:

I received a few lines from you the other day, wanting to know how Helen was getting along, she is well and healthy so far, as any child can be.

She is very fleshy and gets better looking every day, and she begins to know it. I dress her as good as any girl of her age. I often tell her she is too proud. She likes the looking glass very well. She went to S[unday] S[chool] and Church all summer, until the going got too bad, and this Winter the roads were so bad I taught her at home. She won't own the name of Shagrin and wants us to tell people she is our own child, and calls us Papa and Mamma. If any thing happens to her, I will write to you. From,

Lydia B. Wilson

February 15, 1889

[Dear Sir:]

I thought I would write and let you know of our loss. It is with a sad heart I pen these few lines to you. It is just three weeks to-day since my husband died with a shock and all there is in my family is Helen and myself. His children all have their homes and my son is up at Round Lake in a store and all of my friends tell me they dont think it will pay me to keep house. One of Mr. Wilson's daughters lives up at Sand Lake and works in the mill and she says Helen may come up and stay a spell & work in the mill & some of my friends say they will take her this summer & I will let her go a spell if you are willing for me to but I shall look after her as much as I possibly can for she is at the age she needs a good deal of care. I tell her that if she is a good girl it may be that I will live with her some of these days. She wants me to ask you to tell her in your next letter where [her] sisters are & I will write for her to them. I will try to look after her wherever she is & I shall always try to be a mother to her for she seems near to me. Perhaps I will keep house & visit my friends this summer and in the winter Helen & I [can be] together again. Hoping to hear from you soon again. I remain your friend & well wisher. Helen sends her love to you all.

Lydia B. Wilson

*Helen remained with Mrs. Wilson over the next two years. As the following letter indicates, she subsequently married and left to make her own home. If asylum records are accurate, Helen was but sixteen years old at the time.*

October 5, 1890

Dear Sir:

*As it has been some time since I heard from you I will drop you a few lines in regard to Helen saying that she is married and has left me. I did well by her gave her a good out set such as stove, chairs, carpets, and all necessary articles to keep house with and I think that she has done as well as if she had been my own child. She has seemed near to me and I will always be a good friend to her in sickness and health. I will send her marriage notice to you. I told her to give her name Shagrin but she said that she would not and i was sorry she didn't. She was always mad if anyone called her Shagrin. I hope to hear from you.*

*Mrs. L. B. Wilson*


## Ella Brown

Motivation for taking an asylum child on indenture varied from case to case. Some, perhaps most, wanted free labor, others wished only for the loving companionship of a child. Rare were situations like that facing ten-year-old Ella Brown. Intended to replace their own dear lost daughter, Ella's new parents placed high expectations on every facet of the girl's behavior and demeanor. Authorities knew little of Ella's family. She had spent so many years as an inmate at the Children's Home of Amsterdam, New York, before coming to Albany, that information relevant to the child's past had either been lost or left unrecorded. With little experience of family life and confronted with the demands of middle-class society, Ella's indenture (or expected adoption) seemed doomed to failure. Ella's new home was in Valatie, New York.

March 5, 1892

Dear Sir:

[W]e received from your home for Orphan children yesterday a little girl Ella Brown by name for which please accept our thanks. At present we like the appearance of the child very much; she seems very quiet and we think we will like her very much, as she will soon [in a measure] take the place of our only child and daughter who died [at age sixteen on] Jan. 24, 1892.

It is not for a drudge that we want her, but we want that she should become our own daughter. We will send her to school and give her a common school education, also give her instructions on the Piano. Should she prove what we hope she will at the expiration of her trial term . . . we will adopt her as our own.

We have a great many things that our daughter left, which we will give to her for her own amusement. We are trying to love her already and pray to Him who rules the universe to so rule us that we may be wise to bring her up in the love and fear of the Lord.

Please let me know all that you know of the date of her birth, parentage, etc. that may be of use to us. We are members of the Lutheran Church and shall expect her to attend its services and Sabbath School whenever her health will permit.

Now as Ella wants me to say something to you for her I will quote her own words. "I send my love to you and all the girls also to the teachers. At present I feel a little lonesome but think I will like [it] here after a while. Yesterday I went with Mr. Grant on the street to the Post Office. This morning I helped wash the dishes and am now looking over a lot of pictures and eating nuts and apples, Ella."

Ella feels a little homesick just now, but we are trying to make her feel as lively and at home as possible. We will be up to see you in a few weeks and will bring her along too you.

Very respectfully yours,
M. W. Grant

March 20, 1892

Dear Sir:

. . . I now make our weekly report to you of the condition and welfare of Ella Brown the child you have entrusted to our care. We still like her very much; she being obedient, respectful, polite, honest, truthful and obliging. Her health seems to be quite good only complaining a little at one time, and then I think it was caused by change of diet and water. She is now well and enjoying herself. Her eyes seem to be weak when a bright light shines in them. We are undertaking her instruction in reading, writing, spelling, and arithmetic for awhile yet until she becomes better acquainted in the village. She attends church with us and has been twice to Sabbath School. To sum it up all in a Nut shell, we are well pleased with her and I think she is with us, for a caller asked her where she liked it the best and if she wanted to go back again, her reply was that she did not want to go back again and that she wanted always [to] remain with Mr & Mrs Grant. . . . May God bless you for the interest you take in the poor and homeless orphans.

Very respectfully,
M. W. Grant

April 20, 1892

Dear Sir:

I defered making my report earlier as I wanted a day or two more in which to make up my mind what I should report in the case of the girl Ella Brown. We all [a]long were greatly in hope that she would be just the child which we would want, and therefore have reported the bright side of her life here, but am now a little afraid she will not answer our purpose.

1st her eyes seem to be quite weak; 2nd She is very selfish; 3rd Procrastination seems to predominate; 4th She has no taste for learning and prefering to sit idle with her hands in her lap rather than taking a book to study; 5th is gifted with a peculiar temper which is not loveable and which she for the last week or more has liked to show.

Now what we want of a girl is this; not a drudge, but one of a good disposition and that will try to learn, willing to lend a helping hand about the house in doing little chores etc. etc., in fact willing to take hold and try to make herself a young lady. We want to educate her not alone in the common schools, but to one worthy [of] a higher education, as also in music.

We have a Piano in the house which may be used at all times by willing and trusting hands. Ella seems to want to play rather than study and we have told her repeatedly that if she would learn well and that when she had become advanced far enough in her reading so she could read most words at sight, that she could use the Piano, and of course we would get her an instructor on it.

For the first few weeks she done better than now. I am very sorry to make these reports but duty demands it.

We will try her yet a while longer and see what the future will bring forth. In the mean time, please give me some advice how to manage with her to have her become the girl we want. If i had the time to call on you and explain all you would probably understand better my desires in regard to a girl. I would make her as near as I could like my own daughter.

We pray God that he will so temper the mind of Ella that she will so live as to become a good Christian and an ornament to Society.

Respectfully yours,
M. W. Grant

*Ella's behavior improved immediately following Mrs. Grant's letter, "as though she was trying to make amends." Over the long term, however, Ella's final outcome is unknown.*

## Matilda (Tillie) Hoffman

Although there were many exceptions, foster parents most often expressed their long-term investment in an indentured child in monetary, rather than emotional terms. Many children, like fourteen-year-old Tillie Hoffman, understood their position within the home, as labor and not family. She knew that bad behavior could easily result in punishment, dismissal, or loss of even the meanest privileges. Yet try as she might, Tillie seemed repeatedly to displease her foster parents. She had spent eight years in the

Albany asylum before being placed in their home. The girl's mother had died of consumption while she and her two brothers were still in that institution. An older sister who had cared for the mother during her illness subsequently married and made a home of her own. The children's father, a German immigrant and musician, had deserted the family and refused to do anything for them. Tillie had few protectors and her only hope seemed the family of siblings with whom she wished someday to reside. Tillie's placement was in Ballston Spa, New York.

November 6, 1885

Dear Mr. Fuller:

I received your letter last Saturday evening. we have all been busy for awhile. I thought I would drop you a few lines telling you what I intended to do. I am going to be a good girl and try & do what I can for [Mrs. Waldman].* when I am asked to do anything I will do it pleasantly. I am very sorry to act the way I have to Mrs Waldman lately. I hope I shall keep my word as I promised. . . . when she speaks to me I am always going to speak to her and answer pleasantly. I often think the time will come when I had wished I had been good to Mr & Mrs Waldman. I know I shall feel very bad about it so I think I shall like it here & I shall get along all right if I am a good girl. I hope this will be the last time I shall ever have to write to you for acting so. with love to all.

From,
Tillie Hoffman

February 8, 1887

Dear Sir:

I wish that you would write to Matilda & tell her that if she does not do as she is told, that I have a perfect right to punish her as I would one of my own children. She has been advised very badly & is so impudent that I cannot keep her in my family if she continues as she is doing. Now she seems to think that I have no right to correct her in any way & is altogether a very bad and disobedient girl. I have been trying for some time to get her another place but without success so far. I should like to know if I have got to submit to having such a girl in my family & if there is no other way for me to do. I do not think it is right for her to have every thing on her side & me no redress, for it is come to that now that she is really beyond me, unless I am in continual strife with her. I wish, if you can, that you would be on the look-

---

*This letter is in response to a reprimand by Albert Fuller upon reports from Tillie's foster home of the girl's bad behavior.

out for a place for her. She is a capable girl & has been well taught & if she was only different would be invaluable.

Yours very truly,
Mrs. H. G. Waldman

February 17, 1887

Dear Sir:

I received your letter in answer to one of mine about Tillie a few days ago & hasten to answer it. I must say that I am rather surprised at the tone of your letter & cannot quite understand it as you speak as though Tillie had been whipped, now I wish to assure you that such is not the case. she has never been whipped since with us, once about two years ago Mr. Waldman ferruled her for refusing to answer a question that had been put to her all of twenty times & she has had her ears boxed a good many times for impudence; now that is the extent of the punishment & I do not think that you can say that I have not a perfect right to punish her when she is disobedient. I am sure that I should feel as if I had not done my duty by Tillie if I allowed her to go unpunished when she had done wrong. About your taking Tillie, I do not feel able or willing to pay you the $50., as I have had all the trouble of teaching her & now she is really getting useful, I would say to you the same as I did to a lady who talks some of taking her that I will agree to pay $25. when she is eighteen & whoever takes her will pay the other $25. She certainly will be worth $25 [for the 2 1/2 years that is still unexpired] & her clothes for the time. she certainly would go from here with plenty of clothes which she did not have when she came; her only extra luggage then consisted of an old apron & a fine & coarse comb, not even a night dress to put on, on her arrival. Tillie has been doing very much better ever since I wrote you & I could not part with her now as I am without a girl in the kitchen at present. I am inclined to try Tillie for a time longer as I think she is trying to do better, she is very easily influenced by the servants that I have had & a good many of them have made trouble for her by putting her up to not doing as she is told. Tillie is a very foolish girl, for she could have a good place here as long as she would want one if she could only be prevailed upon to curb her bad temper & mind & try to please Mr. Waldman & myself. I am sorry that I have had to apply to you & perhaps things will work themselves out all right.

Yours truly,
Mary L. Waldman

Larrabees Point, Vermont [undated]

Dear Sister:

Think how far I am away from you now. I have been sent away from home for being a very naughty girl to Mrs. Waldman. I am ashamed to have to write and say so. I have thought it all over and have written to them seeing if they will take me back again with them. Oh what a lovely home it was for me if I had only been a little different girl from what i had been before; there was everything there to keep me happy. . . . If they do not want me again I have made up my mind I shall come & live with you until I can get a nice place to work. . . . I can do all kinds of housework but washing which I do not care to do. Why could not Freddie come up here on the train & I could go down with him, or, if I had the money, I would just as soon go alone as to have anyone go with me. . . . Please write back as soon as you can & let me know what you think about it. . . . Send me $2 & I can come right away to you if you wish me to, which I know you will.

[Your sister,]
Tillie

December 22, 1887

Dear [Mr. Fuller] Sir:

I received your letter this morning. I am going to tell you just where I am & how I like it also. Mrs. Waldman has sent me to her Auntie in the country to live with her till I attain the age of 18 years & then she said I might do as I choose about it after that. Now my sister has promised me she would take me to live with her if I should go, which I most certainly would do if you would be glad to have me. Mrs. Waldman has always said that I made trouble with the help she had, but I know I have not done anything of the kind as she thinks I have. Another thing she has always said that I have made her children so saucy that she was sick & tired of me & she must find me another house to live in till I was of age. Now since I have been living out here, I have heard that she has always had trouble keeping her help, & I know she always will if she does not try & do different with them than what she does now. I always said that when I was of age I was going to stay right there & I thought I could go right on with the work & it would be so nice for me & for her also. I do not believe that any girl that was ever taken out of your institution was treated like I have been, or worked so hard as I have done from 6 a.m. till 8 or 9 in the evening. I know I have done my duty while I lived there & they all know the same to, as well as I do. Now I know any young girl will be saucy that has seen as many strange faces as I have seen since I have lived with Mrs. Waldman & how can they help it when some one is always setting them up to do it as I have been set to. I know if I should live in a place where there were only two children in the family I should be contented as well as any where.

From,
Tillie Hoffman

*No record exists regarding Tillie Hoffman's release from her indenture or ultimate reunion with her family.*

## Lottie Van Allen

The majority of children placed in homes by the Albany asylum generally ranged in age from twelve to sixteen years. Blossoming adolescence, a difficult experience under the best of circumstances, proved a volatile life-cycle event for the indentured child. As the natural progression of physical, biological, and emotional changes occurred, these children many times confronted the additional psychological burdens of abandonment, neglect, and physical and sexual abuse.

We know little of the day-to-day circumstances from which they emerged. Nevertheless, the behavior of many indentured children often bordered on the pathological. The basic symptomatology of parental deprivation (or bereavement) surfaced again and again—aggressiveness expressed in the form of stealing or pointless deceit and evasion, a violent acting out either in the form of self-abuse or the abuse of brute animals, and sexual promiscuity.

Asylum officials often explained away such behavior in the context of the times, as simple, yet tragic, heredity. So it was with Lottie Van Allen. She hailed from a long blood line of paupers in Washington County, New York.* Her mother was dead and her father, a farm laborer, incarcerated at the Clinton Prison in upstate New York. Lottie spent four years at the Albany institution. Probably fourteen years old at the time of her indenture, Lottie was described as "intelligent" but not far advanced and her most defining feature that of a deformed or "enlarged" chest. Lottie's indenture was in White Creek, Washington County, New York.

March 29, 1886

Dear Sir:

I do not know whether you will be surprised at the receipt of this letter or not. Perhaps your previous acquaintances with Lottie Van Allen will lead you to expect something of the kind. She is without any exception becoming the worst child I ever saw. The first year she was quite a help to me and my own children were so small that the bad influence of her example was not noticeable. But she has developed worse traits during the past year and I really do not know what course to take with her. No punishment which I consider within the bounds of reason has the least effect upon her. She will tell a lie when the truth would answer the purpose a great deal better and steal when

---

*Lottie was the sister of Mary Van Allen, whose letters appear in the first series of letters.

the same articles could be had for the asking. Besides when I am obliged to be away from home she is constantly telling something to make trouble with the help and her conversation with my own little girl is of a kind which would be least apt to exert a good influence over the mind of any child. Altogether it is a bad piece of business and the question is What can I do? I would like to exchange her for a good honest boy. Please let me hear from you soon.

Yours in haste,
Mrs. L. E. Bridges

April 2, 1886

Dear Madam:

Your favor of the 29th inst. in regard to the girl Lottie Van Allen is at hand and contents noted. I have been looking for just such a letter for many months. I felt just as positive that it would come as of my own existance.

I am sorry for you but we can not exchange with you. I believe that the best thing that you can do is to go before your Justice and have said child committed to the House of Refuge. Since you were here I have some experiences with the older girl [Anna] which confirms my belief in the inherent badness of the Van Allen stock. They appear to want to do right and seem to be sorry when they go wrong but have not strength of will enough to overcome the many very bad traits of character that they have inherited. I believe for the good of others as well as their own good that the only safe plan is for the whole Van Allen tribe to be kept in institutions of some kind all their lives. Otherwise they will be their own ruin and drag others with them.

If some reliable neighbor will assume the bonds that you signed we will permit the transfer. Perhaps if the girl was given to understand that she would be sent to the House of Refuge if she did not change her course it might have a good effect for a time although I have very little faith in any permanent improvement.

There is too much hereditary taint for that. Please drop me a line within a week or too saying what you have decided to do.

Yours respectfully,
Albert D. Fuller

January 31, 1888

Dear Sir:

I received your letter last evening in regard to Lottie Van Allen. I can only say in reply that there is no permanent change.* She is subject to tem-

---

*Lottie remained with the Bridges family for nearly two years after the initial correspondence requesting discharge of the girl from their care.

porary reformations which sometimes last for a day or two and then she falls back into her usual condition. I think the difference between the good she is to me and the care she has been are so evenly balanced that i would require a very close calculation to decide whether I had gained any by her [indenture]. I have done for her the best I could and shall look forward with relief to the time when I shall be through with all responsibilites concerning her. I think her Father's [prison] sentence expires in June and perhaps he will claim her. I shall not offer any opposition in that case. She will tell the most useless lies and the most unreasonable ones of any person old or young that I ever met. She prefers stealing to asking for things that she knows I would be perfectly willing for her to have. The evil seems born in that crooked frame and no power on earth can separate it until the soul is freed from the body. I have taken her to see her aged Grandmother in hopes to kindle up a regard for somebody or something that might result in good. Her brother has also visited her but I have given up hoping for any change. If you have any suggestions to offer I should be pleased to hear from you. The case is beyond any experience I have ever heard of. Hoping to hear from you soon, I remain,

Yours with respect,<br>Mrs. L. E. Bridges

*Asylum records do not indicate when Lottie was to be released from her original indenture nor is it known for certain if she remained until the end of her term. The final bit of information on the girl appears in a letter from one of Lottie's aunts writing to the asylum in the summer of 1893. The girl would have been twenty-one years old at the time. "Lottie was married," her aunt reported, "but she could not let the [men] alone so she got took to [jail] & She is ten times Worse then she ever Was. She lays out Doors nights With them. She had a good man . . . [but] he Was to good for her."*

## Lorenzo Moore

Perhaps the most frequent complaint against asylum children placed out on indenture was their untruthfulness. The persistence of such behavior angered, frustrated, and even shocked many foster parents. At times they would relate in depth to Superintendent Fuller the intricacy of certain deceptions that seemed almost impossible to believe.

Young Lorenzo Moore told frequent and elaborate falsehoods. Most probably illegitimate, he came to the Albany Orphan Asylum at the age of five, a few years after his mother had married. A family friend reported to Albert Fuller some years later her surprise that Lorenzo was still alive, "he was so frail when I saw him before he went to Albany. I did not think he would ever grow up." Lorenzo did grow but at the age of twelve was still a bed wetter. After seven years in the Albany asylum, he lived and worked in three different foster homes. The difficult behavior of his early years, however, eventually eased and he fell into a comfortable and productive life during his third and final indenture.

April 29, 1887

Dear Sir:

Your letter at hand. I take this, my first spare moment, to answer. I was so thankful for those few lines, it seems to take a burden off my shoulder[s]. I will try to answer your questions as truthfully & conscienciously as possible. In the first place the boy [Lorenzo Moore] has enjoyed the best of health, he has not been sick an hour since he has been with us, with the exception of a slight cold. He has attended the church & Sabbath school as regularly as possible, there were some Sundays last winter the roads were so blocked we could not get out & 4 weeks I kept him in for punishment, as I could not conquer him in any other way & I could not make up my mind to whip him. You ask does he appear disposed to do right? In a few things, but I think him the strangest disposition that I ever dealt with. I never knew him to steal anything, not even to take an apple without asking for it. . . . He never uses any bad language such as swearing, not that I have ever heard, but Mr. Fuller he is the biggest liar I ever saw for so young a child, please excuse strong language, for I think of all evils, lying is the very worst, and he will not only tell a lie but he will act a lie. Perhaps you may not understand what I mean so I will give you an example. At Christmas we had company & they staid over night, so it was necessary for us to get up very early on Monday morning in order for them to get . . . to the train. [Mr. Van Zandt] told him not to come to the barn as it was long before daylight, but to stay in the house & help me, but he did not mind one word, he went to the barn & after a half hour or more came to the house & said he had fallen from the scaffold & had hurt himself. Well I have a sister with me [a nurse] so she & myself stripped him to see where he was hurt so as to apply remedies. We could not find so much as a red mark, well we doctored & did all we could but he would not be relieved & he never got black & blue nor any mark, so he deceived me, of course he could not go to school & when I got my eyes open to the deceit, I kept him home from Sabbath school & all places for punishment & told him just as long as he deceived me he could not go any where. Then when he found I was determined he stopped some of his limps & when he started for school again he would go like an old man as far as we could see him; out of our sight he was hanging himself upon the schoolhouse doors by his toes & running as fast as any of the boys. But he never forgot to limp before us. Mr. Fuller if a man grown could act a lie any more perfect I should like to see it done. I have tried my best to teach him right & to break him of little lies, he will stick to a lie right in my face & wont own the truth when I am known to the fact. I admit I dont know how to stop the awful habit. This is only one case, I cant put on paper the whole list, it would take to long. There are other things I have to put up with that I cannot break him of & feel sometimes as though I would like to see you & ask what I shall do. . . . I have threatened more than once to bring him back to you, for he seems determined to have his own way. My kind words never have any effect on him in the way of punishment. I have made a lengthy letter of this, but dont know as I have said all yet that is expected. How I should like to see you face to face. I can talk to so much better advantage.

Yours with respect,
Mrs. Van Zandt

*Returned to the asylum in April of 1888, Lorenzo was eventually placed with a farmer in East Galway, New York, where he and another indentured boy, John, experienced five happy years helping to work the land. Lorenzo kept in frequent contact with Albert Fuller. His final letter in January 1893 indicated that he had left the farm to work in a laundry in Warrensburg where he and John worked side by side "like two brothers." The once brash and deceitful young boy was now a thoroughly reformed twenty-one year old man, by his own reports: "I love to work and I go in the very best company. . . . I never took a glass of liquor in my life and I never will nor smoke and I am doing all I can to help others not to touch it. I should think every body would be ashamed of themselves, wouldn't you?"*

## Jesse Keene

Older children placed out from the asylum on indenture often considered themselves used and felt they should rightfully receive payment for their labor rather than the promise of one hundred dollars, a suit of clothes, and a Bible when they came of age. Perhaps wages would provide them with a concrete expression of their own self-worth. Such may have been the case with Jesse Keene who, after six years at the orphanage, was placed with a farm family in Kinderhook, New York.

At the age of four, Jesse had spent six months at the Albany Orphan Asylum. During that stay, the boy confided to his mother that he was afraid of the big boys and afraid to tell Mr. Fuller. "He . . . used to be so sick that he vomited himself nearly to death." Circumstances forced the boy's mother to request admission again in 1889 when Jesse was nearly eight years old. A younger sister was placed with another family at the time. Hattie Keene had been deserted by her husband, an Irish-born laborer, and by her own report she "was very sickly with the heart disease in the worst form" and was "liable to die at a moments notice." Hattie's deathbed wish to superintendent Albert Fuller was that the boy be retained at the institution for at least a few years and that under no circumstances should he be placed with any of his father's relatives. Abiding by her wishes, Fuller denied a request by Jesse's aunt to take the boy to Saratoga Springs where his father was living nearby and receiving "big wages." Jesse's placement elsewhere did not seem to diminish the boy's desire for his family, however. Two very lengthy and detailed letters from his foster-care providers suggest more than a complaining and dissatisfied nature. They describe instead a frightened, angry, bitter, and perhaps grief-striken child locked inside a budding adolescent.

[Undated, 1895]

Dear Friend [Mrs. Fuller]:

I was glad to hear from you and am sorry to be so neglectful. I have been to school all this winter & read out of the forth reader and I use the monteiths Geography. I attend church and sabbath school regular. I had a very [nice] time Christmas. I got a book off the xmas tree. Mrs & Mr. Walker's folks were all very kind. they gave me a bible, a large over coat, hymnal & some handkercheifs, also thirty cts. mr Walker gave me a dollar & a half. I have two dollars & a half. My guardeans are very kind to me. When you write a gain please tell me how the society is. I send my love to mrs. Charllet Fuller [your sister] and keepe a good share of it your self. please let my teachers read this letter. . . .

Yours respectfully,
Jesse Keene

P.S. Will you please be so kind as to see if you can find out any thing about my pocket book which mr Mc Clellan [the office clerk] put in the desk. my mother gave it to me.

[Undated, 1895]

Dear friend:

yours of the 19th received. I think we have been quite neglecful in not informing you in regard to Jesse. We have spoken of it frequently & Jesse [too]. . . . He has enjoyed good health ever since he came, with the accep- tion of a slight cold. He has attended church & sunday school regular. He did not miss but 1 sunday from the time he came untill Christmas & that from his cold. He received a pretty book on the tree from sunday school. as to eny day school, he has been regular since the 1st December. The blizzard has kept him home for the past two weeks. He has been a very good boy since he came but when cold weather started he would have flown back to Albany if he had had wings. He wanted to come up to spend Thanksgiving if he could have got there. he would not have come back unless you had sent him. He said he was not used to the cold & he could not stand the cold. I told him he ought to have thought of that before he came in the country but now he can go in snow knee deep & go . . . a mile & a half to every day school & seems to enjoy it. I do not think he is as progressive in school as he might be judging from the studies he has but I may not be right as he learns his sabbath school lessons very quickly & he seems to like the Episcopal church very much. he says he is a going to belong to it because his mother was an Episcopalian. I like the way he speaks of His mother very much & he seems to pay a great . . . attention to what the minister says & I do not have to urge him to go to church. . . . I . . . think it is oweing to the Asylum judging from what he has told me. He speaks very kindly of it. But he seems to be very desirous to earn money. I do not know if he will wait until he is twenty one or not. when he first came, if we gave him anything he would want to know if it was agoing to be taken out of his $100.00. If Mr Walker or myself should come to Albany we will bring him. . . . If Jesse should be taken seriously ill I should inform you immediately or if any of his friends are sick & would like to see him I would try to have him go. He told me his Grandmother was living in Troy. It seems strange to me he has so many relatives & they pay so little attention to the child. They could write him if nothing more. He says he would like to see his little sister once more & then he will be satisfied. It will be some few yrs. before I consent to let him go.

Mrs. Adrian Walker

July 16, 1895

Dear friend:

I am writing in regard to Jessie Keene. I am sorry I have to offer any complaint. he is very much dissatisfied at times & he wishes to return to Albany. We have allways spoken well of him & have not told of his faults to any one, only of late & we found out praising him up did not have any influence. His principal work has been ever since he came to help me in the house untill May [?]. He went to school most of the time untill then. He helped me with the dishes & carried the wood & water & gathered . . . eggs when he came home. Only satterday's . . . he helped me with other work but he sputtered from the time he commenced untill he got through unless he happened to be in the right humor & he was so dissatisfied with helping me he said if he could only get out of the house he would not find any fault. as it is very hard work to get hired help & the woman I had left in Oct 1894 on account of sickness with the intention of returning but could not & said she was coming back the first of April if she could, so I did not try to get any one until I saw she could not come. finally a strange woman came along & said she heard my woman was not coming back & she wanted work & she would have to go back if I did not hire her as she was a stranger here. she asked me to try her. so Jessie was delighted to think some one wanted work, but I guess he wished he had never seen her a few days after. I gave him a small task to carry his vessel down when he came down mornings. I would take it back when I went to make his bed. he would allways forget it, so this morning I asked him if he had done it & he said no so I sent him to do it & he would not eat any breakfast. when dinner time came he sat down to the table & the woman said so you think you will eat your dinner so he arose & left the dinner table. I knew he would not come back. I knew his temper but she did not think she had said anything, but he wanted her to understand she must not say anything to him. finally tea time came & we did not put any place on the table for him. he came to the table & did not see any place & walked away. Mr Walker told him he had refused twice to eat that day so we thought it not necessary to put a place for him. In the morning he told me he was very weak. I told him it was his own fault, but if his temper was as weak . . . it might do him some good. That was a good punishment for a few days. so finally I told him to do something else & he began to find fault & this woman said to him, hold your saucy tongue & go in & do as she tell[s] you. It was a lucky thing you fell into her hands. That went on for a few days & I had some cleaning upstairs & I asked him to wash the dinner dishes so the woman could help me. . . . he wanted to know who was a going to dry them. I told [him that] he was. he said he was not agoing to wash the pots & spiders.* I said he should, so he did them all but the spiders. . . . I told the woman she could go down [since] I could finish before tea time. So she came down, Jessie was in the yard & she told him to wash those spiders. He said he would not do it. I wont touch them. She said Mrs. Walker told you to wash them & I wont do your work after you. When I came down I told him to finish his work. he would not wash but one of them. There was only one used dinner time & the other one was left from breakfast & he would not wash it. I made him wash both of them. when tea time came I told Mr. Walker how he a did & he went out in the [evening] & he told the woman to tend to all of [the] dishes but the frying pan, to leave that for Jesse & he turned to me & told me to see that it was done well. That was [too] much for

---

*A spider is a frying pan, originally with attached legs for use over an open fire.

Jesse. so after she had finished the dishes she told him to wash the [frying pan]. he said something back. she said remember what Mr. Walker told you about talking back. I was talking to the hired man not paying much attention to him. he took the pan out of the water & I said Jesse have you washed the bottom well. he said you just sit there & look at me & see if I do it well or not. I was so provoked I steped up to slap his mouth. he dropped the frying pan & dishcloth took hold of both of my arms & was ready for a fight. I let go of him but did not get a chance to slap his face. he backed himself right up against the wall, doubled up both fists and & shoved them right at me ready for a fight, just as he would to a little school boy. I declared I would have nothing to do with him again. that was to much for me. when Mr Walker came home I [told] him what a time we had over the order he left about the frying pan. Mr. Walker was more than angry. He did not think [Jesse] would dare go as far as that. The next day Mr Walker took him & tied him fast [so he could not run]. He asked him if he had [tried to fight] Mrs. Walker. He said he [had] not. he called the hired man & asked him. he said he did not want to get in trouble but if Mrs Walker had not given in I think he would have struck her so Mr Walker gave him a good talking to & he promised not to do it again & then he gave him a good whipping. it is the first & only whipping he has had since he came. we had both told him we would not whip him. He was not our child, but if he had been he would have had more than one, so I guess he thought he would never get one. no matter he did. since he has work out of doors it is just the same. what he likes to do you could not get a better boy & what he dont like he is determined not to do it unless you compel him by force. the men wanted him to learn to milk before harvest so he could help. they gave him one cow & he said he could not, his hands were to small. he would get out of it & get them to finish it. at the same time he could milk but did not want to do it. so Mr Walker told them to leave him two cows to milk, not to touch them no matter how long [Jesse] was. so he sputtered & he cried & he did not get in with his milk untill 9 oclock. so he has milked those two cows ever since and can milk as good as anyone, & then he allways wants to go back to Albany every time we make him do anything he does not want to he allways wants to know if he can come back to Albany. It was just so when he was in the house. We like him. I could do most anything for him if it was not for his temper & dissatisfaction. He is so dissatisfied at times. he seems to think so much about money & he thinks we ought to pay him for what he does. We have two hired men & they take turns in the chores [on Sundays]. so one sunday it so happened they did not come as early as usual. he said if they did not come & he had to do their work he was going to have there share of the money but they came when he got through talking. so it was in the house. I asked him to wash the spittoon one satterday & he said he used to get paid for that in Albany. I have given him money at different times. once in a great while I have [severe] headache[s] & before I had help Jesse was very good to me. he would do anything for me. He would say Mrs Walker you cant do that you are [too] sick. let me do it. I could keep the child & bring him up but he is either so very good or else so very bad. I do not give him any more money for this reason (he has a little over two dollars), I think if he gets enough & has a good chance, he will run away. He is allright now, good as can be. he does not know of my writing. I am writing for the purpose to know if he should continue to remain so dissatisfied & should wish to return to Albany. If we could bring him back—most every one who works with us seems to think he will run away. he would be all right if he received wages but he receives more than he earns. He seems to think a great deal of the $100.00 to start with, but he says he could get that in Albany & stay untill he was 21 yrs. He is the sharpest I ever saw of his age. He does not attend church & sunday school as regular as he did but I think the reason is because he wants long pants & he thinks he will get them by staying. Mr Walker told him he would have had a new suite long ago if he had behaved. Will you kindly inform us if we could return him if should be necessary, but will not unless obliged to. I would not like to have him go away & not know where he went. you will perhaps grow as weary of reading this as I am of writing. but it is entirely private & the one you return will remain private. Please oblige.

I am friend,
Mrs. Adrian Walker

*Jesse Keene ran away from the Walker farm sometime in 1896. He was reported by Saratoga County Superintendent of the Poor as living in Green Island with his father who "was a miserable drunkard & a thief." Fifteen-year-old Jesse was apparently working along with his father in the Green Island railroad car shops at the time.*

## Frank Baldwin

Some children arrived at the Albany asylum thoroughly lacking in any home life. Frank Baldwin spent the first months of his life within the confines of the Albany almshouse where he was born in January of 1869. He came to the orphan asylum before his first birthday and remained there for nearly ten years. His mother, a German immigrant considered somewhat mentally defective, worked in Troy at a collar factory and likely never had any contact with the boy. Frank's first indenture from the asylum at the age of ten did not succeed. On a second placement in the town of Brainard, Rensselaer County, at age thirteen he received fair reports but by his fifteenth birthday an inner rage seemed to spill over in the form of blatant and vicious animal abuse and frequent overt anger.

January 31, 1884

Dear Sir:

I write to you in regard to Frank Baldwin as we have tried to mannage him without complaining to you of him, I have tried my best and cant make him mind for when I need him moast he is mad and wont work. I cannot trust him to do chores to the barn without I am there to see to it. I sent him to put the cattle in the stable. after he got them all in he went pounding a 2 year old heffer so that she dident stand on her leg for half our after word. . . . last winter I was fatting a cow and the men [who] Butchered and skined her along her back [said] it was all [matter ?]. they had to throw away some of the beef. the men said this cow has been hurt. I said no, not that I knew of. some time after, Frank told the boy that worked for me that he had pounded her. last summer I had a 2 year old [cow and] every time [Frank] went after the cows he would keep plagueing [it]. I forbid him to [continue]. he dident mind. he went in the lot one night, commenced walking [the cow], . . . hooked [it] down and then took [it] on his horns and threw [it] over a fence. [the fence?] was all that saved [it] from being killed. [it] was hurt quite bad, [it] got so ugly I had to sell [it]. . . . one morning Frank got mad at the Boy that worked for me because he woulden wait till he got the cows turned away so he could ride one of the horses to the house. so when he come to the house he wouldent eat breakfast. my wife called him four or five times to come and eat. he would say I wont do it. she picked up a whip and whiped him. I told him to cary some milk away, he said I wont do it. I said go get some water and help me grind my [scythe], he said I wont do it. he sat in the barn and on the lot and dident have breakfast, Dinner, or supper. next morning he went to work as useual. he said [that] you . . . had tried to conquer him but you hadent, nor no one would. we have whiped him three times. whiping does no good or nothing else. he is a bad Boy to swear and tell stories. . . . you know something about his disposition your self without saying any. . . . I think you can manage Frank better in the [a]sylum than any where else. if you think we are saying more about him than is true please come out here and inquire how he is treated. Please answer very soon.

Philip Jones

February 15, 1885

Dear Sir:

your letter of the 10 is received. I cannot comply with your wishes in keeping Frank & besides there isent any one that has been to my house & seen him drive my cattle to pasture or handle my teem that would want him. the neighbors tells me more how he treats them than what I have seen my self. he has nearly spoiled one of my horses. he isent safe for an old man like me or a boy to handle. if i say any thing to him [that he must stop plagueing the horse], he tells me he will spoil him so no none can drive him. this morning he went to the barn. I wasent up yet. My Daughter heard him pounding the cattle. she went up there [to] watch him. after he had fed the horses he stood before them with the fork & when they would come to the manger to eat he would go after them with a fork & then he would scare [them] & make [them] jump back. then he went to the cows & went to swearing at them. last harvest I sent him to rake hay with the horse [and] told him not to drive her fast as it was very warm day [and] he might hurt her. he said he would be careful. after he had been gone about ½ hour my daughter thought she would go & see what he was doing. he had tied up the rake so it wouldent drag and was runing the horse through the field as fast as she could go. when my daughter got to him the water driped off of the horse. when I scholded [him] for it he said he knew we would [watch] him & did it on purpus. my cattle kept brakeing out of the field, my neighbor . . . told me . . . he could tell me why they jumped so. he said Frank would let down 1 or 2 of the bars and make the cattle jump over the rest, he would club them till they jumped it. what profit is he to any one. . . .

Yours,
P. H. Jones

February 19, 1885

Dear Sir:

I am in receipt of your letter of the 15th Inst. in regard to the boy Frank Baldwin. Hope that you may be able to find some good person who will be willing to take him. Of course you understand that you are responsible until other papers are drawn. The person that he goes with must assume the same obligations that you did and in writing before we can release you. From your statement of the case the boy deserves to be sent to the house of refuge and I am afraid that it will result in that. Please let me hear from you again as soon as you have found a home for the boy.

Yours hastily,
Albert D. Fuller

*Frank never went to the reformatory. Instead, he was placed in the home
of a nearby farmer probably sometime in 1885 at the age of sixteen. Two years
later, as the following letter reveals, he ran away in a near state of desperation, returning to his former foster home in hopes of finding refuge.*

November 21, 1887

Mr. Fuller Dear Sir:

I have left Frank Burley['s] and am now at Mr. Jones. I could not stay
with him for he did not give me clothes suitable for this cold weather, nothing
but thin pants and old shoes, all to pieces. my feet were wet and cold. I took a
servere cold and have it yet. . . . When I came to Mr Jones, Mrs. Jones
mended some clothes they had for me to put on & Mr Jones got me a pair of
boots. Mr Fuller will you please see Burley & have him pay me for my work
[since] I have been eighteen or get me clothes. . . .

Yours Truly,
Frank Baldwin

## Ella Borden

If children lacked the experience of intimacy before coming to the asylum, they were not necessarily devoid of such contact by the time they left.
Not only the superintendent but the many teachers and attendants, cooks and
groundskeepers, seamstresses, nurses, and office clerks each in their turn
might obtain the confidence of one small child. As a consequence, children
of the asylum faced more than the anxiety of separating from parents. Those
placed out on indenture encountered, as well, the loss of friends, teachers,
and beloved siblings left behind in the institution. Nurturing relationships
formed over weeks, months, or years might abruptly come to an end as the
child was confronted with the task of seeking ties of intimacy in the context
of new family settings.

For many, the asylum had become their true home. Perhaps as any adolescent wishing a measure of independence, there were those anxious to
leave. But once thrust into the harsh reality of life outside the asylum, many
experienced a profound sadness and longing for the comfort and familiarity
of those old surroundings. Time and tender treatment by her new caretakers
eased the pain of transition for young Ella Borden. She eventually found
contentment in her new home in Chatham, New York. Nothing is known of
her long-term outcome, however, nor of her life previous to coming to the
Albany asylum.

May 24, 1888

Mr. Fuller friend dear:

I thought I would drop you a few lines letting you know how I like my place. the family I live with is verry kind to me and I like them verry much. I have nothing to say against my staying with them but one thing, and I will tell you what it is. I am so homesick that I don't know what too do to over come it. I've tried to keep from gating so home sick every day sence I've been here but it does no good. . . . as it is Wednesday evening and its half past nine o'clock and I am verry tired but for all of that I thought that I couldent wait till my week was up to write to you. O Mr Fuller if you will get me a place in Albany, so I will be near by, I would be so glad for if you knew how sorry I am too think that I was so anxious to leave and do for my self, but it is all comming home too me now. I dident realize it before till now. Oh how I miss you all, you can't imagine. so I want to tell you to let you know that I've been a good girl and have tried to do every thing I can too please the family. Mrs Altier feels verry sorry too see that I feel so home sick and so she says that I woulden't feel happy as long as I feel so bad. She says she knows how it is when city girls comes in the country to live, there not verry happy. but she says that she is pleased with everry thing I do because I am so neat in every-thing. she says she would like too have me stay if I felt like I could, so Mr Fuller I thought I would ask you and get your advice but I do hope you will get me a place near by so I could come and see the place, so please excuse my writing for I haven't any ink and my pencil is not sharp. so now will close my letter for I feel sad tonight. please write a long letter and tell me if you will get me another place or not for I would like to know as soon as possable for you know I can get a recemend from these people here. I send my best respects too you all, aspecialy to my brother.

Ella Borden

May 25, 1888

Dear Friend:

Your letter of yesterday came to hand this morning. I can see by it that you are quite homesick, but am not surprised because I expected that you would be. Your new home is a good one and I think you better try to keep it.

You will undoubtedly feel much better within a week or two, after you get better acquainted. Write me again in a couple of weeks. I think by that time you will be feeling all right.

Our people are well as are also all the rest of the children. Hoping always to hear good reports from you I remain,

Your friend,
Albert D. Fuller

June 12, 1888

Dear Mr fuller:

I receaved your glad and welcome letters and was pleased too hear from you, for I was so homesick. but I have over come that feeling. I like my place much more now than I did before. Mrs Altier waited on me last week a Friday and Saturday because I was so sick I could hardly hold my head up, they gave me medicine and now I am well. Mr Fuller how is my Brother and all the folks? is Miss Pogue [in the sewing room] well? tell her I send my best respects to her. I hope all the rest of the Children are well and tell them I send my love to them all. . . . now I will close until and nother time.

Yours Truly,
Ella Borden

*No further correspondence exists in asylum case files from Ella Borden.*

## Anna Milton

Homesickness and longing for the asylum often lasted more than a few short weeks. After returning home to West Troy, New York from a two year stay at the Albany asylum, seventeen-year-old Anna Johnson wrote frequently to Albert Fuller. Her correspondence continued for more than a year. Anna's father was said to be an imbecile and her mother a "bad character." She and her sister Libbie came to the Albany asylum in the winter of 1888, brought there by the Albany County Society for the Prevention of Cruelty to Children.

Not untypically, Anna expressed deep gratitude for the care received at the institution. Her memories of the asylum were perhaps exaggerated, however, when she juxtaposed those recollections against the current state of affairs at home—hard work, sickness, and the death of her sister. Anna's correspondence with Albert Fuller also suggests that asylum children sought continued approval from their temporary keeper even outside the bounds of institutional life. The superintendent in turn both reprimanded and encouraged each child as would any concerned parent.

January 4, 1891

Dear Friend:

I thought I would write to you thinking you would like to hear from me, and how I was getting along. I am well and getting along nicely. I am workeing every day steady. I hope when this reaches you it will find you well. Mr. Fuller I am very sorry for writing those letters that time to May Churchill and I am glad you corrected me for it. I will never do the like again, and I hope you will forgive me for doing it. I should like to come down there again to stay for I never had a better nor happier time in my life than when I was there. I was very sorry after I came away. Since my sisters death I am so lonesome, but she is happier than I am I suppose. How are all the girls getting along. I hope they are well. . . . How is [your daughter] little Ruthie, I should like to see her. I will, now close with my regards to you and all the folks. Good bye.

From,<br>Anna Milton

January 7, 1891

Dear Friend:

Your letter of the 4th Inst. has been received. I was glad to hear from you and also to have you say that you were sorry for writing as you have to May Churchill, but if you were truely sorry for doing it why did you do the same thing over again after I spoke to you about it. I understand that within a comparatively recent period you have been writing to May in an underhanded manner, sending the letters to a girl living on West street by the name of Smith, [the letters] being brought to May by her.

Do you consider such action on your part either honorable or right? You have always pretended to think a great deal of May Churchill. If that is really the case, it certainly does not show good judgement on your part to do things which cause her to act the part of a sneak. You know very well that I havn't the slightest objection to your writing to any one here in the right way. If it is in the right way certainly there is no need of either you or May sending letters in the way you have attempted recently. I hope that you have got through with that sort of business entirely by this time. If you have I would be glad to see you, otherwise not.

I am and always will be interested in your welfare and I want to see you grow up to be an honorable and straightforward girl and have your conduct such that it will bear the closest inspection. I think you understand that such is the case. . . .

Will be glad to hear from you soon. I remain,

Your friend,<br>Albert D. Fuller

September 24, 1891

My Dear friend Mr. Fuller:

I thought I would drop you a few lines to let you know I am getting along. I am feeling quite well now but have been very sick. I hope when this reaches you it will find you and all well. . . . I used to sometimes think the worke hard to do down there but I now am working harder here than ever I did. O how I wish I where down there again. I'should give mostly anything to be there. I started down several times but I thought you were so mad at me that I did'nt get there, but if you now say I can see the girls if I am down I will come with your permission. I will make this as short as I can because my hand is trembling so I canot write anymore. Please remember me to Mrs. Thompson, Mrs. Albert and all the folkes.* I will now close with my regards to all and my kindest rememberance of you Mr Fuller. Answer soon.

From,<br>Anna M. Milton

September 25, 1891

Dear Friend:

Your letter of the 24th inst. is at hand. I was glad to hear from you and pleased to know that you now appreciate the care you had when here. . . . I am perfectly willing you should come and make us a visit here. You can come most any time. You of course know that I had good reason to feel displeased with what you did a while ago, but I certainly have no ill will against you. I remain, with best wishes,

Your friend,<br>Albert D. Fuller

May 4, 1892

Friend Mr. Fuller:

As I had a few leasure moments to my self I thought I would write a few lines to let you know how I am getting along. well I am very well at present but I have been very sick with the Grippe. I was kept in the house an awful long time and I was wishing I was down there to your place all the time, and I would often say to the folks a round me that if I were down there I would never be sick for when I was there I always had my health but now I have not. . . . I have not had a letter from any one there in a long time. I supose they have all forgotten me now. I am comeing down soon to see the girls and folks. I should like to be at my old position yet as a sewing girl. I will close now with saying good bye.

from,<br>Anna Milton

---

*Mrs. Thompson was probably a teacher or attendant in one of the girl's dormitories. Mrs. Albert was the familiar name given to Albert Fuller's wife, Helen, who served as matron of the Albany asylum during her husband's tenure and as acting superintendent after his death.

*Anna Milton's last letter to Albert Fuller is dated October 10, 1892. She reiterated again her sense of gratitude and longing for the asylum: "I am well and hope this will find all of the children the same and my dear friends that were so very kind to me when I was with them. I can never forget their kindness and of yours. I can not speak, for you was too kind to me for me to be in such a hurry [to go] away as I was and I am now very sorry for I did not know where I was coming until I realy got here."*

## Ross Miller

For some children the experience of asylum life was a joyous memory. In such a context, the superintendent might not only emerge as a kindly friend, but as a hero of sorts. Young Ross Miller* never masked his admiration for Albert Fuller nor his happy memories of the "good old asylum." Perhaps Ross was among the lucky ones. He had come from a large, close-knit family. His father, an English immigrant and moulder by trade, had died of pneumonia in 1882. Two years later, at the age of four, Ross came to the Albany asylum for the first time. He stayed only a month but returned the next year on account of his mother's serious illness. She subsequently died and Ross spent the next five years at the institution. Discharged to the care of an older, married sister who lived in Ohio, Ross eventually came to enjoy the boyhood of which most asylum children could only dream.

October 26, 1890

My Dear Friend:

I have not seen you in a long time, but I have not forgotten you. I have wanted to write to you for a long time but have waited until now because I have been very busy. I go to school now every day and am getting along nicely. I have a Third Reader, an Arithmetic, a Geography, a writing book and I have language work and physiology. I have a very nice lady teacher and am trying to be a good boy every day. I think Collinwood, [Ohio] is a nice place. it is eight miles from the large city of Cleveland and I often ride up there on the electric motor cars. it is only a little way to the nice large lake Erie. I went down to the edge of the lake with my brother a few days a go and the water was very rough, I thought it was a sea. There were no vessels on it that day but some days there are a good many vessels and boats sailing there. Some day I am coming out there to see you if I can. I will never forget

---

*Ross Miller was the younger brother of William Miller whose letters regarding his sons LeRoy and Jesse appear in the first series of letters in this volume.

you, and I will always remember your kindness to me. Please give my love to [your daughters] Alice and Gracie and Mrs. Fuller, also Miss Eliza, Miss Anna Burn and Miss Pouge. Please remember me to Hugh W., Ray C., Henry C., Santa S., Spencer C., Archie C., James W., Robert W., Roy C., Arthur R., Libbie K., Etta S., Mamie K., Emma K., Mallowayla M., Nellie D. and all the other boys and girls of the good old Asylum. I would like to see them all. Now I will close this letter with lots of love to you.

From your friend,
Ross Miller

October 31, 1890

Dear Friend:

Your very nice letter of the 26th. inst. has been received. If you could know how glad I was to hear from you would write me again before a great while.

Your letter was a very nice one and I am glad that you wrote it yourself, it seemed just like you and I enjoyed it very much as did other of your friends here. . . . Let us hear from you again before long. Ever-so-many children join in sending much love to you. . . .

Respectfully yours,
Albert D. Fuller

September 11, 1892

Dear Friend:

I started to write to you a long time ago but neglected it. I will write a letter now as I have time. School is very interesting to me. It commenced Tuesday, Sept. 6. My studies are easy for me now. I am studying the Mc Guffey's Fourth Reader. I was twelve years old July 27, 1892. I hope the boys and girls at the asylum are all well, and have not forgotten me. Please tell [them] that I remember them all very well and my place in the Chapel, and in the other school. I send my love to Miss Anna Burns, May Churchill, Miss Eliza Mitchell and the rest of the teachers. I suppose [your daughter] Ruth is a large girl now, I hope she is well. I send my love, and thanks to the dress makers for so kindly keeping me in clothes while I was there. Grapes are ripe out here and there are a great many large fine vineyards all around here. It is a good place for them here by Lake Erie. We have moved and I have a nice pleasant room for my own. It is very nice in Collinwood and I am trying to be a good boy so I can be an honest man, and earn money so I can buy my own clothes and come out to see you and everybody. the Electric Motor cars run past our street. I have earned enough money to buy a pair of slippers, and a hat, and nearly enough money to buy a pair of shoes. I am required by the Sunday School to represent my class Sept. 25, at quarter review. I go to Sunday School every Sunday I can. I am earning money now and then, so by hard work I can soon be able to buy a new suit. The fifteenth of every month I have work to do by drawing packages up from the Depot with my wagon. . . . Now I will close as I see I have written you a long letter. With love for you and all.

Respectfully Your Friend,
Ross L. Miller

September 15, 1892

My Dear Friend:

I was delighted to get your letter of the 11th Inst. It was well written, nicely expressed and gives strong indications that you are going to make a thrifty good man. I like the way you have started out. It is a good thing for boys to commence to earn something when small. They are far more likely to succeed in after life and make far better men; there is no mistake about it. . . . I will take your letter to Miss Burn and let her read it aloud before the children; many of them will remember you. . . . Hoping to hear from you again before a great while, [I] remain with best wishes,

Your friend,
Albert D. Fuller, Superintendent

*No further correspondence exists in case files from young Ross Miller to Albert Fuller.*

## Charles Henderson

Albert Fuller's guiding hand reached far beyond the confines of the institution. At the height of the asylum's operation, just prior to his death, Fuller had governance over six hundred indentured children. He provided counsel and encouragement to many of them through his letters and they in turn responded favorably with honest efforts to please their former keeper. Nevertheless, some children, like Charles Henderson, faced far too many temptations and ultimately failed. Charles had spent eight years with Albert Fuller at the Albany asylum. He was brought there at the age of three by an uncle because his stepfather, a stovemounter, refused to support him. The boy's own father had died in Germany before his mother immigrated to this country. In 1886 Charles was indentured to a New York City physician for what was intended to be a period of ten years. The boy was just eleven years old at the time.

October 7, 1886

[Dear Mr. Fuller Sir]:

   i like this place verry well. i hope your folks are all right. i can not rite verry good becase i dident go to school the last year i was theare. i wish you Would rite me a letter some day.

Charles Henderson


October 11, 1886

[Dear Friend]:

   I was very glad to receive your letter of the 7th instant and especially to know that you are liking your new home so well. I hope you will remember all I told you in regard to your conduct while you are with Mr. Van Sanford.

   The Doctor and Mrs. Van Sanford I know to be very kind people and they will be good to you if you only do right. Be faithful to them—be honest—be truthful—do whatever they tell you promptly and the very best you know how. Keep good control of your temper and always be polite in your deportment.

   It will certainly be for your best interest to give heed to all the above points. Do not be influenced by others in the Doctor's employ who may be disposed to be slack or unfaithful to him.

   Hoping to always hear the best of reports from you. I remain,

[Your Friend],

Albert D. Fuller, Superintendent


December 1886

Dear sir:

   i am verry glad you have goten me this place. as you have not heard from me fore a long time. it is true when you told me they were very kind people. they are going to let me see the show [Buffalo Bill]. . . . i do not have much to do. And i hope you are geting along very good and i would like to no about Willie H. i am very thankful fore what you and Mrs. Albert fuller [have done for me]. I am verry sory that i did not show you how thankful [I was]. i have not much time to rite. i want to rite to my Aunt & Uncle, Grammother, Cousins, & mother. When ever you rite to me please tell me how many years I was there. I think it was eight years i was there. if there is any way i can help you i wish you would tell me. one way, keep my place and be good.

From,

Charles Henderson

April 4, 1887

Dear Sir:

I hope you are fealing well. i am very glad to let you know that i am still trying to do my best. . . . I go to the pray[er] Meeting evry thursday night with Edie. when i was there i dident make good use of my school. Now i want to go to school. it seems that boys are never sadfied, I mean my self as much as any body. i have not much time now. i guess i'll have to stop. . . . i will write soon again. the Doc is very busy now, now it['s] nine o'clock. i have to sit in the hall till 1 oclock. i do not mind it. i do not idle the time. when i sit in the hall i read my books. when i was there i did not like to learn my sunday school lesson. now i love to go to sunday school and learn my lesson and read books. please remember me to Mrs. Howe my teacher. i am very sory to not have a little more to say.

your truely friend,
Charles Henderson

April 8, 1887

Dear Friend:

Your letter of the 4th inst. has been received and I can assure you I was very glad indeed to hear from you and above all to know that you are trying to make a man of yourself. I am glad that you are liking to read, if you make a good selection of the books that you read it will be a good thing for you.

You must have a good deal of leasure time and you can improve yourself a good deal by reading and study. all the children are in good health, we have no sickness at all now. Let us hear from you again after a while. With best wishes, I remain,

Your friend,
Albert D. Fuller

October 24, 1887

Dear Mr Fuller:

I thought i would write you a few lines. I am geting along very nicely. And so is Joseph D . . . And so are the other boys. the Dr and Mrs. Van Sanford were at Watch Hill this summer. And i had a very good time. And had nothing to do all summer. Joe's family were away and we two boys were together all the time and went to Coney Island and had a good time. And a great many other nice places. And i hope all your family and your self are all well. And hope all the boys and girls are well. Please remember me to all the boys And School Teachers. I am still trying to do my best.

Yours Respectfully,
Charles Henderson

October 30, 1887

My dear Mr Fuller:

I am very sorry to be obliged to send you a bad report about Charles, but things have come to such a pass that I cant stand him in the house any longer. When I returned this fall I found him much [changed]. . . . He was listless, impudent, lied to me, idle and in fact useless. I discovered soon that he practiced self-abuse; consequently thought that the changes in him was in consequence of it. So I had a long and earnest talk with him, he seemed sorry & promised to mend his ways, which he did for a week or so, but he has since become so much worse that I have given it up. He is vulgar in his conversation and has told most disgusting lies about my servant girls to new servants who have come into the house that he has demoralized the entire house hold. He is also not honest, has taken orders and gone to the store and obtained goods for them and his lies when detected have been simply fearful. I have always been kind & considerate to the boy & tried to do what was right by him, but this is no place for him, as he is soon to go from bad to worse if left to himself. I write this at length that you may know his true character. what shall I do with him? send him back to you or discharge him. the first seems the only course for if left to himself he will certainly go to the bad in the city. A place on a farm is in my opinion the only salvation for him, for I can not possibly keep him. As I said I am sorry to trouble you with this but there seems no other course. . . . Trusting to have an early and favorable reply. believe me,

Sincerely Yours,
S. O. Van Sanford

November 11, 1887

Dear Friend:

I received a letter about two weeks since from Dr. Van Sanford in regard to you, which has caused me a great deal of anxiety and pain. You know Charles that I am your friend and want you to succeed in life and grow up a useful, honest and pure minded man. I think you want this yourself, but I am inclined to believe that you have in some way, recently been led into ways which will sooner or later bring destruction if you continue. You promised me faithfully when you went to New York, to do right in every respect, and to be true to the doctor's interests and not to meddle in any with his other help. I dont think that you have intended to break this promise, but very evidently have.

Now I want you to take a new start, first, stop any filthy habit of self abuse you may have formed which habit has been the means of ruining thousands of people and sending many thousands others to Idiot and Insane asylums. 2nd. Obey the Dr. and Mrs. Van Sanford promptly and pleasantly. 3rd. Be pleasant and agreeable with the other help, but do not meddle with their affairs or have any more to do with them than is necessary. 4th. Be honest and truthful and feel above doing anything that is low and mean.

You have already promised to carry out these rules, noted above, I am very sorry that you have failed, but it is not yet too late to start in once more and I want you too. Drop me a line at once on receipt of this letter, stating what your intentions are in regard to renewing the promise you have already made me. I remain your friend,

Albert D. Fuller

*Charles ran away from his indenture on January 12, 1888. He was not quite thirteen years old at the time. Albert Fuller attempted to track his whereabouts but was unsuccessful. The boy likely drifted around New York City and cared for himself, ending up for a brief time at the Young Men's Christian Association in that city.*

## Frank Gifford

A child's dependence on asylum caretakers often extended beyond adolescence into young adulthood. Indentured children, in particular, might end their term at the age of eighteen or twenty-one with one hundred dollars, a Bible, and a new suit of clothes, but with nowhere to go. Even after years of labor within a foster home, many former asylum children had little if any preparation for a self-sufficient life and no one to counsel them on how best to support themselves.

There were those, however, who felt anxious to end their "contracts" so that they might work for wages or pursue other professions. Probably the majority of indentured children sent out from the Albany asylum were placed in the country. As they came of age, there were those who found the long-term prospects of country life and farming less than appealing. More exciting goals beckoned, even if not in their own best interest.

Frank Gifford looked to Albert Fuller less for direction than assent. He knew his own mind and would not be dissuaded. Frank had lived in the orphan asylum from the age of four, having been left there by his father, who, officials said, showed no interest in the family. The boy's mother had died of heart disease. Indentured for the first time at the age of twelve, Frank eventually ran away, back to the asylum. Placed a second time in West Milton, New York, at the age of fifteen, the boy seemed to find contentment and pride in his work. He once wrote to Albert Fuller, "I can plow now, reap, drag & cultivate or anything most." The pull of another kind of life, however, proved too great.

August 23, 1890

Dear Sir:

I thought that I would write you. I am going to leave here my next birthday, I will be 18 years old. Mr. Roberts is willing that I should if you are willing. I dont want to farm . . . and I do not want to learn a trade but I do want to enlist as a soldier in the regular army if I can. Mr. Roberts says that I have been very good since I had a little fuss when you came up here. If you want to know more about me please write Mr. Roberts and he will tell. I am well and hope that you are well. I have stopped all cursing. Tell the boys that I am well . . . .

Yours truly,
Frank Gifford

September 1, 1890

Dear Sir:

I am at home and received your letter and much pleased with it. I thank you very much for your offer to help. I am doing well here, but I do not like the farm work and I think that which I spoke of will suit me best, to enlist, and with your help I think I can. I guess I will stop writing. Good bye. Excuse poor writing.

Yours truly,
Frank Gifford

David's Island, Company B, April 18, 1891

Dear Sir:

I thought I would write you a few lines to let you know that I am well and I hope you are all well. I have got right where I wanted to get for a good while. I am in the Army; I enlisted in Buffalo, N.Y. I have to stay here three months on this island to drill. I wanted to get here in the winter when I was there and now I have got here and find it just as you said, a life full of hardships, but now I have got it easy for what I will have I suppose.

There are 500 men on this Island, about 200 are going away this week. . . . I am not quite heavy enough yet for a soldier. I weigh 122 pounds. I would give anything if I could get out of here. If I could get out of here now I would go home and study down to work. I would give the world if I knew how I could get out. Will you try and help me to get out? I remain, as ever,

Frank Gifford

*Frank did "get out" of the army although the circumstances of his discharge are unknown. Having ventured out on his own and failed, he turned once again to the only true parent he had ever known. The following letter sent from West Troy, New York, was his last to Albert Fuller.*

*December 8, 1892*

*Dear Sir:*

*I thought I would write a few lines and ask you if you could give . . . any information as to me getting a job of work. I am out of work now. If you will help me I will be obliged to you. Mr Fuller if you know of anything I could get let me know. I do not like to lay idle long. I will be 21 years of age on the 30th of Nov. I will end this.*

*Respectfully yours,*
*Frank Gifford*

## Julia Newbury

Young girls on the verge of womanhood were perhaps the most vulnerable of all asylum children, especially those with little or no parental guidance. Albert Fuller counseled these girls in stern yet fatherly tones. Once they left the asylum, however, his only means of control was to speak to their conscience. Many became promiscuous and showed little remorse for tarnished reputations. Others, like Julia Newbury, would deny such behavior until no longer able to persist in their lies.

Julia was brought to the Albany asylum by poor-law authorities in February of 1883 at the age of thirteen. She had a number of younger sisters and brothers. Both her mother and father were in jail. Upon his release from prison, Julia's father threatened to obtain possession of the girl "at all hazards." But Albert Fuller believed that going back to her parents would be Julia's ruin, at least until they could show conclusively that they had reformed thoroughly. The chaos that must have surrounded Julia's young life led her to perpetuate such an existence. Over the long term, however, the tragic outcome of her behavior, and perhaps the loving guidance of her former caretaker, allowed her to escape the consequences of fate. The following letters were written during and just following Julia's second indenture with a family in South Ballston, New York.

December 12, 1887

Dear Friend:

Just a line to let you know that i am not feeling very good and i thought I would write and ask you what i had better get. i have such a pain in my

head, first i will be burning up and then i will be freezing. Mrs. Van Olin
thinks that it is some sickness comeing on me so i thought i had better write
to you and see if you couldn't tell me what to get for it. For i dont want to
pay a Dr. bill. i haven't been feeling very well since i have been here. will
you please write rite away. i wrote to you that day i came home and have not
receive answer yet. So i will have to close by saying good night hopeing this
will find you well. . . . So good by. love to all. hope you can read this.

Yours Truly,
Julia Newbury

December 15, 1887

Dear Friend Julia:

Your letters have been received, I am sorry that you are not feeling well.
If you are much sick you had better see a doctor at once. If only a little sick,
it might be well for you to take some quinine, from [the] description of your
symptoms I would think it would be a good remedy; take 2 grains of quinine
at each meal for say four days. I think they will help you and in doses mentioned could do you no possible harm.

We are all well and everything is going on here all right. The girls wish
to be remembered to you. The pills I spoke of, you can [buy at] any Drug
Store, either one or two grains each. I have put your money in the Albany
Savings Bank.* I hope you will remember your promise to me when you
were here in regard to being a good girl.

Your Friend,
Albert D. Fuller

January 15, 1888

Dear Friend [Mr. Fuller]:

your kind and welcome letter has been receive, allways being glad to
hear from you. I am feeling a good [d]eal better. . . . I am taking German
lessons twice a week from our nabor. They are German people and they are
learning me how to speak in German. I find it pretty heard to learn. How
much interest are you geting on the money. I have not for got my promise,
but i am trying to ful fill it. what do you think [the] Churchill folks says
about me.† they started a story that there isn't any truth in it. they say that i
have been to the White church and a number of other places with a gentle
man. . . . I thank you very much for your Christmas present. I surpose you
will get tired of answering my letter for i write so often. I wish to be remem-

---

*The money Albert Fuller refers to is partial payment made on Julia's first indenture.
†Julia's first indenture had been with the "Churchill folks."

bered to the girls. would you go and see Churchill folks if you was in my place. i went to Schenectady and got me a new hat, i am going again next week and get me a new [dress]. I remain,

Yours Truly,
Julia Newbury

[Undated]

dear Sir:

I thought I would write and let you know about Julia Newbury's conduct. she has been going to see a german family and she has been tauld not to and she will not listan. she is a nice girl and I like her and I do not like to see her do so, and I thought you aught to know about it and write and tell her to do better. she goes to see a german boy in the family. Mrs Van Olin has tould her she could find better company then them. she will not listan to Mrs Van Olin the lady she works for, and she has got a good home there. . . . I tell you of this as a friend and for her own good and hope you will write and tell her to do better. she will not listan to any one. I am,

Yours truly,
[Unsigned]

February 3, 1888

Dear Friend:

I have just received a letter which does not speak very well of your conduct and makes me feel badly.

The letter states that you are not trying to please . . . the woman that you are working for and pay little heed to what she tells you. Also that there is a German family living near them and that there is a young man or boy in the family and that you are running after him all the time.

Now Julia you know what is right and if you are doing the things mentioned you know that you are doing wrong and ought to stop at once. Dont spoil your whole life for the sake of having your own way. Please let me hear from you soon.

Your friend,
Albert D. Fuller

February 11, 1888

Dear Friend Mr Fuller:

I received your kind letter and was glad to hear from you. I intended to have written before but have neglected it. you must excuse me this time and I will try and do better next time, was very much surprised to hear you got a letter. some things are true and some are not. I will own that I have been their and some other places. I went to church Sunday and Mrs Van Olin and I went to schenectady Wednesday to do some trading. I got me two new dresses and we had a [nice] ride. . . . Mrs Van Olin called to Mr Churchill and they never asked how I was or never spoke my name so I dont think I will go to see them. I will close so good by. love to all.

Yours Truly,<br>Julia Newbury

February 14, 1888

Dear Friend:

Your letter bearing date Feb. 11 has only just reached me. I hope the information which you say is true and was to your discredit, will not be repeated. I think you really want to be a good girl but are sometimes indiscrete in your actions. Please use more care in that direction in the future. . . . I hope you will write to me frequently letting me know how you are getting along. With kind regards, I remain,

Your friend,<br>Albert D. Fuller

February 17, 1888

Mr Fuller:

I thought I would write and let you know about Julia Newbury. she is not doing as I want her to. she is going to see a German family that lives near us and she goes there every Sunday night and two or three times in the week and I do not think it is right for her to do so. I have tould her for her own good and I can not have her do so. she will have a bad name and there is know young ladyes for her to go to see there. if there was it would not be so bad but she goes to see the boy. I tell her for her good not to do so but she will not listan to me. I like Julia. she is a good girl to work and trys to please me in some things. I tell her what is right as I would my daughter. I thought you ought to know about it and would like to know. she says she is not going to work for me this Summer if she does not get two dollars a week. I do not think Julia can earn that a week and another thing, my work is not hard and she has it very easy Indeed, and I tell her I will do well by her if she will stay. I have got her a good many things all ready since she has been hear. I do not think Mr [Churchill's] folks did well by her when she was there. Julia is [a] very changeable girl. I tell you of this as a friend. please do not let her know I send this. hope you will write and give her some good advise, and tell her what is right. I am very sorry I halfto write such a letter about her but she is young and she ought to be very careful about her name and listan to people that are older than her self. I remain,

Yours truly,
Mrs Van Olin

P.S. she went down there last Sunday and staid all night and thay are setting her up and I do not think that is right. I for got to tell of this befor. I ment to.

February 29, 1888

Dear Friend:

I received your kind and welcome letter, always being glad to here from you. Will you pleas tell me what the people state to you that i visit that family for. Well i dont think that the people can say much more for that family [is going to move away] and then i think i will have a little piece. I have been quite sick for the last week, So i have not been able to do harden any thing. i heard that Mr Churchill and Mrs. Van Olin wrote to you. i want to know. I often wished i was dead for i [dont] have any thing to live for, only for people [who] try to make me trouble. . . . love to all. pleas excuse short letter and hast[e].

Yours Truly,
Julia Newbury

March 2, 1888

Dear Friend:

Your letter of the 29th has just been received. I was sorry to learn that you had been sick, glad to know that you are getting better. . . . Mrs. Churchill has never written to me since you left them, neither has Mr. Churchill, that is to my knowledge. I had one letter about you to which no name was signed, so dont know who wrote it. The letters carried the idea that you were making love to a boy who lived with this German family. That you kept going there and even staying over night and that your object was simply to get a chance to see him although you gave other reasons for going.

I dont think that any one wants to make you trouble. these people probably thought that you were doing yourself harm by running after this boy and if you were you certainly were doing what you ought not I think myself. There is no need of wishing yourself dead only do what you know is right and proper and you will get along well and be happy, anyone as young and strong as you has much to be thankful for. I hope you will write me again before long. I am always glad to hear from you.

Your friend,
Albert D. Fuller

May 11, 1888

Dear Friend:

Your letter of the 9 inst. is just before me asking me to send you 15 dollars.

I think you are very foolish to remove your money from the bank. It seems to me that a strong girl like yourself who is earning fair wages ought to be able to clothe herself comfortably without drawing upon the money she has in the bank to do it. How much better it would be for you to add to this little saving that you have instead of drawing from it.

Of course if you are suffering for clothing, we will send you the money, but I do not think such can be the case. I think you had better reconsider the matter, and allow your money to remain where it is drawing interest, and try and add more to it occasionally. If you do not comence saving while you are young and strong and form that habit, you probably will never have more than what you wear upon your back . . .

[Your Friend,]
Albert D. Fuller

May 14, 1888

Mr. Fuller:

I thought I would write a few lines to you to let you know that I have discharged Julia Newbury. She would not do as I wanted her to, and was very saucy to me. I told her to do some thing, and she said she would not, so I tould her she could go. she is not the kind of a girl I thought she was. she is the taulk of the people around hear. I never saw a girl like her. if you knew some things she has done you would be very much surprised. she is a very wild girl for her age. she went down to the next house to the germand family and thay shut her and a fellow in a room for a[n] hour and would not let them out and I think any one that will let any one do so [there] is something the matter with them. I thought I would tell you of this as you ought to know. I tryed to do everything I could for Julia and have her do what is right. but i could not get her to do so. she will tell things that are not so. She tould me that she had sent to you for money. I do not think she needed it as I have payed her right along, and before it was time to. she wanted it befor she earned it. i have written this as I thought you ought to know about it. no more. I remain,

Yours Truly,
Mrs Van Olin

May 15, 1888

Dear Friend:

I am very sorry to learn that your conduct has been such recently that the people with whom you are living have been obliged to discharge you. I can now see why you want the money that you sent for.

I understand that you have always been paid promptly, and if you had behaved yourself and made proper use of your money you would not be in want. I enclose check for fifteen dollars as you request. I send it in the form of a check because it will be safer. The store-keeper I have no doubt will give you the money for it.

Hoping to hear a better report from you before long, I remain,

Your friend,
Albert D. Fuller

Nursery and Child's Hospital, Staten Island, New York
March 4, 1889

Dear Sir:

I write you these few lines to let you know that I would like that money you have of mine. have you heard from [my sisters] Martha or Lucy lately. pleas let me know how they are getting along. pleas send the money right away for i nead it very much.

From Yours,
Julia Newbury

March 5, 1889

Dear Friend:

Your letter of the 4th inst. is before me stating that you would like to have me send you the balance of money in my hands belonging to you. I think that I have about $26.00. Will look the matter up this morning and mail you a check this afternoon. What are you doing at the nursery? How long have you been there. Please write us again giving this information. I hope that you are well and conducting yourself in the right way. I heard from your sisters only a few days since. They are quite well. I also learned that you had gone to New York, but did not get your address. I remain,

Yours respectfully,
Albert D. Fuller

Mt. Vernon, New York, April 29, 1889

Dear Sir:

I received your kind and welcome letter some time since, being glad to here from you. i received the check all right and i am very much oblige to you for makeing you so much trouble. i am very sorry that i did not take your advice and do what you told me. you ask me what i was doing at the [nursery]. i will tell you i have got a little baby and i am trying to take care of it. it is a girl and she is three monts old. you dont know how bad i feel about it. pleas dont tell any body so it wont get back where i used to live. i hope that [my sister] Libbie will do better for i dont want her to know it. . . . i would like to see you, you must excuse me for the first time that was the reason i did not write.

Julia Newbury

May 6, 1889

Dear Friend:

Your letter acknowledging the receipt of check for balance of money I held in trust for you is at hand.

I was exceedingly sorry to learn of your trouble but hope it will be such a lesson to you that you will from this out try and lead a better life. I hear from your sisters occasionally but will not say anything to them about your trouble.

Everything is going on here about as usual. Have a very large family just now over four hundred children. The winter however has been a good one and we have had hardly any sickness. Hoping to hear from you again before long I remain.

Your friend,<br>Albert D. Fuller

*Julia's correspondence continued for another four years. She obtained work as a clerk in a store in New York City, fell in love, and eventually married. During this time, she became substitute parent to her younger siblings, removing the smallest ones from her mother's home after finding that they had been misused. They were in a terrible condition, she said, "their heads were sore and dirty and they had the itch." Her final letter to Albert Fuller revealed not only the difficulties of raising children from such circumstances, but her continued reliance on her former keeper and friend when facing major obstacles in her young life. Julia apparently did not know that Fuller had died just six weeks previous.*

August 11, 1893

[Dear Friend]:

*Just a few lines to ask you to do me a favor. I have had the children in the [Five Points Mission] and they would not keep them for me. I have kept them for over a year and they are more trouble now than when I brought them*

*down. I've had whiskey in the house for medical purposes and I find that they*
*have been using it when I've been out and they have been doing things that I*
*dont care to mention on paper. If you let me know when I can see you or if*
*you should come to the city I would be pleased to have you call. Will you be*
*kind enough to let me know if you can take them for me or if you know of a*
*place where I could put them. they wont be taken in school for one, so they*
*run the streets and I cant do anything with them. Will you be kind enough to*
*answer by return of post and kindly oblige.*

Mrs. Paul Black [formerly Julia Newbury]


## Jennie Riley

As far as it was in his power, Albert Fuller never abandoned a needy child. Once they were brought under his guardianship, he remained steadfast in his commitment to them. The children sensed this and turned to him repeatedly in times of distress. Abused and fearing abandonment, Jennie Riley wrote to Albert Fuller in a state of utter desperation. With swift and decisive action he traveled to the outskirts of New York City to find the girl and assess the situation. One can only imagine Jennie's response when she opened the door to find her former keeper, her friend, and in this case her savior. It is no wonder that in her fantasies she considered Albert Fuller her true parent.

Jennie's parents brought her and a brother, Sammie, to the Albany asylum in August of 1878. Jennie was eight years old at the time. A three-year-old sister, Sophia, was admitted a few years later along with an infant brother who subsequently died in the institution. While in the asylum, Jennie contracted scarlet fever and over a period of years lost her hearing and eventually became profoundly deaf. An Irish immigrant and bookkeeper by profession, Jennie's father died in a Boston hospital in the spring of 1885 after years of heavy drinking. Her mother, Jane, was said also to be severely intemperate.

Over a period of twelve years, the children's mother wrote frequently to the asylum, but appears never to have visited them. She lived in New York City and worked there in between bouts of unexplained illnesses. Sometime in 1890, Jane Riley became obsessed with the thought of obtaining custody of her children, now twenty, eighteen, and fifteen years of age, and bringing them to her sister's home in Ireland. At the time, Jennie and her siblings had long been placed out from the asylum on indenture. Jennie ultimately made the trip to Ireland. The following correspondence took place after her abrupt return to this country.

October 13, 1890

Mr Fuller Dear Sir and Ladies all:

I suppose you have been waiting to recieve a letter from me. I could not write before because I had not the chance. I have been to Ireland and they sent me back. they are to poor to keep me. they did not know I was coming till they got the telegram. they did not want me at all. I have been very sick of ship fever for nearly 3 weeks. it was bitterly cold, my feet were badly blistered and swollen so I could hardly walk on them. I have the heart disese which is very painful. there was much suffering on the ship coming over nearly every body had the ship fever. I had it the worst of all. I am staying at a ladys house [in Long Island City] with my mother. she is not good to me. she treats me very badly and often strikes me. last night she doubled her fist and hit me a fearful blow on the left temple. I am in constant fear of her all the time. please help me Mr Fuller. she is going to desert me. send a message to [my brother] Sammie and tell him to come fore me. what is to become of me. God only knows. please befriend me Mr Fuller. . . . I have no other friend to appeal to but you. Please send Sammie for me. . . . I am so sick I cant write very well as my hand is so weak and pains. Good bye from your true and loving friend.

Miss Jennie Riley

October 23, 1890

Dear Sir:

Trusting to God you are well and all under your care. I am sorrow I was not in . . . when you came. I was out trying to get the money to send [Jennie] up to you but I believe it was God that sent you here to take her away. You can do what you please with her for I never want to see her face dead or alive and that is hard for a mother to say. She made to much trouble and scandal for me both before she went and when she come back, for my sister wrote me all and said she wouldn't have her there on no account for she had to much of a scandalious tongue, writing over paper every time her back was turn. You know Mr. Fuller the old country is not like here, but had she known enough to behaviour herself she would be made a good christian girl . . . like her sister is. . . . She said I was no more than a stranger to her and that's all I intend to be from this out. Every place I took her, and I always took her in respectable places, she scandalized me fearful behind my back. . . . She wished the Tuesday morning I went out that the cars might run over me or something else might happen to me. . . . When I had her boarding in Mrs Allen's and when I'd go to see her she slam the door in my face. But Mr. Fuller your not to blame for if I had taken your advice I would not have this trouble but I did it all for the best. . . . I can be blamed but not shamed. . . . She is gone now and thak God for it. But I respect you for you always respected me and you done your duty. . . .

Yours Respectfully,
Mrs. Jane Riley

November 4, 1890

Dear Mrs. Richardson:*
Your favor of the 24th ult. is before me. I had many doubts about its being best for Jennie to go to Ireland but her friends there and the mother especially pressed the matter so strongly that I did what I could to further that project, although I had many doubts as to its being best. I am sorry that it has proved so unfortunate for all of you.

About four weeks ago I received a letter from Jennie stating that she was in Long Island City and imploring of me to come and get her. This was the first intimation I had received from any source of her return. The letter was written in such a way that I felt it my duty to protect the girl from trouble which might come to her in her exposed condition from the public place in which she was living.

I went myself to Long Island City, saw Jennie and endeavored to find her mother but could not do so, although I made diligent search. I was fully convinced it was not safe to leave the girl there, although I think the people were kind to her. It was in a Saloon and Liquor store where she would be brought in contact with the more viscious elements. I therefore brought her back to the asylum with me.

She is in excellent physical condition now. I think the voyage over wore on her somewhat as she was rather thin in flesh. Since her return I have made application to a Deaf Mute Institution for her admission and have just received notice that she has been accepted for a term of five years; I will take her to place mentioned within a few days. It is located within about 100 miles of Albany. . . .

It is our endeavor to protect as far as possible any children who may have at any time been inmates of this institution and we shall so do in Jennie's case. Of course we do this no matter what the character of the child may be. . . . From what I learned of the mother I felt that she was at times in unfit condition to be the guardian of the girl otherwise would have left her in Long Island City. . . . I remain,

Yours respectfully,
Albert D. Fuller

*Mrs. Richardson was Jennie's aunt; she lived in Bainbridge, Ireland.

Deaf Mute Institute, April 16, 1892

[Dear Friend]:

In your last [letter] to me you spoke of having recieved a letter from my mother inquireing after Sammie and I. Why did she write? Was it through any apparent interest in us? Not much. It was only through mere curiosity. You see I wrote a letter to a girl named Maggie Allen of Long Island City in respon[se] to one which she wrote to me and as she knows my mother I suppose she went and told her. So she wrote to you inquireing about us. I never tell any one here I have a mother. They think that I am your adopted daughter. Well I let them think. Sammie is old enough to take care of himself, and as for me well I am all right, she need not bother her head about us. I hope you have not answered her letter yet. I am not going to write to Maggie Allen again. When you write please do not mention [my mother] in your letters again. I never think of her if I can help it and I do not like to be reminded of her. I can say no more. I beg to be excused. . . .

Yours very truly,
Miss Jennie Riley

*Jennie spent many years at the Deaf Mute Institute in Rome, New York, eventually becoming a teacher at that institution. She continued an extensive correspondence with Albert Fuller and with his wife, Helen, after Fuller's death. Jennie also remained in close contact with her brother Sammie and sister Sophia. They visited each other often. A final letter to the Albany asylum, dated 1935, indicated that their association was lifelong. The letter, from Sophia, requested verification of their ages from the asylum so that she and Jennie might apply for a joint life insurance policy. Jennie was sixty-five years old at the time.*

# Conclusion

What a different story these letters tell of poor families of the late nineteenth century and the huge impersonal institutions that served them. As a body of evidence, this correspondence fits poorly into much of the current theory on lower-class family relations of the last century, theory that continues to emphasize instrumentality over sentimentality in the parent-child bond. Neither does this material lend strong support to suppositions of "social control" as an integral component of late-nineteenth-century institutionalized social welfare.

Perhaps foremost, the letters of this volume strongly suggest that lower-class families were not simply passive recipients of a legacy of social welfare set in motion earlier in the century. To the greatest extent possible they acted rationally and with forethought in developing clearly defined strategies for survival during times of crisis. In large measure, they consciously used nineteenth-century institutions to meet their needs and to advance their own interests. In the case of the asylum, that "self-interest" was nothing more, nor nothing less, than the care and betterment of their progeny. As portrayed by the families of the Albany asylum, the institution itself was no mere mechanism for separating poor children from their parents and breaking hereditary lines of pauperism. Rather, the orphan asylum in many ways provided an instrument for keeping families together during times of economic crisis, sickness, and death.

Seen from this perspective, the asylum superintendent fades from view as a tyrannical, controlling, and self-righteous disciplinarian and reappears as a benevolent caretaker serving as family intermediary, befriending both parent and child caught up in a nightmare of separation, abrupt change, and loss. Both viewpoints, of course, are somewhat distorted by a literary and historical focus on the worst and the best of late-nineteenth-century child-care providers. In fact, most asylum superintendents likely practiced a blend of benevolent care and despotism. In an era before the specialization of social work, the nature of the role itself invested administrators with power, knowl-

167

edge, and wisdom often far beyond their innate capacities. Whether they desired it or not, the institution lent instant charisma to those who by choice or by fate took up the reins of leadership.

Albert Fuller held the admiration of perhaps thousands of parents and children with whom he had contact over the years. At the time of his death he was eulogized in highly sentimental terms. His capacity for love was almost legendary. Some even went so far as to say that "he died of love" as he ministered to the hearts and needs of his charges. But Albert Fuller had his blemishes as well. He was steeped in a culture that believed in the power of eugenics and the evils of masturbation. He considered some children totally without hope. He knew others whom he believed should never be returned to the influences of pauperism from which they had emerged no matter how strong the attachment between parent and child. Yet there can be no denying that Albert Fuller did his utmost to maintain the bonds of family despite a system that seemed designed specifically to thrust poor families apart. He operated his own institution as a huge family and not solely on the basis of the need for discipline, control, and routine. He allowed children their individuality and parents their due respect. He had an abiding love for the asylum children and counted himself among their friends.

For their part, the children of the Albany asylum generally did not constitute a subset of the emotionally impoverished or maternally deprived. Their ability to form trusting and loving relationships outside the family circle with asylum personnel, with peers, and with substitute caretakers lends powerful support to new theories that children of the asylum succeeded first and foremost in developing confident and trusting attachments at home. Despite environments of utter deprivation and often the loss of at least one parent through death or desertion, and despite a separation that must have surely felt like complete abandonment to many, these children exhibited a remarkable resiliency not only in their ability to trust and confide in new caregivers but to forge close and loving bonds.

Certainly, to many children the institution represented something bigger than life, greater and more powerful than anything that they had yet experienced in their young lives. It was "as big as a city" to some. Yet, it was not, as has too often been portrayed, a wholly negative nor a physically, emotionally, or intellectually confining experience. The asylum instead became a safe haven offering the child a variety of experiences, lessons, and expectations that would guide them through to adulthood. And for a time, at least, the asylum child experienced freedom from material want and even enjoyed the pleasures of childhood in the shared experiences of special outings, celebrations, and holidays. Despite the rigid environment of congregate care, these children were no mere numbers but individuals with definable identities, free to maintain personal possessions, to speak on their own behalf, and to communicate with family and friends.

For their part, the parents appear to have maintained powerful attachments to their children, bonds that seem to have intensified rather than diminished by the very act of separation. In no way do the parents represented here view their children primarily as economic assets. On the contrary, they articulate a well-defined sense of the child as "precious," an attitude of sentimentality toward children that some conjecture did not filter down to the lower classes until well after the turn of the century. Constrained by circumstances and by asylum policy to monthly visits, parents saw their children infrequently if at all, but through gifts and letters and photographs, they shared, no matter how meagerly, in their lives, experiences, and development.

Even those parents in the most impoverished circumstances do not emerge from the Albany asylum correspondence as indifferent or abusive. Fathers as well as mothers are gentle and sentimental in expression and both exhibit an intensity of emotion toward the child that, for the period of the late nineteenth century, is remarkably middle class in tone. Parental affections are not only apparent but oftentimes effusive, the pain of their loss extreme. These families clearly place the child at the center of their lives, a focus perhaps exaggerated by the realities of separation.

In few ways do the parents represented in this volume exhibit the resignation and apathy that poverty status is said to imply. It is their often conscious and direct use of the orphan asylum to meet their goals of child rearing that makes the most persuasive argument in this regard. Their values appear almost starkly middle class when parents exhort their children to excel in their learning; when they press their children to maintain high standards of obedience, morality, and self sufficiency; and when they take very pronounced risks in breaking up the family in order to achieve even the most modest goals. Their frame of reference (even among the poorest families) becomes the future, as true happiness awaits a hoped-for reunion of family members at some indistinct moment months, if not years, in the future. Postponement of gratification, at least in the matter of satisfaction of familial attachments, becomes a way of life.

Parental involvement in the emotional lives of asylum children, then, did not cease with the child's surrender to the institution nor with their "permanent" placement within foster families. Neither did parental rights and responsibilities abate. Physical separation did not put an end to parents' protracted efforts to raise their children right. If not through daily child rearing, they achieved what they could by frequent and direct correspondence with the child or by way of their intermediary, the asylum superintendent. Though many of the children received letters sent by parents, sometimes carrying the valued article around in their pockets for days until the words began to fade, many probably did not. Some children simply were too young to understand. Others might easily have been disturbed by hearing from a parent who proved inconsistent in care and affections or who might never again be able to provide for the child.

Although a parent's actual role in the socialization process and the frequency of interaction between parent and asylum child can only be surmised, it is perhaps their perceived role that is of most interest and importance. The perception, even the belief, no matter how ill-founded, that they had a significant part to play kept parents involved, concerned, and actively pursuing the training, the betterment, and the care of their young. Their lives allowed for little else. Those who might have participated enthusiastically in the "cult of domesticity" as it was being played out in middle-class homes and suburbs across the country did the best they could with the resources at hand. The asylum became their sanctuary and for many a means to a better end.

Middle-class attachments, attitudes, and expectations, if they did exist among the lower classes, certainly did not translate into middle-class lifestyles or behavior, however. Though we are allowed only a brief glimpse into their lives, the struggles that these families faced certainly did not cease once parents and children were reunited. Their material lives and homes remained modest at best, deplorable at worst. Many children continued to live in surroundings of dirt, drunkenness, and destitution (the "three terrible D's"). Fathers and mothers worked when, where, and if they could. Life was precarious and their poverty was a simple and tragic fact of life. Yet the significance of family, the strength of parent-child bonding, and the parental aspirations exhibited here seem to transcend rather than to fit comfortably within the bounds of class. There are differences, of course, but perhaps differences more firmly rooted in material culture than in class-based attitudes, values, and outlooks. The pervasiveness of poverty in late-nineteenth-century America made attainment of middle-class material life an impossibility for many, but certainly not so the attainment of a fruitful and satisfying emotional life.

# Epilogue

The first White House Conference on the Care of Dependent Children held in Washington, D.C., in 1909 culminated more than a half century of debate over the relative merits of child placement versus institutional care. At the time, however, neither viewpoint prevailed. Instead, conference delegates adopted a three-tiered plan of action to tackle the problem of child dependency. At the apex would be care in the child's own home, followed by foster care, if necessary, and the orphan asylum as the place of last resort. Conferees unanimously agreed that under no circumstances should a child be taken away from parents simply because of poverty.

The 1909 conference represented a first step in the slow process of federal involvement in combating the problem of child dependency. Child welfare workers of all persuasions and denominations rallied together at White House Conferences on Children about every ten years following that first successful conclave. Although the conferences often served primarily symbolic functions, they nevertheless laid the groundwork for significant legislation in the areas of mothers' pensions, child labor, aid to dependent children, pre-school education, and foster care. It was that first White House conference, however, that seems to have turned the tide of child welfare reform in the United States.

The origins of new policy directives, which emphasized the importance of familial attachments and bonds of kinship, are nevertheless unclear. Care for dependent children in their own homes had little, if any, currency in the official debate before 1909. State and national charity agencies and organizations continued to operate under the assumption (implied or stated) that separating poor children from their families was necessary, if not desirable. In contrast, on-the-ground practitioners of child care, in particular poor-law officials and asylum superintendents, understood perhaps better than the more distant philanthropic reformers of the day that destitution and neglect were by no means exclusively moral issues. Caught up as they were in the day-to-day economic realities of late-nineteenth-century American society, purveyors of

171

child welfare, men such as Albert Fuller, knew from experience that familial bonds and parental attachments clearly transcended the bounds of class.

To a large extent, the Albany Orphan Asylum foreshadowed changes in child welfare after the turn of the century. Certainly its entry into the modern era mirrored the trends of the times as well. Not satisfied to remain mired in nineteenth-century congregate care, the Board of Managers rebuilt the entire facility in 1906, adopting the new progressive cottage plan. Following the path of numerous other institutions, the Albany home ultimately evolved into a residential treatment center for emotionally troubled youth and continues to function in that capacity today. Reflected in these changes was the twentieth-century shift of attention to the child and the child's own family in the treatment process, the operative word now being "treatment" rather than custodial care or the simple provision of basic physical needs, as it had been in the past.

The first and greatest object of the new social work was "individualizing" the child. At the Albany home this meant a drastic reduction in total numbers. In 1907 the Board of Managers cut the population of children in half and those from counties outside Albany were returned for placement elsewhere. Under the new system, a series of small brick cottages accommodating only twenty-five to thirty children were erected, replacing the huge ponderous asylum structure of a former era where hundreds of children lived, ate, slept, played, and prayed. The crux of the matter was architecture as it had been nearly a century before. But a new design concept prevailed, one that was intended to reduce the physical plant to a more human scale. Family life, reformers believed, could easily be replicated in the small cottage building, whereas it was increasingly untenable within the confines of the institution.

The deficiencies of large-scale congregate care had already become evident by the time of Albert Fuller's death in 1893. Helen Fuller succeeded her husband as superintendent, serving for nearly a decade until her resignation in 1902. Her departure came on the heels of an investigation of the Albany Orphan Asylum by the New York State Board of Charities. Charges included eleven counts of careless and negligent management, particularly in the area of maintaining adequate precautions against the spread of contagious disease among the children. Inspectors graded education at the home as inadequate and condemned the standard practice of having the children come in regular order and proceed in a body to different functions such as meals, work, chapel, and bed.[1]

Helen Fuller answered all charges and the institution was subsequently exonerated with the provision that certain changes be carried out. But management of the asylum had seriously deteriorated in the years following the loss of Albert Fuller's strong administration. Deficiencies both in management and discipline were rampant, as Helen Fuller's successor reported. He found that discipline among the employees was very bad, that even the coachman and night watchman had disputed his orders, and that the largest boy in the institution had refused "peremptorily and profanely" to do work that he had ordered, "this being a colored boy of 18 years of age who had left the institution and returned." In a few cases the superintendent caught boys on the fence begging. The teachers had very short hours of work, four hours a day, which was not long enough, and he found one man in charge of 124 boys, too many for anyone to manage. Of this number, sixty were little boys who should have been under the charge of a woman. He reported further that the children were put to bed too early, about six o'clock; that they ought not have been put to bed until they were tired. And he found some walking about the institution who called themselves "somnambulists."[2]

The state board's criticism of the Albany asylum came about not only as a result of more progressive directions in institutional child care but in direct response to actual problems and conditions at the home. In the years following the state's investigation, dramatic changes ensued not only in the physical plant and daily routine but in the treatment of the children themselves. The institution now operated within a system of "expression" rather than what many had perceived as "repression," a system that allowed the children to dress dissimilarly, to play freely on the grounds without supervision, and to associate openly with children on the outside. They were given opportunities to know stores, libraries, churches, schools, and other features of life in the surrounding community as children in normal homes would have known them, and perhaps most important, they could now visit parents, friends, and relatives and even spend lengthy vacation times at home.

In contrast to earlier philosophies of child care, "good" child welfare work after the turn of the century would now mean a constant regard both for the child's family and for the child as part of his or her family. By the mid-twentieth century, child-care workers could reflect back on the "crudities of the previous century" as having resulted from treatment of the child too exclusively in isolation, with little or no regard for emotional bonds or for the various other ties, whether assets or liabilities, that may have existed in the child's relationship with his or her family. Albert Fuller, of course, had known this and operated the Albany Orphan Asylum by such rules of thumb. Perhaps he was a man before his time. A half century after his death, a study of children's institutions by Howard W. Hopkirk, executive director of the Child Welfare League of America and a former superintendent of the Albany Orphan Asylum, emphasized the significance of the parent-child bond and pointed to the fact that even parents who had died continued to wield a powerful influence in a child's development. "Indeed the hopes of the dead parent may sometimes be more respected by the child than the hopes and ideals of all those whom he knows among the living."[3] Even neglected and ill-treated children identify with and value their own parents above all else.

As we approach the end of the century, "family preservation" has become the catchword in child welfare circles. But it is clearly not a new concept. The only difference is that after decades of deinstitutionalization the country is coming full circle to debate once again the relative merits of group care over in-home or family care. The resurgence of interest in residential treatment or the "orphanage idea" stems from the fact that child dependency today is less a result of poverty and more directly an outcome of drug and alcohol addiction, child abuse, and mental and emotional illness. Should children be removed from environments of physical and mental anguish or should they be part of a process that preserves the sanctity of the home at all costs? This will be the child welfare issue for the twenty-first century, one that, as in the past, will likely not be debated by the children and families most in need.

Notes
Suggested Reading
Bibliography

# Notes

## Introduction

1. Samuel Rezneck, *Business Depressions and Financial Panics: Essays in American Business and Economic History* (Westport, Conn.: Greenwood, 1971), 15–16.

2. Henry George, *Progress and Poverty*, abridged, (New York: Vanguard Press, 1924), 5. See Stuart M. Blumin, *The Emergence of the Middle Class: Social Experience in the American City, 1760–1900* (New York: Cambridge Univ. Press, 1989), 138–91 and 230–57, on the integrated spatial organization of class in antebellum urban centers such as New York and Philadelphia. American cities underwent a greater physical segregation based on class and consumption patterns much later in the nineteenth century.

3. Billy G. Smith, *The "Lower Sort": Philadelphia's Laboring People 1750–1800* (Ithaca: Cornell Univ. Press, 1990), 92–125; Christine Stansell, *City of Women: Sex and Class in New York: 1789–1860* (New York: Knopf, 1986), 6–8; Stephan Thernstrom, *Poverty and Progress: Social Mobility in a Nineteenth Century City* (New York: Atheneum, 1977), 192–224; Blumin, *Emergence of the Middle Class*, 39–40.

4. Michael B. Katz, *In the Shadow of the Poorhouse: A Social History of Welfare in America* (New York: Basic Books, 1986), 5–6.

5. According to Michael B. Katz, *Poverty and Policy in American History* (New York: Academic Press, 1983), 10, "No one has precise figures for the proportion of wage workers at different points in American history. As an example, though, one historian points to an increase in the proportion of laborers—the people who were most unambiguously wage workers—in New York City's work force from 5.5% to 27.4% between 1796 and 1855. Other research shows clearly that by the mid-nineteenth century most artisans in North American cities were wage workers." See also, Brian Greenberg, *Worker and Community: Response to Industrialization in a Nineteenth-Century American City: Albany, New York 1850–1884* (Albany: State Univ. of New York Press, 1985), 11, who states that a permanent wage-earning class in America emerged during industrialization and that by 1870 two out of every three productively engaged workers were wage earners.

6. By definition, cyclical unemployment is loss of work as a result of recurring economic depressions. Seasonal unemployment is self-evident. Structural unemployment involves the process whereby new machine techniques replace old human skills. Melvyn Dubofsky, *Industrialism and the American Worker: 1865–1920* (New York: Thomas Y. Crowell, 1975), 20–21; Katz, *Poverty and Policy*, 9–14; Daniel J. Walkowitz, *Worker City, Company Town: Iron and Cotton-Worker Protest in Troy and Cohoes, New York, 1855–1884* (Urbana: Univ. of Illinois Press, 1978), 143–46; David Rosner and Gerald Markowitz, eds., *Dying for Work: Worker's Safety and Health in Twentieth Century America* (Bloomington: Indiana Univ. Press, 1987), xi.

7. Richard B. Stott, *Workers in the Metropolis: Class, Ethnicity, and Youth in Ante-bellum New York City* (Ithaca: Cornell Univ. Press, 1990), 87–122; Walkowitz, *Worker City, Company Town*, 145; Thernstrom, *Poverty and Progress*, 17–23.

8. Stott, *Workers in the Metropolis*, 96–107; Thernstrom, *Poverty and Progress*, 21–23; Walkowitz, *Worker City, Company Town*, 145; Alice Kessler-Harris, *Out to Work: A History of Wage Earning Women in the United States* (New York: Oxford Univ. Press, 1982), 119–22; on the family life course and family strategies see John Modell, "Patterns of Consumption, Accul-turation, and Family Income Strategies in Late Nineteenth-Century America," in *Family and Population in Nineteenth Century America*, ed. Tamara K. Hareven and Maris A. Vinovskis (Princeton: Princeton Univ. Press, 1978), 206–40; and Tamara K. Hareven, "Themes in the Historical Development of the Family," in *Review of Child Development Research*, ed. Ross D. Parke (Chicago: Univ. of Chicago Press, 1984), 137–78.

9. Katz, *Poverty and Policy*, 11–12; Stansell, *City of Women*, 12–18; Kessler-Harris, *Out to Work*, 122.

10. Faye Dudden, *Serving Women: Household Service in Nineteenth Century America* (Middletown, Conn.: Wesleyan Univ. Press, 1983); Katz, *Poverty and Policy*, 11–12. The eco-nomic and social strictures of single motherhood in the period of the late nineteenth and early twentieth centuries are adeptly discussed by Linda Gordon, *Heroes of Their Own Lives: The Politics and History of Family Violence, Boston 1880–1960* (New York: Viking Penguin, 1988), 82–115.

11. A declining maternal mortality from the 1880s reduced the likelihood of widowers raising children. See Ross D. Parke and Peter N. Stearns, "Fathers and Child Rearing," in *Children in Time and Place: Developmental and Historical Insights*, ed. Glen H. Elder, Jr., John Modell, and Ross D. Parke (New York: Cambridge Univ. Press, 1993), 149. Despite this trend, families in impoverished circumstances still likely grappled with higher instances of maternal sickness, death, and desertion than did their middle-class counterparts. Most children admitted to orphan asylums in the late nineteenth century, for instance, were actually "half-orphans," having one surviving parent. At the Albany Orphan Asylum, according to the superintendent's report for the year 1893, nearly 60 percent of a total of 844 children supported by the institution in that year were half-orphans. Of this number more than one-fifth came from homes in which the father was the sole surviving parent. See Helen Fuller, *Superintendent's Report for the Year 1893*, in Parsons Child and Family Center Collection, SC17377 (hereafter cited as "Parsons Collection"), box 2, Manuscripts and Special Collections, New York State Library, Albany, N.Y.

12. For a discussion of the historical arguments underlying the poverty question in the United States from the mid-nineteenth century through the 1920s see David Ward, *Poverty, Ethnicity, and the American City, 1840–1925: Changing Conceptions of the Slum and the Ghetto* (New York: Cambridge Univ. Press, 1989).

13. Thomas L. Kinkead, "Report of the Committee on the Care of Defective, Dependent, Delinquent and Neglected Children," in the *Proceedings of the New York State Conference of Charities and Correction*, First annual session, Nov. 20–22, 1900 (Albany, N.Y.: J. B. Lyon Co., 1901), 125, (hereafter cited as 1 *New York Conference* [1900]); Betty Reid Mandell, *Welfare America: Controlling the Dangerous Classes* (Englewood Cliffs, N.J.: Prentice-Hall, 1975), 9.

14. Statistical and narrative reports on the various agencies, asylums, and institutions are included in the annual reports of the New York State Board of Charities for the years 1867–1900. See, in particular, statistical tables, vols. 1–34, (hereafter cited as 1–34 *State Board* [1867–1900]).

15. Katz, *In the Shadow of the Poorhouse*, 58–84.

16. David J. Rothman, *The Discovery of the Asylum: Social Order and Disorder in the New Republic* (Glenview, Ill.: Scott, Foresman, 1971), xviii, 19.

17. Walter I. Trattner, ed., *Social Welfare or Social Control: Some Historical Reflections on Regulating the Poor* (Knoxville: Univ. of Tennessee Press, 1983); Katz, *Poverty and Policy*, 183–237. For a brief discussion of the debate over social control specifically with regard to orphan asylums see Nurith Zmora, *Orphanages Reconsidered: Child Care Institutions in Progressive Era Baltimore* (Philadelphia: Temple Univ. Press, 1994), 5–6.

18. Rothman, *Discovery of the Asylum*, xix

19. See Katz, *Poverty and Policy*, 55–156 and his chapter on "New York's Tramps and the Problem of Causal Attribution," 157–81; Gregg J. Duncan, *Years of Poverty Years of Plenty: The Changing Economic Fortunes of American Workers and Families* (Ann Arbor: Univ. of Michigan Survey Research Center, Institute for Social Research, 1984); Gordon, *Heroes of Their Own Lives*, 6, 83.

20. Hareven, "Themes in the Historical Development of the Family," 146–51; Oscar Handlin, *The Uprooted: The Epic Story of the Great Migrations that Made the American People*, 2d ed. (Boston: Little, Brown, 1973), 152–79; John Bodnar, *The Transplanted: A History of Immigrants in Urban America* (Bloomington: Indiana Univ. Press, 1985).

21. Katz, *In the Shadow of the Poorhouse*, 36–57.

22. See: 4–34 *State Board* (1870–1900).

23. Hastings H. Hart, "The Care of the Dependent Child in the Family," in *Care of Dependent Children in the Late Nineteenth and Early Twentieth Centuries*, ed. Robert Bremner (New York: Arno, 1974), 467.

24. Ibid., 466–67.

25. Marian J. Morton, "Homes for Poverty's Children: Cleveland's Orphanages, 1851–1933," *Ohio History* 98 (1989): 5.

26. These figures and others cited below for the Albany Orphan Asylum are based on the author's analysis of a random sample of 540 children admitted to the Albany Orphan Asylum in the period 1877–1903. See Judith Dulberger, "Refuge or Repressor: The Role of the Orphan Asylum in the Lives of Poor Children and Their Families in Late-Nineteenth Century America" (Ph.D diss., Carnegie Mellon Univ., 1988), 135–80. Other studies corroborate the point. See Morton, "Homes for Poverty's Children," 8; Susan Whitelaw Downs and Michael W. Sherraden, "The Orphan Asylum in the Nineteenth Century," *Social Service Review* 57 (1983), 277; and Zmora, *Orphanages Reconsidered*, 9–10.

27. Board payments by parents provided some assurance that children would not be placed out on indenture and that they would be returned to their own families upon a parent's request. However, as was the case at the Albany Orphan Asylum, parents often lagged in their monthly obligations and were forced to rely on the good graces of the superintendent or turn to county poor law officials for relief. See Zmora, *Orphanages Reconsidered*, 52–54.

28. Statewide, as many as 75 percent of asylum children returned to their own families upon discharge from an orphan asylum. See 1 *New York Conference* (1900), 123–24; and William Pryor Letchworth, "History of Child Saving," in 27 *State Board* (1893), 102; and Morton, "Homes for Poverty's Children," 12. The question of legal surrender of a child differed from state to state and institution to institution. Many asylums did, in fact, demand official surrender. See, for instance, Clare L. McCausland, *Children of Circumstance: A History of the first 125 Years of Chicago Child Care Society* (Chicago: R. R. Donnelly, 1976), 20–21; and Downs and Sherraden, "The Orphan Asylum in the Nineteenth Century," 280.

29. "An Act to Provide for the Better Care of Pauper and Destitute Children," *Laws of New York* (Apr. 24, 1875), chap. 173. The use of the asylum by poor-law officials in the disposition of dependent children reflected the general tendency to move along the lines of least resistance. At the time of the passage of the state's Children's Law, a small network of orphan asylums already existed. The network had evolved over a period of a quarter century, encouraged largely

by lump-sum state appropriations to orphan asylums in the early years. Poor-law authorities looking to place dependent children turned most readily to the orphan asylum because it involved a minimum of effort. Placement of children in foster homes, a more complicated and time consuming process, was much less frequently employed. In order to be eligible for state funds a child had to be admitted to an asylum under direct authorization of county poor-law officials. For a further discussion of the subsidy system see Homer Folks, *The Care of Destitute, Neglected, and Delinquent Children* (1902; reprint, New York: Arno, 1971), 69–78; and Homer Folks, "The New York System of Caring for Dependent Children," in 1 *New York Conference* (1900), 129–47; for a comparison of the subsidy system with other state child-care systems see, Homer Folks, "The Removal of Children From Almshouses," in *Proceedings of the National Conference of Charities and Correction*, Twenty-first annual session, May 23–29, 1894, 123–32, (hereafter cited as 21 *National Conference* [1894]).

30. 21 *National Conference* (1894), 126–28; William O. Stillman, "Children as Public Charges," in 1 *New York Conference* (1900), 155.

31. 1 *New York Conference* (1900), 163.

32. Ibid.

33. See, for instance, Josephine Shaw Lowell, "Report Upon the Care of Dependent Children in the City of New York and Elsewhere," in 23 *State Board* (1889), 182–84. On the issue of day care or day nurseries see Gordon, *Heroes of Their Own Lives*, 103.

34. For a brief discussion of the emotions involved in parting with children sent to orphan asylums around the turn of the century see Zmora, *Orphanages Reconsidered*, 68–69.

35. Henry P. Phelps, *Story of the Albany Orphan Asylum* (Albany, N.Y.: Albany Engraving Co., 1893).

36. Albert Fuller to James O. Fanning (Secretary State Board of Charities), Apr. 21, 1889, New York State Board of Charities Correspondence 1867–1902, vol. 34, p. 370–71, ser. #A1977, New York State Archives, Albany, N.Y.

37. Albert Fuller, *Superintendent's Report for the Year 1888*, (unpaginated), Parsons Collection, box 2. Business rationale was not the only justification for covering a larger geographical area. An added benefit was the possibility of breaking up nests of pauperism by putting considerable distance between a child and an unsuitable home environment. Fuller to Fanning, Apr. 21, 1889.

38. For a more detailed statistical analysis of familial characteristics see Dulberger, "Refuge or Repressor," 135–80.

39. Ibid.; Fuller to Fanning, Aug. 22, 1884, p. 68.

40. Thomas M. Mulry, "The Home or the Institution," in 25 *National Conference* (1898), 362.

41. Albert D. Fuller, *Report to the Trustees of the Albany Orphan Asylum for the Year 1889* (unpaginated), Parsons Collection, box 2. Each child placed out on indenture underwent a trial period of six weeks, sometimes more. Under the stipulations of each indenture agreement, children were to receive certain protections. Persons applying for children promised to furnish suitable food, clothing, and health care. They were also to provide a good common school education and to instruct the child in a trade (usually farmwork or housework), and to teach them the religious principles of the Bible. At the end of an indenture, at eighteen or twenty-one years of age, the foster family was to send the child off with a suit of clothes, a new Bible, and the sum of one hundred dollars for boys and fifty dollars for girls. Albert Fuller traveled the state frequently checking on the physical and emotional condition of his indentured children. He perhaps anticipated the concept of "aftercare," which was not a common practice among asylum administrators at this time.

42. *Albany Sunday Telegram*, June 25, 1893.

43. 21 *National Conference* (1894), 128.

44. See, for instance, Gary Polster, *Inside Looking Out: The Cleveland Jewish Orphan Asylum, 1868–1924* (Kent, Ohio: Kent State Univ. Press, 1990).

45. Fuller's efforts to maintain the ties of family were perhaps not so untypical. See, for instance, Zmora, *Orphanages Reconsidered*, 11 and chap. five.

46. "In Memoriam, Albert D. Fuller" (1893), unpublished booklet, Parsons Collection.

47. Albert Fuller, "Superintendent's Report for the Year 1889."

48. Katz, *Poverty and Policy*, 196.

## Parents and Children

1. For a discussion on the concept of the cult of domesticity see: Carl Degler, *At Odds: Women and the Family in America from the Revolution to the Present* (New York: Oxford Univ. Press, 1980); Mary Ryan, *Cradle of the Middle Class: The Family in Oneida County, New York, 1790–1865* (New York: Cambridge Univ. Press, 1981), especially chaps. 4 and 5; Robert Griswold, *Family and Divorce in California, 1850–1900: Victorian Illusions and Everyday Realities* (Albany: State Univ. of New York Press, 1982), with a particularly useful discussion on family precepts, spousal expectations, and parent-child relations; Blumin, *Emergence of the Middle Class*; and, John Demos, *Past, Present, and Personal: The Family and the Life Course in American History* (New York: Oxford Univ. Press, 1986), especially chaps. 2, 3, and 5.

2. Ryan, *Cradle of the Middle Class*, 157–62; Griswold, *Family and Divorce*, 166.

3. Ibid.; Elder, et al., *Children in Time and Place*, chap. 7.

4. The phrase "haven in a heartless world" is taken from Christopher Lasch, *Haven in a Heartless World: The Family Besieged* (New York: Basic Books, 1977). See also Demos, *Past, Present, and Personal*, 34. For a discussion of the growth of the American suburb in relation to the concept of physical and emotional haven see: Kenneth T. Jackson, *Crabgrass Frontiers: The Suburbanization Of America* (New York: Oxford Univ. Press, 1985).

## Children Outside the Asylum

1. Steven Mintz and Susan Kellogg, *Domestic Revolutions: A Social History of American Family Life* (New York: Free Press, 1988), 45–57; John Demos, *A Little Commonwealth: Family Life in Plymouth Colony* (New York: Oxford Univ. Press, 1970); Demos, *Past, Present, and Personal*, 92–109; Degler, *At Odds*, 66–85; and Elder, et al., *Children in Time and Place*, 8–11.

2. Joseph Kett, *Rites of Passage: Adolescence in America 1790 to the Present* (New York: Basic Books, 1977), 44–158; Mintz and Kellogg, *Domestic Revolutions*, 60–62.

3. Ryan, *Cradle of the Middle Class*, 191–210; Kett, *Rites of Passage*, 138.

4. See for instance, Jerome Kagan, *The Nature of the Child* (New York: Basic Books, 1984) and Elder et al., *Children in Time and Place*, for a review of literature on the recent collaboration between historians and psychologists.

5. Erik Erikson pioneered a developmental theory based on parent-child interaction in the first five stages of life. See, Erik H. Erikson, *Childhood and Society*, 2nd ed. rev. (New York: W. W. Norton, 1963), 247–74; refer also to any standard psychology text, for example, John Janeway Conger, *Adolescence and Youth: Psychological Development in a Changing World*, 4th ed. (New York: Harper-Collins, 1991).

6. Lloyd deMause, "The Evolution of Childhood," in Lloyd deMause, ed., *The History of Childhood* (New York: Psychohistory Press, 1974), 1–73; Henry Ebel, "The Evolution of Childhood Reconsidered," *Journal of Psychohistory* 5 (1977): 66–80. See also Viviana A.

Zelizer, *Pricing the Priceless Child: The Changing Social Value of Children* (New York: Basic Books, 1985).

7. See Linda A. Pollock *Forgotten Children: Parent-Child Relations from 1500–1900* (New York: Cambridge Univ. Press, 1983), 23–43. For a historical critique of assertions made by authors such as Lloyd deMause, see Demos, *Past, Present, and Personal*, 68–91.

8. See, for instance, John Bowlby, *Attachment and Loss*, vol. 2 (New York: Basic Books, 1973), 245–312. For a discussion of the stages of grieving as experienced by young children who have lost a parent through death or separation see, Claudia L. Jewett, *Helping Children Cope with Separation and Loss* (Harvard, Mass.: Harvard Common Press, 1982), especially chaps. 2 and 3.

9. Much of the literature on adoption of older children refers to this initial period of good behavior as the "honeymoon period." According to Jewett it is "that time following relocation from one family to another or from family to institution when the child is no trouble, fits in easily, is eager to please. Many times this 'see how good I am' phase grows out of the attempt to please the caretaking parent as well as to demonstrate magically to the absent parent that the child will do anything even be good, if only the parent will return and reclaim him" (*Helping Children Cope*, 30).

10. According to psychologist Bowlby, the more secure a child's attachment to his principal figure (usually a parent), the more uninhibited is he likely to be in developing attachments to other individuals (*Attachment and Loss*, vol. 1, 308).

## Epilogue

1. *Albany Argus*, Oct. 21, 1901.

2. Helen Fuller, "Superintendent's Report for the Year 1901," (unpaginated), Parsons Collection, box 2; Board of Managers, minutes, special meeting, Dec. 5, 1902, Parsons Collection, box 1, vol. 1.

3. Howard Hopkirk, *Institutions Serving Children* (New York: Russell Sage Foundation, 1944), 131–34.

# Suggested Reading

Following is a selective survey of sources relevant to the study of the orphan asylum. The list extends beyond the scope of this volume but may be helpful to readers who wish to pursue the topic further. Not an exhaustive bibliography, it is merely suggestive of the sources available for investigation and offers a look at some of the current literature on subjects of related interest. The history of the asylum is much more than the history of legislated child care and philanthropic child-saving efforts of a former era. To fully understand the orphan asylum, its place in history, and its impact both on society as a whole and on the individuals and families it served, requires a multidisciplinary perspective. Issues of class, work, poverty, child rearing, and child development are as much a part of the story of the asylum as the motives, policies, and architectural designs of the asylum builders.

In studying the history of the asylum, it may be useful to adopt theories from the social sciences, for example on the subject of parent-child relationships, when attempting to draw conclusions from often very limited written resources. In view of the fact that most asylums served also as placement agents, the contemporary literature on foster care and adoption is pertinent as well. Newly emerging research models that unite social history and child development also can hold particular relevance to a study of the asylum experience, as might current theoretical models on abuse, neglect, and abandonment. The removal of children from their homes, whether placed ultimately in asylums or with other families, also raises the question of the psychological ramifications of separation and loss. The significance of the grieving process therefore should be acknowledged in any study that goes beyond the public realm to consider the children and families of the asylum.

Interestingly, an interdisciplinary perspective is suggested in Larry Benson's recent compilation, *Orphaned Children: A Bibliography* (Vance Bibliographies, 1991). For the most part, however, much of the historical literature on the nineteenth-century orphan asylum falls within the broader context of studies on "scientific charity" and the rise of institutionalized social welfare, works that often lump the orphanage together with an analysis of insane asylums, poorhouses, and prisons. A good deal of this material focuses on the issue of social welfare or benevolence versus social control, a topic that has declined in currency over the last decade. In contrast to these more sweeping monographs, a number of case studies, comparative overviews, and commemorative histories provide a detailed look at the inner world of individual

183

orphan asylums. Sociologists and those in the social work professions as well delve into the topic of the orphanage in clinical studies, textbooks, and journal articles. Nineteenth-century child-care reformers and commentators have also left a vast pool of primary materials for use by historians, a product of their perennial debates over the relative merits of institutional care versus home placement. Finally, in contrast to the more scholarly and academic literature, published reminiscences and autobiographies by former asylum inmates provide perhaps the only first-person accounts of the emotional consequences of institutionalized child care of the last century.

## A Census of Child Saving

How many children actually lived within the confines of orphan asylums in the last century? There is really no conclusive answer. Compiling information and aggregate statistics on orphanages in the United States before 1880 is a difficult task. Until the 1870s and 1880s, most dependent children received care along with their parents in the poorhouse or through outdoor relief, indenture, or apprenticeship. A 1902 report by Homer Folks, then Secretary of the New York State Charities Aid Association, *The Care of Destitute, Neglected, and Delinquent Children* (1902. Reprint, Arno Press, 1971), is one of the more frequently cited contemporary accounts on the history of the orphan asylum and other "child-saving" activities for the entire period of the nineteenth century. Folks discusses the various state systems of public and private asylum care instituted after legislated removal of children from poorhouses and offers some suggestive, though by no means thorough, statistics on the number of children's institutions founded through the 1870s.

A useful companion piece is William Pryor Letchworth's survey, "Orphan Asylums and Other Institutions" in the *Ninth Annual Report of the New York State Board of Charities for the year 1876*. A commissioner to the New York State Board of Charities at the time, Letchworth catalogued over 130 orphan asylums, reformatories, and special-needs institutions in New York State that together provided care to more than 17,000 children. At least two-thirds of the facilities he visited were private orphan asylums that served the largest population of dependent children in any state of the union at the time. Subsequently published by the New York State Board of Charities under the title *Homes for Homeless Children: A Report on Orphan Asylums and Other Institutions for the Care of Children* (1903. Reprint, Arno Press, 1974), Letchworth's compendium portrayed the asylum as the ideal alternative to almshouse care and set the stage for the proliferation of children's institutions in New York State through the turn of the century.

Statistical abstracts from the United States census offer the best and only aggregate picture on orphan asylum populations and child dependency for the period of the late nineteenth and early twentieth centuries. Unfortunately, variations in classification terminology from census to census and unstandardized data collection at the local level makes gross figures questionable and any attempt at trend analysis problematic, if not impossible. The first U.S. census of poverty, homelessness, and welfare dependency was issued by the Government Printing Office in Washington, D.C., in 1888 as a *Report on the Defective, Dependent and Delinquent Classes of the Popula-*

*tion of the United States as Returned at the Tenth Census, 1880*. This was followed by a second survey of dependency in 1892, *Report on Crime, Pauperism, and Benevolence in the United States at the Eleventh Census, 1890*. Special reports under such titles as *Benevolent Institutions* and *Children Under Institutional Care* were issued by the U.S. Census Bureau intermittently over the next four decades, in 1910, 1913, 1927, and 1935.

State charity board reports offer perhaps better and much more detailed and comprehensive statistical summaries on orphan asylums and dependent populations than the Federal census, as do annual reports of county superintendents of the poor. As in the case of the New York State Board of Charities, annual reports also often include such social data on asylum children as orphan status, age, sex, and length of incarceration. Likely the best materials for studying the numbers and characteristics of orphan asylum children are retained in the administrative records of individual institutions. Although standardized recordkeeping varied from state to state and institution to institution, this data remains the primary source for reconstructing demographic profiles on asylum children and on their families. Case files, registration and admission books, and discharge and placement records are common to most extant collections. Additionally, superintendent's reports, board of trustees' minutes, and promotional documents establish the policies under which individual institutions operated and the day-to-day routine of life.

While case files and registration books offer the richest source of data on children and families served by late-nineteenth- and early-twentieth-century orphan asylums, the issue of confidentiality still precludes the use of many collections for publication despite the passage of time. The Parsons Children and Family Center Collection of the former Albany Orphan Asylum, now maintained by the New York State Library Manuscripts and Special Collections Division, is unusual in its accessibility for publication, but confidentiality is still carefully monitored.

## The Orphan Asylum vs. Home Placement

Despite its high stature in contrast to the poorhouse, the orphan asylum was nevertheless a hotly debated issue almost from the time of its inception. For nearly a century, home placement and foster care advocates vehemently argued their points in the public arena with staunch supporters of the orphan asylum. Beginning in the 1860s and 1870s, state charity boards fueled the debate with findings of special studies and official surveys published in annual reports. The pages of the proceedings of the National Conference of Charities and Corrections and individual state conferences bristle with the controversy as well. After the turn of the century, decennial White House conferences on children and youth continued the debate at the national level and added to it discussion of issues regarding child labor, health, education and welfare.

In the early 1970s, Arno Press published more than fifty volumes of reprinted essays, commentaries, monographs, and reports from state and national charity proceedings under the series title "Children and Youth: Social Problems and Social Policy." One edition from that series, *Care of Dependent Children in the Late Nine-*

*teenth and Early Twentieth Centuries* (1974), includes reprints from the National Conference of Charities and Correction under such titles as: "The Shady Side of the 'Placing-Out System,'" "Placing Out Children: Dangers of Careless Methods," "Children's Homes in Ohio," and "What Do you Know of the Children After They Leave Your Home or Institution? Do you Supervise Them?"

The debate surrounding institutional care versus foster care continued in various forms throughout the first few decades of the twentieth century. Sociologists and those in the new social work professions provided perhaps a more balanced view than the philanthropic reformers of the previous generation had done, by stating the pros and cons of each system succinctly within the context of statistical findings. Bias nevertheless prevailed. For instance, in his study of nine Jewish asylums and placement agencies in New York and Chicago, *Institutional Care and Placing-Out: The Place of Each in the Care of Dependent Children* (The Marks Nathan Jewish Orphan Home, 1930), Elias Trotzkey clearly favored the asylum over foster care. Published the very same year, Henry Thurston's work, *The Dependent Child: A Story of Changing Aims and Methods in the Care of Dependent Children* (1930. Reprint, Arno Press, 1974), though not quantitative, nevertheless offered a dispassionate overview of the history of child care through the early twentieth century, concluding in the end only that each system, from almshouse care to the orphan asylum to boarding homes and foster care, had its failings. Thurston made no pretence to having the "ideal" formula, but suggested that the ideal existed in suiting each action to the real needs of the individual child, a therapeutic approach that, if it was to err, did so in favor of family preservation.

Nearly fifteen years after the Trotzkey and Thurston studies, Howard Hopkirk, Executive Director of the Child Welfare League of America, documented the trend in child welfare circles away from institutional care in his book, *Institutions Serving Children* (Russell Sage Foundation, 1944). But Hopkirk's report underscored, as well, the persistence of asylum care, which he believed was here to stay. Though clearly a solution of last resort, still no one called for complete abolition of the orphan asylum at this time, only the need for self-criticism, analysis, and change within the existing array of institutional alternatives.

Hopkirk's work brought to culmination more than three decades of social surveys that began with the pioneering Pittsburgh Survey in 1907 and included important work by such public and private agencies as the United States Children's Bureau and the Child Welfare League of America. Hopkirk cites a number of leading child-care advocates, among them past presidents of the Child Welfare League of America, who undertook the social analysis of child welfare and children's institutions during this period. They included Carl Carstens, Henry Thurston, Hastings H. Hart, and John M. Cooper, the last of whom published the findings of one of the more comprehensive and carefully defined studies of the period, *Children's Institutions: A Study of Programs and Policies in Catholic Children's Institutions in the United States* (Dolphin Press, 1931). As with Thurston and others of the period, Cooper was not looking to condemn the institution as such, but to ascertain the best practices in actual use and place at the disposal of each institution the best experience of all.

## Case Studies

Much of the current historical literature on the orphan asylum is less an indictment of the century-old system of institutional child care or an exegesis on the variety of competing systems than an attempt to understand the asylum's function within the larger society. Nurith Zmora's *Orphanages Reconsidered: Child Care Institutions in Progressive Era Baltimore* (Temple Univ. Press, 1994) is a rare comparative analysis of three religious and ethnically diverse early-twentieth-century Baltimore orphanages. Utilizing case files, institutional sources, and children's letters, Zmora emphasizes the importance of the progressive-era asylum as refuge for impoverished families, often single-headed households, and its role as a "boarding school" of sorts for the poor. Reena Sigman Friedman's book, *These Are Our Children: Jewish Orphanages in the United States, 1880–1925* (Univ. Press of New England, 1994), is another among the few very recent comparative studies of American orphan life. In this work, Friedman analyzes the impact of Jewish children's institutions on American Jewish communal life and the place of the orphanage in inculcating both Jewish and American values. Ironically, though not always the case, many ethnic and religiously affiliated orphanages served a dual function, on the one hand of Americanizing the children of the poor at a time of massive immigration, while on the other hand maintaining the thread of cultural identity.

Other recent historical monographs on the orphan asylum fall within the category of case studies and offer very detailed chronological accounts of the origins, mission, policies, programs, and procedures of individual orphan asylums. These histories may be considered commentaries on the "cult of personality" that to a large extent defined the asylum experience in the late nineteenth century. As superintendents and boards of trustees changed, so too did the daily lives of the children. Food, discipline, nurture, education, and maintenance of family ties often hinged on the character and philosophical bent of individual administrators.

For instance, the tyranny of asylum life is portrayed in the tenure of such men as Samuel Wolfenstein in Gary Polster's book, *Inside Looking Out: The Cleveland Jewish Orphan Asylum 1868–1924* (Kent, Ohio: Kent State Univ. Press, 1990). Serving for thirty-five years, from 1878 to 1913, Wolfenstein, as did many administrators of the time, sought to inculcate the children of the poor with middle-class values. The waves of East European Orthodox Jews arriving in Cleveland in the 1880s and 1890s caused particular fear of an anti-Semitic backlash among the city's more established and assimilated German Jews who had come to Cleveland a generation earlier. As the asylum began to fill with the children of these impoverished newcomers, Wolfenstein initiated more coercive measures and established a policy of isolating the children inside the orphanage where he could socialize, that is Americanize, them correctly without any competing or distracting influences. A harsh disciplinarian, he exacted obedience and loyalty from the children through guilt and shame and degraded the Orthodox religious background of the orphans to their faces, deliberately trying to wipe clean the slate of cultural heritage.

As suggested by the title of Hyman Bogen's book, *The Luckiest Orphans: A*

*History of the Hebrew Orphan Asylum of New York* (Univ. of Illinois Press, 1992), asylum life could be a blessing, provided one could weather the storm of changing leadership as superintendents would come and go, sometimes annually. Although many of the orphanage case studies focus on the motives of asylum founders and practitioners through a recounting of the procession of superintendents and matrons, they point as well to one of the more surprising aspects of the story of the asylum, which is that many of the orphans were not without parents. As the children within the system of foster care today are often referred to as "orphans of the living," so too were the children of the asylum.

In the absence of other alternatives, poor families often looked to the asylum as a source of food, shelter, healthcare, and education for their young. To a large extent, the late-nineteenth-century orphan asylum served as refuge for children of the poor, as the title of Marian J. Morton's article implies: "Homes for Poverty's Children: Cleveland's Orphanages, 1851–1933" in *Ohio History* 98 (1989): 5–22. Parents faced with destitution saw orphanages as solutions to immediate circumstances. Relinquishing control of the child was only a temporary measure, until the family could get back on its feet. In their study of the Protestant Orphan Asylum in St. Louis, Missouri, "The Orphan Asylum in the Nineteenth Century" in *Social Service Review* 57, no. 2 (1983): 273–90, Susan Whitelaw Downs and Michael W. Sherraden agree with Morton and suggest further that the development of the orphan asylum can best be understood as a response to the social and economic problems of transiency. "Traditional urban poverty played a part in creating candidates for admission, but the users [of the asylum] were not simply the poor—they were the poor in motion."

Although much of this current literature is revisionist, even some of the more traditional works and commemorative institutional histories underscore this point. Clare L. McCausland's *Children of Circumstance: A History of the First 125 Years (1849–1974) of Chicago Child Care Society* (Chicago: R. R. Donnelly, 1976) places the asylum experience within the context of the evolution of modern social welfare, while at the same time recounting the story of how the orphanage met the needs of a rapidly growing metropolis and its newly arriving families. McCausland also discusses the practice of indenture or child placement, which was a secondary function of most orphanages in disposing of older children who could not return to their own homes. Child placement often became a primary mission of some institutions, particularly in the early years, as recounted in Daniel I. Hurley's *A History of the Children's Home of Cincinnati 1864–1869* (Children's Home of Cincinnati, 1989). Although child placement agencies and organizations proved serious competition for institutions, little has been written about foster care and indenture in the nineteenth century aside from historical studies dealing with placement of urban youth on Western farms, a practice initiated by Charles Loring Brace and the Children's Aid Society in the 1850s. See for instance, Marilyn Irvin Holt, *The Orphan Trains: Placing Out in America* (Univ. of Nebraska Press, 1992).

## Benevolence vs. Social Control

The orphan asylum has often been placed within a larger body of historical literature on the evolution of American child welfare that focuses not only on the dependent child but also on the juvenile delinquent. Peter C. Holloran's book, *Boston's Wayward Children: Social Services for Homeless Children, 1830–1930* (Fairleigh Dickinson Univ. Press, 1989), is a reminder that child welfare was very much a complex system of care of which the orphanage was only a part. Holloran also demonstrates that institutions established by the ruling elite were supplemented or supplanted by parallel welfare networks established by various immigrant and religious working-class groups.

Whether mainstream or alternative programs or institutions, until very recently historians have discussed child welfare or "child saving" of the last century largely within the context of the social-control impulses of the time. Two works dealing with juvenile delinquency set the theoretical stage for much of the historical literature on child welfare published throughout the 1970s and 1980s. Anthony M. Platt's *The Child Savers: The Invention of Delinquency* (Univ. of Chicago Press, 1969) and Steven Schlossman's *Love and the American Delinquent: The Theory and Practice of Progressive Juvenile Justice, 1825–1920* (Univ. of Chicago Press, 1977) both look at the social roots of the "rule makers" and their role in delinquent reform. Unlike Platt, however, the importance of Schlossman's study is probably not so much in its contribution to the "reform-as-social control" literature as in the connections the author makes between juvenile reform and changes in prevailing attitudes of child rearing, child nurture, and the nature of the child.

Two other volumes stand out as the pioneering works in social control theory. David Rothman's *Discovery of the Asylum: Social Order and Disorder in the New Republic* (Little, Brown, 1971) and Paul Boyer's *Urban Masses and Moral Order in America* (Harvard Univ. Press, 1978) both argue persuasively that a moral or social control tradition dominated welfare reform throughout the nineteenth century. Boyer investigates private and voluntary reform of the era, including evangelical Protestant philanthropy and scientific charity, while Rothman looks to the institutional creations of the times—the almshouse, mental hospital, orphan asylum, and penitentiary. Despite the different focus, both authors arrive at similar conclusions, that a predominating ideology of moral and social control emerged among social thinkers early in the nineteenth century as a result of a pervasive fear of the city and concern over increasing poverty and family disintegration caused by the larger forces of urbanization, industrialization, and immigration.

In a second book, David Rothman chronicles the abuses and failures of nineteenth-century social institutions and efforts to improve them during the Progressive Era. In *Conscience and Convenience: The Asylum and Its Alternatives in Progressive America* (Little, Brown, 1980), Rothman continues the emphasis on the theme of social control but he admits that there were often mixed motives among sponsors of institutional reform. According to LeRoy Ashby in *Saving the Waifs: Reformers and Dependent Children, 1890–1917* (Temple Univ. Press, 1984), the child savers of the period often responded to genuinely tragic conditions with considerable sensitivity and a driving desire to do good. These estimable concerns often were translated into the creation of "anti-institution institutions" such as farm schools and junior republics founded by radical thinkers and institutional innovators of the day.

Both historians and social scientists have developed and used the concept of social control as a theoretical construct. Frances Fox Piven and Richard Cloward perhaps set in motion a debate on the issue between historians and sociologists in *Regulating the Poor: The Functions of Public Welfare* (Pantheon Books, 1971). The authors contend that poor relief has always been an instrument of social and labor discipline extended in times of acute distress or potential violence to pacify the poor and withdrawn during periods of labor scarcity when the poor are anxious for work. A somewhat more radical stance is taken in a book edited by Betty Reid Mandell, *Welfare in America: Controlling the "Dangerous Classes"* (Prentice-Hall, 1975), on the delivery of welfare services in late-twentieth-century America.

In the decade following the presentation of the Piven and Cloward thesis, historians began to explore in some depth the contradictions between concepts of humanitarianism and social control within the context of American social welfare. For instance, Susan Tiffin, in *In Whose Best Interest?: Child Welfare Reform in the Progressive Era* (Greenwood, 1982), attempts to postulate the reasons for the accelerated interest throughout the progressive era in dependent and neglected children. In the process she cautions against a too broad application of social control theory. Some historians, she points out, define the concept so broadly as to make it virtually identical with "socialization." Tiffin states as well that, although control issues cannot be denied, for instance in the case of mothers' pensions, those who concerned themselves with child saving at the turn of the century might more aptly be viewed as having tried to achieve a dual objective of social order *and* social justice.

Walter Trattner and other contributing authors, in *Social Welfare or Social Control: Some Historical Reflections on Regulating the Poor* (Univ. of Tennessee Press, 1983), reiterate this point. Whether in the case of outdoor relief, mothers' pensions, children's institutions, or old-age benefits, historians are cautioned against the tendency to give too much credit to the governing elite for clear thinking and assuming that they had more power to control events and people than was actually the case. Additionally, as Trattner points out in his introduction, social welfare history up to the mid-1980s focused primarily on the providers or benefactors rather than on the recipients of aid. Historians have raised few questions regarding the role of the poor in the whole process, their culture and lifestyles, their reactions to or feelings toward the system and their efforts to accommodate to or undermine the system as a whole.

In response to such concerns, Michael B. Katz forged ahead in the 1980s in reshaping the historiography of poverty. In so doing he called for the introduction of new methodologies that would allow historians to rewrite the history of dependency from the bottom up. In *Poverty and Policy in American History* (Academic Press, 1983), Katz calls upon historians to reverse their perspective and to look at the lives and experiences of the poor themselves, not at the activity of their custodians on their behalf. He suggests looking specifically at the statistical demography and case files of institutional populations rather than at official reports about these groups.

In addition to important new methodological perspectives, Katz's work has been significant for its success in refuting long-held stereotypes about the nature of poor, dependent populations. Based on a detailed demographic analysis of inmates in the Erie County (New York) Poorhouse, he has gone far toward dispelling certain myths about the chronic nature and intergenerational character of poverty and dependency. Katz credibly contends that, rather than being the exception, economic dependence was a predictable and recurring aspect of working-class life in the last century—a condition perpetuated by low wages and irregular work. In his broad synthesis on the history of social welfare, *In the Shadow of the Poorhouse: A Social History of Welfare in America* (Basic Books, 1986), Katz maintains this line of reasoning, stating that no clear boundary separated ordinary working people from those in need of help throughout the period of the nineteenth century because periodic destitution was essentially a structural result of the great social and economic transformations taking place in American life. Though there are clear qualitative differences separating the past from the present, particularly in regard to urban poverty, there are continuities of experience between the "dangerous classes" of last century and today's "underclass." A masterful discussion of the distinctions and continuities that inform the underclass debate today can be found in a recent volume edited by Katz, *The Underclass Debate: Views from History* (Princeton Univ. Press, 1993).

## The Nature of Work

To look at the orphan asylum or any other social welfare institution of the late nineteenth century from the bottom up, it is necessary to understand the nature of work in the industrial era. With the emergence of the new labor history in recent decades, the conditions of working-class life have been much more clearly defined. Rejecting the economism and institutional framework that dominated the writing of labor history since the turn of the century, historians more recently have sought to re-create the experiences of working people in their private lives, workplaces, and communities. The objective of both the new social history and the new labor history, say J. Carroll Moody and Alice Kessler-Harris in *Perspectives on American Labor History: The Problem of Synthesis* (Northern Illinois Univ. Press, 1989), is to bring to center stage the history of inarticulate, subordinate, and ordinary people.

Stephan Thernstrom's pathbreaking work, *Poverty and Progress: Social Mobility in a Nineteenth Century City* (Atheneum, 1977) established the precarious nature of work in the nineteenth century and the inability of laboring families to be self-supporting even with a fully employed breadwinner year round. The labor of women and children became essential to survival and intermittent dependence on kin or public assistance was a simple fact of life. A later work by Thernstrom points to the distinction commentators make today between the "mass" poverty of yesterday and the "class" poverty of today. After combing through a vast array of primary source materials, Thernstrom is left with the impression that the entire working-class population of the previous century lived barely above, if not actually below, the margin of subsistence. See "Poverty in Historical Perspective" in *On Understanding Poverty: Perspectives from the Social Sciences* (Basic Books, 1969), edited by Daniel Patrick Moynihan.

In a similar vein, Melvyn Dubofsky's *Industrialism and the American Worker: 1865–1920* (Thomas Y. Crowell, 1975) documents the growth of the industrial labor force in America throughout the late nineteenth century. He speaks of the "economic treadmill" that trapped most workers at that time, a result of periodic depressions, technological displacement, and cyclical unemployment. In addition, the miserable conditions of working class life—long hours, ravages of industrial accidents, and job insecurity—plagued both men and women.

A number of monographs have been published over the last decade or so on women in the workforce. The most notable among them is Alice Kessler-Harris's *Out to Work: A History of Wage Earning Women in the United States* (Oxford Univ. Press, 1982). A previous work by the same author is titled *Women Have Always Worked: A Historical Overview* (Feminist Press, 1981). Among other things, Kessler-Harris points to the prevalence of domestic service as the most ready employment option for women before World War I. Faye Dudden studies the topic of domestic service in the nineteenth century as well, portraying it as demanding and demeaning work in her book *Serving Women: Household Service in Nineteenth Century America* (Wesleyan Univ. Press, 1983). Dudden supports Kessler-Harris's thesis that women's willingness to enter domestic service seems to have reflected above all the lack of alternative employment opportunities in a predominantly patriarchal economy.

Barbara Mayer Wertheimer's *We Were There: The Story of Working Women in America* (Pantheon Books, 1977) provides a documentary on women's wages and women's work in other service and industrial sectors of the economy—in steam laundries, canning factories, book binderies, packing houses, and sweatshops. In *City of Women: Sex and Class in New York 1789–1860* (Knopf, 1986), author Christine Stansell traces the changing structure of women's work to the early nineteenth century and finds single women, especially single mothers, struggling to survive, many times turning to prostitution as the closest employment at hand.

Other studies on work in the nineteenth century are perhaps as much an account of the dimensions of poverty and the spartan material lives of the laboring classes as they are an analysis of jobs, wages, work routine, changing technologies, and labor movements. Among these studies are Daniel J. Walkowitz's *Worker City, Company Town: Iron and Cotton-Worker Protest in Troy and Cohoes, New York, 1855–1884* (Univ. of Illinois Press, 1978); Richard B. Stott's *Workers in the Metropolis: Class, Ethnicity, and Youth in Antebellum New York City* (Cornell Univ. Press, 1990), though his emphasis is on the cheerier and more masculine side of working-class experience and culture; and Billy G. Smith, who in fact dates the phenomenon of working-class poverty to the period of the late eighteenth century in *The "Lower Sort": Philadelphia's Laboring People, 1750–1800* (Cornell Univ. Press, 1990).

## Family Ideas and Ideologies

Americans have always been torn over the issue of the causes of poverty. Who is to blame? As a nation, we have vacillated along with the prevailing political climate and laid blame at one time or another on morality, environment, or economics, and sometimes on a combination of all three. Amos Warner, in his often cited 1894 study, *American Charities: A Study in Philanthropy and Economics* (Reprint, Transaction Publishers, 1989), marveled at the large number of children living in poverty at the end of the nineteenth century. One hundred years ago, Warner considered the leading cause of incipient pauperism to be the weakness of childhood and, by way of association, the family. Then as now, parents were viewed as the culprits either through direct negligence, lax supervision, or immoral influences. Yet aside from aggregate statistics on material life or assumptions based on the nature of work and wage structures in the past, little is known of poor families of the last century, how they raised their children, what the nature of affective relationships might have been between parent and offspring and husbands and wives, why such large numbers of families were compelled to seek institutional solutions to problems of poverty, sickness, and death, and what those choices meant in emotional terms.

The literature on the middle class family, in contrast, is abundant to an extreme. Studies focusing on the "cult of domesticity," the rise of companionate marriage, and changes in the family life course provide a dominant theme within the literature on American social history. Steven Mintz and Susan Kellogg have compiled a nice synthesis and broad-sweeping historical overview of the history of the American family in *Domestic Revolutions: A Social History of American Family Life* (Free Press, 1988). In an earlier work, Carl Degler adeptly chronicles the demographic trends and changing dynamic within the American home over the past two centuries in his book *At Odds: Women and the Family in America from the Revolution to the Present* (Oxford Univ. Press, 1980). The evolution of the ideology of the "woman's sphere," a concept at the core of the new domesticity of the nineteenth century, is well documented in two important books, Nancy Cott's *The Bonds of Womanhood: "Woman's Sphere" in New England, 1780–1835* (Yale Univ. Press, 1977) and Mary Ryan's *Cradle of the Middle Class: The Family in Oneida County, New York, 1790–1865* (Cambridge Univ. Press, 1981).

Other works on the American family that provide a look at changes in the family life course since the early nineteenth century include, for instance, John Demos's *Past, Present, and Personal: The Family and the Life Course in American History* (Oxford Univ. Press, 1986). Demos discusses a variety of issues in entertaining language, among them the changing images of the family since Colonial times. Tamara Haraven provides a synthesis on much of the demographic-based research on the family in a chapter on "Themes in the Historical Development of the Family" in *Review of Child Development Research*, vol. 7, edited by Ross D. Parke (Univ. of Chicago Press, 1984: 137–78).

Many of these sources discuss the prescriptive ideals of the modern American family, in particular the heightened emphasis placed on parenthood and childhood and the growing dominance of "separate spheres" for work and home. But again, as Robert L. Griswold points out in *Family and Divorce in California, 1850–1890: Victorian Illusions and Everyday Realities* (State Univ. of New York Press, 1982), most studies of the nineteenth-century family have relied upon the written records left behind by members of the literate classes. Little is known of how the working and dependent poor perceived their proper sex roles or how such parents viewed their children. In a departure from reliance on middle-class source materials, Griswold utilizes divorce court records in an attempt to discern how companionate ideals and affective bonding between parents and children were translated into reality for those who left few if any written accounts. For a later period, Beverly Stadum turns to the case files of the Associated Charities in Minneapolis, Minnesota, in her book, *Poor Women and Their Families: Hard Working Charity Cases, 1900–1930* (State Univ. of New York Press, 1992). Stadum finds that economic privation often pushed women's roles beyond the confines of the prevailing family ethic or "ideal" and blurred the boundaries of what was appropriate female behavior. Yet, although poverty severely strained emotional bonds, and domestic peace and harmony became a fiction in many families caught in the webb of chronic illness, malnutrition, desertion, violence, and despair, the poor maintained a certain vitality and hopefulness as they pursued multiple strategies for survival.

## The Children of The Poor

The changing nature of childhood and the primary significance of child rearing in the new companionate household are well documented in the historical literature on family. A profound shift occurred in the perceived economic and sentimental value of children in the nineteenth century. According to Viviana A. Zelizer, in *Pricing the Priceless Child: The Changing Social Value of Children* (Basic Books, 1985), by the end of the century there had emerged a new middle-class view of the child as economically "worthless" but emotionally "priceless." In the industrial era, however, the increased need within working-class households for the assistance and wages of children resulted in a cultural lag of sorts. The children of the poor essentially were left behind until compulsory education and child labor laws in the 1920s and 1930s removed them from the labor force and they too became "precious," at least within the confines of their own homes.

The sense of "public love" for children did not necessarily parallel the new "parental love," however, as W. Norton Grubb and Marvin Lazerson point out in *Broken Promises: How Americans Fail Their Children* (Basic Books, 1982). Americans, they say, have consistently articulated the sanctity of the private family and reaffirmed private responsibility for child rearing while at the same time adopting policies and supporting institutions that assert that families cannot be private. The state's appropriation of child-care functions, beginning in the nineteenth century in schools, clinics, juvenile courts, public institutions, and other agencies of socialization, has not usually resulted in fair and effective treatment for all children, however, especially those whose families are economically dependent. Part of the problem, the authors conclude, comes from parents themselves, whose love for their own children does not necessarily translate into a love for all children.

The legal doctrine of "parens patriae" evolved throughout the nineteenth century into a conception of "limited public responsibility" for children only under the conditions of familial disorganization and pathology. But, according to Christopher Lasch in *Haven in a Heartless World: The Family Besieged* (Basic Books, 1977), by the late nineteenth century reformers were working to remove children from the influence of their families altogether and "society" was now to take the place of the private family and the benevolent, nurturing mother in the raising of the child. Of course, the level and quality of care was skewed by class and by each family's ability to pay the high costs of health and psychiatric care and the fees for additional "professional" services now necessary to raise children in a modern society.

In the opinion of some authors such as Lloyd deMause in *The History of Child-hood* (Psychohistory Press, 1974), parental love and good parenting are very recent phenomena. The author asserts not only that abuse and psychological projection char-acterized the parent-child relationship for hundreds of years but that, in fact, person-ality changes brought about through successive generations of parent-child interactions represents the central force in historical change. His sweeping, radical, and rather grim thesis has met a good deal of resistance not only from historians but those in the social sciences and even academicians who look to sociobiological theory in understanding or explaining historical change. Linda Pollock, for instance, in *For-gotten Children: Parent-Child Relations from 1500–1900* (Cambridge Univ. Press, 1983), views the prevalent systematic ill-treatment of children in past societies as highly unlikely. Extrapolating from current theories on child abuse, she suggests that, under such conditions, the intergenerational reproduction of deficient and dysfunc-tional adults would surely have resulted. Few people, Pollock says, would be prepared to claim that past societies were composed largely of less-than-competent adults. In contrast to deMause, then, Pollock sees parental attitudes toward children and the affectional bond as essentially invariant over time.

Two anthologies by N. Ray Hiner and Joseph M. Hawes, *Growing Up in Amer-ica: Children in Historical Perspective* (Univ. of Illinois Press, 1985) and *American Childhood: A Research Guide and Historical Handbook* (Greenwood Press, 1985), document the historiography of childhood up to the mid-1980s, presenting much of the new scholarship written after Robert Bremner's massive three-volume documen-tary history on public policy, *Children and Youth in America: A Documentary History* (Harvard Univ. Press, 1970–74). Although the contributors to the Hiner and Hawes volumes do address changing mentalities and variations in childhood experience over time, the focus is less that of "sentiments" history or the changing psychology of parent-child relations than the more traditional treatment of institutional policies, largely educational and social welfare, established over the past two hundred years to manage children's lives.

A critical and probing analysis of recent literature on the history of childhood by both sentiments historians and historians of public policy is Bruce Bellingham's re-view, "The History of Childhood Since the 'Invention of Childhood': Some Issues in the Eighties," in *Journal of Family History* 13, no. 3 (1988): 347–58. Bellingham directs perhaps his harshest criticism against those historians who concentrate on the "official processing of children" and tend to lose sight of the personal lives and actions of children and parents within the larger apparatus of public welfare, that is, their ability and willingness to act on their own behalf.

Bellingham's case study of the New York Children's Aid Society (CAS) for the 1850s responds to the need for new methodologies and a refocusing of perspective in studying child welfare policies of the last century. In "'Little Wanderers': A Socio-

Historical Study of the Nineteenth Century Origins of Child Fostering and Adoption Reform" (Ph.D. diss. Univ. of Pennsylvania, 1984), Bellingham finds that, contrary to more traditional historical interpretations of mid-nineteenth-century policies to place poor urban children with farm families out West, the actual pattern of foster care in this period was one of "shared parenting," favoring the family of origin. Placement of children even thousands of miles distant did not preclude their continued contact with or ultimate return to their own families.

## Paradigms from the Social Sciences

With few exceptions, neither the historical literature on childhood nor that on the family speaks to the internal dynamics of poor families, the emotional and psychic content of their lives, or their personal response to the conditions of nineteenth-century working-class life. Solutions to poverty very often meant familial separation, either for the short term or for the long term. Poor single parents, particularly women, faced the meanest circumstances. Societal expectations that assumed full employment and family wages for men and full-time domesticity for women placed poor single mothers in a double bind in which their very lifestyle became suspect.

In *Heroes of Their Own Lives: The Politics and History of Family Violence: Boston 1880–1960* (Viking, 1988), historian Linda Gordon finds that single mothers were consistently overrepresented in cases of family violence, particularly child neglect, reported by Boston social work agencies for the period 1890–1920. Despite the numbers, Gordon reminds us that many of the defining aspects of child neglect, such as lack of supervision, were in fact essential to the survival of households headed by women. Even the case workers of the period themselves had a difficult time distinguishing between child deprivation caused by poverty on the one hand and neglect stemming from parental indifference or hostility on the other. According to Gordon, even incompetent mothers wanted to be with their children and vehemently protested their forcible removal from the family home for placement in institutions or foster homes.

The strong sense of attachment to their children exhibited by otherwise negligent parents presented a quandary to social workers and charity providers of the last century, as it does today. Despite strong and obvious bonds of affection, lower-class family ties went on trial repeatedly throughout the late nineteenth and early twentieth centuries. Beginning in the 1920s, parent-child relationships became the object of scrutiny by sociologists and family therapists. Urie Bronfenbrenner's ambitious comparative synthesis of twenty-five years of disparate research published in 1958 took a major step toward the development of a theory of class differential child rearing and parent-child relations. In "Socialization and Social Class Through Time and Space," in *Readings in Social Psychology* (Holt, Rinehart and Winston, 1958), edited by Eleanor E. Maccoby, Bronfenbrenner focuses on a number of child-rearing variables such as breast feeding, weaning, and toilet training, and on such broad topics of interest to researchers as the "emotional quality" of the parent-child bond in middle-class and working-class households. He concedes that the age of the child may have some bearing on parental affection, but otherwise the empirical evidence supports the view that both middle-class mothers and fathers typically have warmer, more affectionate relationships with their children than do working-class parents.

Much of the sociological literature suggests that the concept of the "precious" child has never been fully absorbed by the lower classes. Other studies through the 1960s and 1970s supported Bronfenbrenner's finding of a positive relationship between social class and parental affection and involvement, for instance, Viktor Gecas's follow-up study to Bronfenbrenner's work, "The Influence of Social Class on Socialization," in *Contemporary Theories About the Family: Research Based Theories* (Free Press, 1979) edited by Wesley R. Burr. According to Gecas, perhaps no issue in socialization is more controversial than the nature of poverty socialization. Borrowing from the "culture of poverty" school, he theorizes the self-perpetuating and intergenerational nature of poverty. Individuals who grow up in an environment of deprivation exhibit strong feelings of fatalism, helplessness, dependence, and inferiority as well as a strong present-time orientation with relatively little ability to defer gratification and plan for the future. As a consequence, lower-class parents are not only low on expressions of affection but, by virtue of a number of interrelated cultural deficits, they are also low on achievement motivation.

Much of the pioneering work on class-differential child rearing and parent-child relationships has focused on the organization of work and its bearing on interpersonal family relationships over time. Daniel Miller and Guy E. Swanson, in *The Changing American Parent* (John Wiley and Sons, 1958), argued in the 1950s in support of the notion that certain organizational or work settings create pressures for certain types of child-rearing practices. Building on this body of theory, later work by sociologist Melvin Kohn broke away from the study of technique in childrearing practices—breast feeding, weaning, toilet training, etc.—and focused instead on the place of parental values in the study of class-based socialization.

In *Class and Conformity: A Study of Values, With a Reassessment* (2nd ed. revised, Chicago Univ. Press, 1977), Kohn posits the dichotomy between the self-directed orientation of middle-class parents and the more conformist attitudes of working-class families, but stresses that class differences regarding parental values are less a matter of kind than of emphasis. Parents of all social ranks deem it important that their children be happy, considerate, obedient, and dependable and to act in ways that show a decent respect for the rights of others. Middle-class parents are more likely to emphasize self-directed behavior, however, and thus they dwell on certain values at the expense of others, for example self-control and consideration, as opposed to obedience and neatness, which Kohn finds are values most often emphasized by working-class parents.

Whatever the nature of those relationships, parent-child bonds are likely strong among all social classes. The child's attachment to its natural parents, for instance, at times exceeds all reasoning, as in the case of negligent and abusive parents. In *Maternal Care and Mental Health and Deprivation of Maternal Care: A Reassessment of Its Effects* (Schocken Books, 1966), psychologist John Bowlby contends that a child's attachment to a parent may not be predicated at all on the existence of a loving and nurturing maternal presence. Rather, attachment may only be a process of instinct, for how can we explain the abused child's strong attachment and loyalty to the abusing parent?

Many children who populated the nation's orphan asylums in the late nineteenth and early twentieth centuries came from abusive and negligent environments. Their numbers were likely small in proportion to the overall population of asylum children, however. More commonly, it was the economic, physical, and emotional stresses of poverty that led all too often to familial disorganization and separation of parent and child. Poor asylum children left few written records to chronicle their response to such life circumstances. As adults, some former asylum inmates poured out their experiences in autobiographical works. Eileen Simpson, in *Orphans: Real and Imaginary* (Weidenfeld and Nicolson, 1987), tells both her story and that of other well-known orphans from the past in a chapter on "Orphans in Autobiography." Simpson admits to a certain "vein of sadness" that she carried throughout her life both from a sense of loss and abandonment and the shame she felt at having been an orphan.

Separation of children from parents, whether through death, desertion, illness, or divorce, can result in a grief and sadness that is lifelong. At the least, asylum children must have experienced a profound sense of loss tinged with rage, fantasy, and ultimately dour resignation. John Bowlby's important three-volume study, *Attachment and Loss* (Basic Books, 1969–80), has contributed to a better understanding of the grieving process in young children and how it can affect their adult lives. Children in hospitals, in foster care, and in asylums, even children adopted at birth, can experience a syndrome of psychological and behavioral problems all with roots in the sense of abandonment resulting from parental loss. An introduction to Bowlby's attachment theory can be found in two small collections of his lectures, *The Making and Breaking of Affectional Bonds* (Tavistock Publications, 1979) and *A Secure Base: Parent-Child Attachment and Healthy Human Development* (Basic Books, 1988).

Claudia L. Jewett identifies three stages of grieving experienced by children in her book, *Helping Children Cope with Separation and Loss* (Harvard Common Press, 1982). Each phase is accompanied by certain emotions and behaviors, she says, that need to be acknowledged and understood if substitute caretakers are to help the child through the process. Early grief, with its shock and numbing, results in mechanical and lifeless motion often broken by outbursts of panic. Denial and disbelief emerge in this phase and can manifest themselves through hyperactivity. The yearning and pining evident in the second phase of acute grief is often recycled by visits from the separated parent. Children are restless, searching, and preoccupied with intense thoughts about lost family members. Episodes of sadness, anger, guilt, and rage may recur until the child accepts the loss and begins the process of integration and reorganization in the final phase of grieving.

As Jewett points out, losing a parent to death or separation strikes a blow at a child's developing sense of trust and self-esteem. Those who have never experienced a stable and secure relationship with a parent or caretaker are most at risk. Recent studies of children in foster care conclude that the most pervasive, chronic problem in foster care is just that, a child's poor self-concept. Robert L. Geiser, in *The Illusion of*

*Caring: Children in Foster Care* (Beacon Press, 1973), suggests the kinds of questions that such children must ask themselves repeatedly: Why am I here? Who am I? What will happen to me? Am I worth caring for? As Alfred Kadushin reminds us in *Adopting Older Children* (Columbia Univ. Press, 1970), the child in foster care is in psychological limbo belonging fully neither to his own family nor the family of his new caretakers. Additionally, children in such circumstances have lost not only parents, but siblings, who are often important sources of emotional support.

In the absence of adequate records that might touch on the emotional content of the lives of orphanage children of the last century, the contemporary literature on adoption and foster care seems relevant and useful. The locus of care is different today, but not so the experience of separation and loss. The "adopted child syndrome," for instance, with its distinct pattern of symptoms, personality dynamics, and behavior problems, all revolving around a basic lack of trust, can prove informative in studies on the asylum child. Though the term "syndrome" should not imply pathology, says Jean Lifton in *Lost and Found: The Adoption Experience* (updated ed., Perennial Library, 1988), adopted children often exhibit pathological behaviors as they mature to adulthood, for example, pathological lying, stealing, truancy, rebellious disruptive behavior toward authority figures, threatened and actual running away, sexual promiscuity, shallowness of attachment, and lack of meaningful relationships.

This cluster of behaviors is really no different than those reported by foster care providers today or by child savers of the previous century. Ultimately, to understand the psychology of foster care, adoption, or the asylum experience from the perspective of the child, it is crucial to first recognize and appreciate the unique role played by loss and grieving in the search for self. See, for instance, David M. Brodzinsky, Marshall D. Schechter, and Robin Marantz Henig, *Being Adopted: The Lifelong Search for Self* (Doubleday, 1992).

Much of the sociological literature on family and children, as well as many of the broad sweeping developmental theories of psychologists such as Erik Erikson, who expounds his theory in *Childhood and Society* (W. W. Norton, 1963), underscore the importance of continuity and "connectedness" in the process of psychological growth. The implication is that the circumstances and experiences of infancy and childhood cannot easily be erased. Contrary to theorists such as Erikson, or Benjamin Bloom in his book *Stability and Change in Human Characteristics* (John Wiley, 1964), psychologist Jerome Kagan rejects the notion that the process of development is so stringently "continuous" throughout the life course. If, for instance, as he states in *The Nature of the Child* (Basic Books, 1984), a child's environment becomes benevolent after the period of infancy, then outcomes based on emotions experienced repeatedly during infancy will not necessarily predetermine adult psychosis. At the center of his argument is the premise that intervention can alter ultimate behavioral and attitudinal outcomes, a premise central to the rise of institutional child welfare in the period of the late nineteenth century. Finally, Kagan suggests that major forces throughout the life course, such as schooling, historical circumstances, or unexpected and unpredictable events can very often supersede the experiences of childhood. He concedes, however, that a child's class membership, unlike the temporary loss of a parent or a brief period of tension in the home, represents a continuous set of experiences, and for that reason class status has a powerful influence on the child.

Yet, despite certain continuities, there are those who are beginning to question the traditional assumption that the developmental processes of childhood are universally applicable. According to some authors, psychosocial development and other life changes may very well be shaped by imperatives of historical change. Major social transformations, such as the industrialization of American society, or significant society-wide events, such as wars and economic depressions, can have a definite influence on life patterns and how different cohorts come of age over time. Contributors to the recent volume *Children in Time and Place: Developmental and Historical Insights* (Cambridge Univ. Press, 1993), edited by Glen H. Elder, Jr., John Modell, and Ross D. Parke, call for a collaboration between historians and developmental psychologists, who together should be set with the express objective of ferreting out the question of variability in human development over time and exploring the implications of societal change for children's growth and life chances both in the past and today.

## Decline and Resurgence of the Asylum

More than a topic of intellectual curiosity or antiquarian interest, the orphan asylum or "orphanage idea" is receiving increasing attention in child welfare circles today. The decline of the institutional focus of child saving is well documented in studies by Martin Wolins and Irving Piliavin, *Institution or Foster Family: A Century of Debate* (Child Welfare League of America, 1964) and Seth Low, *America's Children and Youth in Institutions: 1950–1960–1964*, Children's Bureau Publication Number 435 (Government Printing Office, 1965). A complex set of variables, including state and federal welfare policies, obsolescence of outdated facilities, changing attitudes regarding dependency, and demographic trends of the late twentieth century, to one extent or another all led to the abolition of asylum care in the United States by the 1960s. Marshall B. Jones in his article, "Decline of the American Orphanage, 1941–1980" in *Social Service Review* 67, no. 3 (1993): 459–79, suggests additional causes, primarily the rising cost of institutional care resulting from increasingly stringent regulations regarding the physical environment and the number and training of child-care personnel considered essential for efficient and effective operation of a facility. The decline in the number of institutions and the proportion of children in institutional care also coincided with a movement toward professional, treatment-oriented care in the twentieth century. Many asylums closed their doors, others reorganized as treatment centers for emotionally disturbed youth and continue in the capacity today.

Although by the time of the first White House Conference on Children in 1909 no one defended the large congregate-care institution in principle, the asylum died a slow death as the foster care system, mothers' pensions, AFDC, and other child care programs expanded to fill the void. Today, those alternatives, which offered so much promise a generation or two ago, are now the subject of harsh criticism. The ideology of "family preservation" hailed at the turn of the century as child-welfare dogma, is now undergoing serious reconsideration and deliberation. In response, articles in defense of the orphanage or group living are appearing with frequency in popular and academic journals and in the mass media as we approach the twenty-first century. Mary-Lou Weisman's article, "When Parents Are Not in the Best Interests of the Child" in *Atlantic Monthly*, July 1994: 43–63 and Linda L. Creighton's piece, "The New Orphanages" in *U.S. News and World Report* 109, no. 14 (1990): 37–41, suggest that group homes and residential treatment centers may well be the wave of the future in providing the constancy of care and the safe haven for needy children that the foster-care system has failed to deliver.

# Bibliography

## Primary Sources

*Albany Argus*, Oct. 21, 1901.

*Albany Sunday Telegram*, June 25, 1893.

Board of Managers, Albany Orphan Asylum. Minutes. Special Meeting, December 5, 1902. Parsons Child and Family Center Collection, SC17377, box 1, vol. 1. Manuscripts and Special Collections Division, New York State Library, Albany, N.Y.

Folks, Homer. "The New York System of Caring for Dependent Children." In *Proceedings of the New York State Conference of Charities and Correction*. First annual session (1900), 129–47. Albany, N.Y.: J. B. Lyon Co., 1901.

———. "The Removal of Children from Almshouses." In *Proceedings of the National Conference of Charities and Correction*. Twenty-first annual session (1894), 123–32. Boston: Press of George H. Ellis, 1894.

Fuller, Albert. Letter to James O. Fanning (Secretary State Board of Charities), Aug. 22, 1884 and Apr. 21, 1889. New York State Board of Charities Correspondence 1867–1902, ser. #A1977, vol. 34, pp. 68, 370–71. New York State Archives, Albany, N.Y.

———. *Superintendent's Report for the Year 1888*. Parsons Child and Family Center Collection, SC17377, box 2. Manuscripts and Special Collections Division, New York State Library, Albany, N.Y.

———. *Superintendent's Report for the Year 1889*. Parsons Child and Family Center Collection, SC17377, box 2. Manuscripts and Special Collections Division, New York State Library, Albany, N.Y.

Fuller, Helen. *Superintendent's Report for the Year 1893*. Parsons Child and Family Center Collection, SC17377, box 2. Manuscripts and Special Collections Division, New York State Library, Albany, N.Y.

———. *Superintendent's Report for the Year 1901*, Parsons Child and Family Center Collection, SC17377, box 2. Manuscripts and Special Collections Division, New York State Library, Albany, N.Y.

"In Memoriam: Albert Fuller." Unpublished booklet (1893). Parsons Child and Family Center Collection, SC17377. Manuscripts and Special Collections Division, New York State Library, Albany, N.Y.

Kinkead, Thomas L. "Report of the Committee on the Care of Defective, Dependent, Delinquent and Neglected Children." In *Proceedings of the New York State Conference of Charities and Correction*. First annual session (1900), 121–29. Albany, N.Y.: J. B. Lyon Co., 1901.

Letchworth, William Pryor. "History of Child Saving." In New York State Board of Charities, *Twenty-Seventh Annual Report* (1893), 102.

Lowell, Josephine Shaw. "Report Upon the Care of Dependent Children in the City of New York and Elsewhere." In New York State Board of Charities, *Twenty-Third Annual Report* (1889), 182–84.

Mulry, Thomas M. "The Home or the Institution." In *Proceedings of the National Conference of Charities and Correction*, Twenty-fifth Annual Session (1898), 362–66.

New York State, *Laws of New York* (Apr. 24, 1875).

New York State Board of Charities, *Annual Report*. 34 vols. (1867–1900).

New York State Conference of Charities and Correction. *Proceedings* (1900).

Stillman, William O. "Children as Public Charges." In *Proceedings of the New York State Conference of Charities and Correction*. First annual session (1900), 147–67. Albany, N.Y.: J. B. Lyon Co., 1901.

## Books and Articles

Blumin, Stuart M. *The Emergence of the Middle Class: Social Experience in the American City, 1760–1900*. New York: Cambridge Univ. Press, 1989.

Bodnar, John. *The Transplanted: A History of Immigrants in Urban America*. Bloomington: Indiana Univ. Press, 1985.

Bowlby, John. *Attachment and Loss*. Vol. 2. New York: Basic Books, 1973.

Conger, John Janeway. *Adolescence and Youth: Psychological Development in a Changing World*. 4th ed. New York: Harper-Collins, 1991.

Degler, Carl. *At Odds: Women and the Family in America from the Revolution to the Present*. New York: Oxford Univ. Press, 1980.

DeMause, Lloyd, "The Evolution of Childhood." In *The History of Childhood*, edited by Lloyd deMause, 1–73. New York: Psychohistory Press, 1974.

Demos, John. *Past, Present, and Personal: The Family and the Life Course in American History*. New York: Oxford Univ. Press, 1986.

———. *A Little Commonwealth: Family Life in Plymouth Colony*. New York: Oxford Univ. Press, 1970.

Downs, Susan Whitelaw, and Michael W. Sherraden. "The Orphan Asylum in the Nineteenth Century." *Social Service Review* 57 (1983): 273–90.

Dubofsky, Melvyn. *Industrialism and the American Worker: 1865–1920*. New York: Thomas Y. Crowell, 1975.

Dudden, Faye. *Serving Women: Household Service in Nineteenth Century America*. Middletown, Conn.: Wesleyan Univ. Press, 1983.

Dulberger, Judith. "Refuge or Repressor: The Role of the Orphan Asylum in the Lives of Poor Children and Their Families in Late-Nineteenth Century America." Ph.D. diss., Carnegie Mellon Univ., 1988.

Duncan, Gregg J. *Years of Poverty Years of Plenty: The Changing Economic Fortunes of American Workers and Families*. Ann Arbor: Univ. of Michigan Survey Research Center, Institute for Social Research, 1984.

Ebel, Henry. "The Evolution of Childhood Reconsidered." *Journal of Psychohistory* 5 (1977):66–80.

Elder, Glen H., Jr.; John Modell; and Ross D. Parke; eds. *Children in Time and Place: Developmental and Historical Insights*. New York: Cambridge Univ. Press, 1993.

Erikson, Erik H. *Childhood and Society*. 2nd Ed. Rev. New York: W. W. Norton, 1963.

Folks, Homer. *The Care of Destitute, Neglected, and Delinquent Children*. 1902. Reprint, New York: Arno, 1971.

George, Henry. *Progress and Poverty*. Abridged. New York: Vanguard Press, 1924.

Gordon, Linda. *Heroes of Their Own Lives: The Politics and History of Family Violence, Boston 1880–1960*. New York: Viking Penguin, 1988.

Greenberg, Brian. *Worker and Community: Response to Industrialization in a Nineteenth-Century American City: Albany, New York 1850–1884*. Albany: State Univ. of New York Press, 1985.

Griswold, Robert. *Family and Divorce in California, 1850–1900: Victorian Illusions and Everyday Realities*. Albany: State Univ. of New York Press, 1982.

Handlin, Oscar. *The Uprooted: The Epic Story of the Great Migrations that Made the American People*. 2nd ed. Boston: Little, Brown, 1973.

Hareven, Tamara K. "Themes in the Historical Development of the Family." In *Review of Child Development Research*, vol. 7, edited by Ross D. Parke, 137–78. Chicago: Univ. of Chicago Press, 1984.

Hart, Hastings H. "The Care of the Dependent Child in the Family." In *Care of Dependent Children in the Late Nineteenth and Early Twentieth Centuries*, edited by Robert Bremner, 464–72. New York: Arno, 1974.

Hopkirk, Howard. *Institutions Serving Children*. New York: Russell Sage Foundation, 1944.

Jackson, Kenneth T. *Crabgrass Frontiers: The Suburbanization of America*. New York: Oxford Univ. Press, 1985.

Jewett, Claudia L. *Helping Children Cope with Separation and Loss*. Harvard, Mass.: Harvard Common Press, 1982.

Kagan, Jerome. *The Nature of the Child*. New York: Basic Books, 1984.

Katz, Michael B. *In the Shadow of the Poorhouse: A Social History of Welfare in America*. New York: Basic Books, 1986.

———. *Poverty and Policy in American History*. New York: Academic Press, 1983.

Kessler-Harris, Alice. *Out to Work: A History of Wage Earning Women in the United States*. New York: Oxford Univ. Press, 1982.

Kett, Joseph. *Rites of Passage: Adolescence in America 1790 to the Present*. New York: Basic Books, 1977.

Lasch, Christopher. *Haven in a Heartless World: The Family Besieged*. New York: Basic Books, 1977.

Mandell, Betty Reid. *Welfare in America: Controlling the "Dangerous Classes."* Englewood Cliffs, N.J.: Prentice-Hall, 1975.

McCausland, Clare L. *Children of Circumstance: A History of the First 125 Years of Chicago Child Care Society.* Chicago: R. R. Donnelly, 1976.

Mintz, Steven, and Susan Kellogg. *Domestic Revolutions: A Social History of American Family Life.* New York: Free Press, 1988.

Modell, John. "Patterns of Consumption, Acculturation, and Family Income Strategies in Late Nineteenth-Century America." In *Family and Population in Nineteenth Century America*, edited by Tamara K. Hareven and Maris A. Vinovskis, 206–40. Princeton: Princeton Univ. Press, 1978.

Morton, Marian J. "Homes for Poverty's Children: Cleveland's Orphanages, 1851–1933." *Ohio History* 98 (1989): 5–22.

Parke, Ross D., and Peter N. Stearns. "Fathers and Child Rearing." In *Children in Time and Place: Developmental and Historical Insights*, edited by Glen H. Elder, Jr., John Modell, and Ross D. Parke, 147–70. New York: Cambridge Univ. Press, 1993.

Phelps, Henry P. *Story of the Albany Orphan Asylum.* Albany N.Y.: Albany Engraving Co., 1893.

Pollock, Linda A. *Forgotten Children: Parent-Child Relations from 1500–1900.* New York: Cambridge Univ. Press, 1983.

Polster, Gary. *Inside Looking Out: The Cleveland Jewish Orphan Asylum, 1868–1924.* Kent, Ohio: Kent State Univ. Press, 1990.

Rezneck, Samuel. *Business Depressions and Financial Panics: Essays in American Business and Economic History.* Westport, Conn.: Greenwood, 1971.

Rosner, David, and Gerald Markowitz, eds. *Dying for Work: Workers' Safety and Health in Twentieth Century America.* Bloomington: Indiana Univ. Press, 1987.

Rothman David J. *The Discovery of the Asylum: Social Order and Disorder in the New Republic.* Glenview, Ill.: Scott, Foresman, 1971.

Ryan, Mary. *Cradle of the Middle Class: The Family in Oneida County, New York, 1790–1865.* New York: Cambridge Univ. Press, 1981.

Smith, Billy G. *The "Lower Sort": Philadelphia's Laboring People, 1750–1800.* Ithaca: Cornell Univ. Press, 1990.

Stansell, Christine. *City of Women: Sex and Class in New York: 1789–1860.* New York: Knopf, 1986.

Stott, Richard B. *Workers in the Metropolis: Class, Ethnicity, and Youth in Antebellum New York City.* Ithaca: Cornell Univ. Press, 1990.

Thernstrom, Stephan. *Poverty and Progress: Social Mobility in a Nineteenth Century City.* New York: Atheneum, 1977.

Trattner, Walter I., ed. *Social Welfare or Social Control: Some Historical Reflections on Regulating the Poor.* Knoxville: Univ. of Tennessee Press, 1983.

Walkowitz, Daniel J. *Worker City, Company Town: Iron and Cotton-Worker Protest in Troy and Cohoes, New York, 1855–1884.* Urbana: Univ. of Illinois Press, 1978.

Ward, David. *Poverty, Ethnicity, and the American City, 1840–1925: Changing Conceptions of the Slum and the Ghetto.* New York: Cambridge Univ. Press, 1989.

Zelizer, Viviana A. *Pricing the Priceless Child: The Changing Social Value of Children.* New York: Basic Books, 1985.

Zmora, Nurith. *Orphanages Reconsidered: Child Care Institutions in Progressive Era Baltimore.* Philadelphia: Temple Univ. Press, 1994.